GunDigest® PRESENTS
GUNSMITHING THE

MW01259723

BUILDING THE PERFORMANCE AR

PATRICK SWEENEY

Published by

Gun Digest® Books, an imprint of Caribou Media
Gun Digest Media, P.O. Box 12219, Zephyr Cove, NV 89448
www.gundigest.com

To order books or other products visit us online at **www.gundigeststore.com**

CAUTION: Technical data presented here, particularly technical data on handloading and on firearms adjustment and alteration, inevitably reflects individual experience with particular equipment and components under specific circumstances the reader cannot duplicate exactly. Such data presentations therefore should be used for guidance only and with caution. Caribou Media accepts no responsibility for results obtained using these data.

ISBN-13: 978-1-946267-28-3
ISBN-10: 1-946267-28-7

Cover & Design by Tom Nelsen
Edited by Corrina Peterson

Printed in the United States of America

10 9 8 7 6 5 4 3 2 1

Related Titles from GunDigest Books

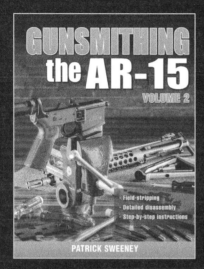
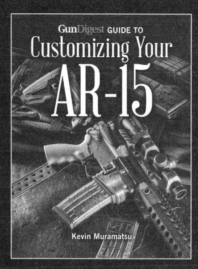
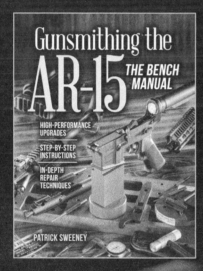
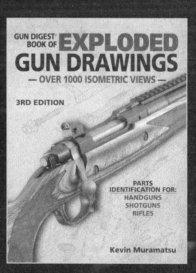

Dedication

For Felicia, because no one deserves more credit and respect for putting up with a cranky, knowledge-laden firearms expert who can drag any conversation around to "Did you know Mauser did…."

She has been by my side during this whole writing experience, and that should be enough to get her nominated for sainthood.

Thank you.

And for the two poodle dudes, who soldier on into their elder years, still eager to get out into the world and sniff and search, and mark.

Last, the hummingbirds. Yep, the feeder produced another season's worth of drama, family-building and excitement.

Contents

Introduction

Why this book? Simple: the world has adjusted to a new normal, a different crazy, and whole new outlook. What do I mean by that? Simple: every-one who wanted an AR-15 now has one. Consider the production of AR-15-type rifles during four time periods. The first is the Colt-only time, from its introduction in the late 1960s until the middle 1980s.

In some ways rifles are like cameras. Yes, the pros use the best, but the pros also use them to earn money. (In ARs, it is to enforce the law or take the fight to the enemy.) You don't need to spend three grand for a "name" AR when you can build one for a third of that. And you can build exactly what you want or need, for sport, competition, hunting or, yes, defense.

Colt was then (and for most of its time so far making ARs) interested in selling them to the government. Whatever they sold to the rest of us seemed to come as an afterthought. It's as if the Colt factory said one Wednesday during lunch, "OK, we've fulfilled the government contracts, let's build commercial guns until quitting time on Friday, and call it good." That change started in the 1980s.

The second era came in the 1980s, when we started to see aftermarket manufacturers that were not just making small parts for Colt. We started to see bare uppers and lowers available, which we used as the basis

for building up rifles from surplus parts, or "surplus" parts.

Mostly, people built pretty much what Colt was making, with some minor changes. Most of what was built were A2 clones and lightweight carbines, since Colt either wasn't interested in making and selling them to us, or they made so few it really didn't matter.

This manufacturing base was accelerated in the third period with various attempted "assault weapon" bans, and then went into high gear with the moronically-worded AWB of 1994. During those times, we bought whatever could be bought, and modified it however we wished, making some truly interesting and different ARs. But, despite the attempt to ban, prohibit, eliminate, delegitimate the AR during this time, and the interest in owning, the buying didn't really take off.

What did come out of this era, before the AWB and in the early years, was what some called the "franken-gun." As in, Frankenstein's monster. Parts from various sources that more-or-less fit, and more-or-less matched in color, were slapped together. I recall one maker of lowers who couldn't seem to get the dye correct on their parts, and as a result, a lot of lowers came through with a slight, but noticeable, purple cast to them.

We had to be good at building, because the makers had not settled down to agreed-upon dimensions. Back then, it wasn't unusual to find an upper and lower "fit" that didn't. The pin holes just could not be made to line up. Or the fit was so loose that the upper visibly wobbled on the lower.

The fourth period is the one just ended. Starting with 9/11 and hitting high gear in 2004 with the sunset of the AWB/94, AR sales went off the charts. Anyone who made anything AR could sell it. People who wanted one, but could never find the time, money, interest or need, suddenly had to have an AR. Along with this came panic buying of ammunition, and the various, lurching shortages of rifles and ammo kept the buying at a fever pitch.

Along with this, interest in 3-gun and multi-gun competition increased dramatically.

We are now in the fifth period of AR buying and ownership. Sales have not only eased up, but slumped, as the artificially increased demand has slackened, and the manufacturers who are out of luck are, well, out of luck. Not because they are bad at business, but for a variety of reasons. Perhaps they bet too heavily on Madame Clinton becoming president. Or they have too much inventory and not enough sales to pay the bills. Or worse yet, they made that inventory on borrowed money and can't pay the monthly note.

Worst of all, they borrowed money to expand the plant, they stocked up on inventory, and now they have to pay for the loan on the new plant, the new machinery and the new inventory. A bigger company with a diversified product line can sit on the slow-moving AR-15 inventory, sell it in due time, and shift production to making what is selling. That's why you are seeing (or have been seeing, depending on when you read this, and how long it takes for the adjustment to happen) ARs offered for sale cheap, at prices that just barely cover the cost of the materials and labor. Maybe not even then.

You will, if you read the firearms trade journals or get email news, learn of com-

The armed forces do not obsess over the AR (M16 or M4) because they have a lot of other tools, some of them a whole lot bigger, with which to deal with problems.

panies closing their doors. These things happen, it is part of the market economy. It is still a bad thing for the companies involved, but it also means smoking hot deals on ARs for the near future.

The cost of ARs has gotten so low, and will likely be so for some time to come, that it is not really cost-effective to build one from a box of parts. Let's take as an example a recent email I received on wholesalers selling to retailers. The price they quoted on an AR was so low that the quality-name rifle would have retailed for $600. The lesser brand, next to it in the ad, would have

sold for $500, retail. Yes, this was a product-moving sale, to clear out excess, but still. And even when moved, the regular price will not have moved up much from that. Yes, it is a vanilla-plain AR-15, but it is a ready-to-go rifle, fully functional and with a factory warranty. The question you have to ask yourself is this: could you build that rifle, sourcing the parts, for that or less? If you can't beat that price, don't build the base rifle, buy it and then modify it.

Let me repeat that: Don't Build A Rifle. At least not from a box of parts. Not if you can get a ready-to-go rifle, close enough to what you want, and only have to change a few things on it.

That's the approach I'll be taking for builds in this book, assuming that I can start from an existing, working rifle.

So, again, why this book?

The number of AR rifles made and sold since the turn of the century is greater than those made in the entire 20th century. That's right, a fifteen-year period, basically, compared to an over thirty-year period, and it isn't even close. A lot of people have ARs, and a lot of those are your basic M4gery.

M4gery? Pronounced "em-for-gery" it describes a non-SBR carbine with a 16" barrel, a telescoping stock, a flat-top upper receiver, and all in black. It's chambered in .223/5.56, with an M4 barrel. Well, often with an M4-profile barrel, but a lot of times, not. In the early part of the 21st century it would have had plastic handguards, and after about 2006 or 2007 it would have more often come with some sort of quad-rail handguard.

This is a good, solid (mostly) basic rifle with which one can learn a lot about marksmanship and competition, and do a great deal of training with and not be hampered by equipment.

But, it isn't the best for a bunch of uses.

Oh, I've gone out prairie dog shooting with just such a rifle. It was fun, it was productive, but I was under no illusion that it was the most effective tool to use at the time.

Ditto using an M4gery for competition. Yes, it may be your go-to rifle in case of TEOTWAWKI, but then again, it isn't the best tool for that, either.

There are a lot of people who own an AR, perhaps an AR unfired in the closet, who want to get out and use it. After the first few times, they will want something that is a bit more efficient for the task they have selected. Building an AR for your needs is not like it used to be, in the first few periods of AR buying. There are few now who expect that their first AR will be one they build from a box of parts.

And, I've already written that book, or books that will lead you through that process.

No, people now want to build on an existing one, to re-build a worn one, or upgrade a still useful but not as-useful rifle they already have. Again, that's what I'll do in the pages of this book.

The modularity of the AR is a big help here. Let's say you have an M4gery and you want more. Or, you have, as some do, an M4gery and extras. You can push the two pins out, take the upper off, slap on a different one and press the pins back.

In fact, you could have a whole suite of ARs on one receiver. One example would be the plain-jane M4gery that you put together and take to the range with your friends or relatives. They love to blast, they even (thank goodness) bring ammo, but you don't want that wear on your match barrel. Then, for the club 3-gun or multi-gun match, you take off the M4 upper, place on your Open or Limited Tactical upper, and head out. You can, if you want, swap out the plain plastic stock for the custom-fitted one you use in matches.

Since your brother-in-law knows nothing about triggers, you could have left your match trigger in the lower this whole time.

Then when it is time for a weekend of shooting prairie dogs, you take the competition upper off, put on the varminter with its high-power scope, and pack the appropriate ammo.

If you have a spare trigger packet, you can swap uppers again, drop in the heavier trigger, and go off to shoot in a Service Rifle match.

You can have, with just one (or maybe two) lowers, a dozen different rifles.

Building those uppers, or building period or end-user correct firearms, is now what a lot of AR owners want. And they are building them on the base rifle that they bought at a fire-sale price, because

they are cheap now. Or, they are building them on the expensive rifle they bought during one of the earlier panic buys, and have found they want something a little (or a lot) different.

Which is why we're here.

Building rifles for these uses calls for a different background of knowledge. One example is mil-spec. For the guys who simply have to have what the end-users have

While an M4 clone might not be the best tool for varmint reduction, it will get the job done. If you have fun while reducing the vermin population, that's a double-bonus. Use the opportunity to learn what you'd like to make the day more fun or more effective, then build it and do it again.

in the dusty places of the world, mil-spec is the be-all and end-all. I hate to break it to you, guys, but the Grand Master in multi-gun competition sneers at your mil-spec gear. He wants more. The NRA High Power High Master shudders in horror at the thought of using a mere mil-spec barrel in his rifle.

There are better materials, better products, and we're here to talk about them.

So, let's get to it, and let's keep in mind that there is no such thing as a bad AR rifle. Oh, there are inaccurate ones, unreliable ones, and even those with a poor cost-to-performance ratio. But there are no bad ones. That's the trap the anti-gunners want to lure us into. "Bad gun, bad gun." B-S.

Rifles are tools. Tools are as good or bad as the person using them.

Be a good person, and use effective tools. ■

CHAPTER 1

What the AR-15 Rifle is Made Of

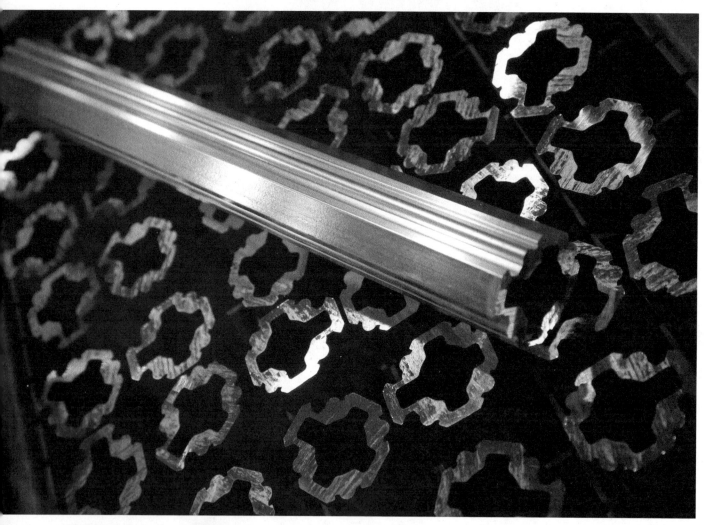

The big advantage of 6061 as an alloy is its willingness to be extruded. Yes, this tube of aluminum was squirted out of an extrusion machine just like toothpaste out of a tube.

Steel, aluminum and plastic make up the AR-15, with a few odds and ends of glass, such as in optics, and brass and lead, the ammo. But, what are they? What do they do, and what goes into them? If you are to make wise decisions selecting and building your AR, you need to know these things. Otherwise you'll fall prey to the most confident person who asserts they know what is what.

The first two, steel and aluminum, are both metals, but the comparisons pretty much stop there. It may be obvious, but it bears repeating: you would not make an aircraft out of steel, and you would not make a skyscraper out of aluminum. There is a place and a reason for each in the AR.

BIG AND STRONG: STEEL

The most abundant element of planet earth is not iron. The interior of our home, as you might remember from school, is hot. The deeper you go, the hotter it gets, and

it isn't that far down, relatively speaking, before things get molten. Molten, but compressed, and thus in a more plastic state than we'd think. You can consider the planet as basically a molten ball of iron, with a cooled crust of solidified slag (non-iron) on the surface. Yep, that slag is where we live. Iron ranks first if you go by mass, but it is the fourth most common element in or on the planet.

In the beginning, the earth was not livable. The surface was devoid of life, and the atmosphere contained no oxygen. The early atmosphere consisted of ammonia, hydrogen, methane and water vapor; not anything we can use, and not anything that causes problems for iron. Given time (the planet has been here some four and a half billion years) life began, and after a billion or so years, that life began producing a toxic, corrosive byproduct: oxygen.

We had water all along, although it took some time to cool the crust and form oceans. The ability of water to dissolve chemicals had over time created a solution, pre-oxygen, that was very high in dissolved iron. Iron-rich oceans we had. Had there been life, it would not have suffered from anemia. When the oxygen content of the

air reached a high enough value, it began reacting with the dissolved iron in the sea water. Basically, the oceans rusted. The oxidized iron precipitated out of the solution, known as the seas, and fell to the sea floor. The iron ore deposits we now mine are the sea beds of long ago, where that oxidized

Once forged, steel is machined into shape, which can require removing just a little steel, or sometimes a lot. Here is a forged 1911 frame, showing that lots of steel has to come off.

Steel is amazing, it can be worked in a variety of ways, including forging. Here a heated piece of steel is fed into the forging dies. This is hot, hard work that requires a good deal of skill to do correctly.

Rail ladders keep the edges from chewing your hands, gloves and gear, somewhat, but they still add even more bulk than the rails create. Quad rails are so 20th century.

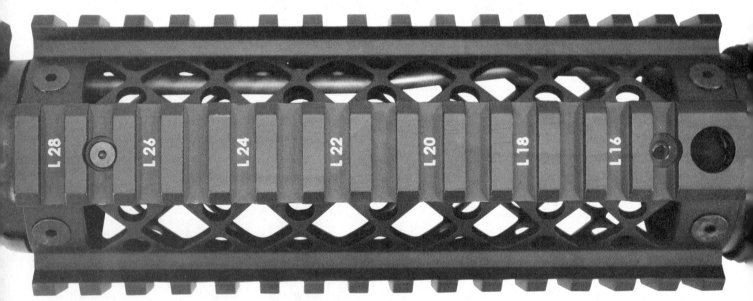

Quad rails were a big advance in the very early 1990s, but since then we've moved on. Still, they have their uses, as long as the bulk isn't a problem.

iron fell out of solution in the oceans and settled on the seabed. Since then, the layers of iron oxide have been flooded, moved, mixed and otherwise jumbled around. (The rusting went on for hundreds of millions of years, which is a pretty short period in the time expanse of the planet. After all, in 4.5 billion years, a hundred million is just over two percent of the time.)

The percentage of usable iron in iron ore can vary a great deal. The amount of iron can be as little as 5% or over 20. As the steel business is a slim-margin business (we'll get into that shortly) the purity matters a great deal. One ore deposit in particular, in western Australia, is immense and rich. The ore there is so pure that a ton of ore can be schlepped directly into a steel mill, no pre-refining needed, and then produce 1,200 pounds of iron. That's 60% purity, compared to half that in earlier-mined ore deposits. (Lucky Aussies.)

In that regard, iron ore is kind of like marble, the building product. Real marble is really, really cheap. After all, you simply dig it out of the ground from pits that can have deposits hundreds of feet deep. Marble is cheap, but moving it costs money. So, if you are ever traveling and you find that even the cheapest hotel you stay at has full-marble bathrooms, you know there is a marble quarry nearby. Shipping iron ore costs money, after all, the stuff is heavy, just like marble.

When the auto industry reigned supreme in America, the Mesabi Range in Minnesota, at only 20% purity, was plenty good enough as a source of ore. The auto companies took that ore, known as taconite, and partially refined it "up north." By upping the purity just a bit, to 30% or so, and then binding it with a substance they could burn off, they "pelletized" it. The taconite pellets (the term also came to be used for the partially-refined product) could be poured into ships, and poured out at the other end of the shipping line into the mills. The business was so lucrative, and required such economies of scale, that immensely long freighters cruised the Great Lakes, carrying huge payloads of taconite.

Maybe you've heard the song "Wreck of the Edmund Fitzgerald" by Gordon Lightfoot? (It was a big hit in 1976, second on the charts only to Rod Stewart's Tonight's the Night.) The Edmund Fitzgerald was the largest freighter when she left the slips, at 729 feet, in 1958. With a draft of 25 feet, she hit shoals in a storm on Lake Superior in November of 1975 and sank with the loss of all hands. The payload was 8,700 tons of taconite.

BURNING OUT IMPURITIES

Ore has to be purified, and that takes heat. In the early uses of iron, that happened in small batches and with relatively low heat. There's only so much you can do with a wood fire, or even a really big charcoal one. You need coal to produce the heat needed to make steel. You need heat to burn out the impurities, create pure iron and then introduce the alloying ingredients. That took a big leap forward with the Bessemer process, back in the mid-19th century. By

blowing air, later oxygen, through a big-enough furnace to make it worthwhile, the process created tons of pure iron, and then steel, where earlier methods had produced a few hundred pounds. And, due to the size and advances in technology, the lot-to-lot consistency was much better. Suddenly, in the middle and end of the 19th century, the world could have lots of really high-grade metal.

To produce more heat and a cleaner burn, steel mills of a couple of generations ago took the preliminary step of producing

High Pressure O_2 is blown over and through the molten iron, oxidizing the impurities, which are converted to a molten slag and removed.

"coke." Coke is simply coal with the impurities burned out if it, to produce hotter heat, and purer iron and thus steel, and to do so with less effort in the bottleneck of steel production – the furnace.

Now, back to the subject of small margins and low profits. Back in the 1960s or so, various ex-colonial countries and former third-world countries determined that the way to move themselves up in the world was to make things that people wanted, things and materials that people would actually pay for. Not just raw materials, but finished, or semi-finished products. The 19th century economic model for empires and colonies was to extract resources from said colonies, use them to produce finished goods, and then sell them back to the colonies. It takes a large amount of the profits from raw goods to purchase a small amount of finished goods. This is a perfect economic model to keep colonies and former colonies downtrodden and poor. (Hey, I'm a capitalist, myself, I'm just pointing out the numbers here.)

Why buy steel from the empire, when you could make it yourself and sell it to others at a good markup? Steel not being the only commodity thus considered. What happened was a massive increase in steel-production capacity, running headlong into the economic disruptions of the oil embargos of the 1970s. Steel companies, many of them overseas being state-owned, found that the profit margin was slim, if not negative. And some countries, such as China, continue to produce even though the net profit margin is negative, both because they need the steel and because they need to employ people. (And in the instance of China, produce without emissions controls, because installing those would make the bottom line even worse.)

As a result, an efficient steel mill operates on a profit margin that makes a modern supermarket look like winning the lottery. I was once at a museum in Naples, Italy, that had a modern art exhibit. The exhibition was by the artist Serra. It consisted of cubes of steel, some as large as chest-high. I really don't get modern art, and I looked at it thinking, "This is simply $435 a ton, delivery extra. How is this art?" Which probably explains why I'm not rich. After a spike in steel prices just before the recession of 2008, steel prices have fluctuated up and down around the same basic price for over a decade. This makes accountants crazy. If inflation is going up at a "modest" 2% and your profit margin is 3%, you have to cut costs every year, year after year, just to stay in business. And then some politician says you have to install fifty million dollars worth of exhaust scrubbers? But I digress.

FERROUS ALLOYS

OK, we all know what steel is, right? Do we? Steel, at its most basic, is iron with carbon in it. Which is kind of like saying cooking is taking food and holding it over some heat. How much? How close? How long? However, all steel is not steel. You see, steel is a particular crystalline form of iron, with not just carbon in it, but particular forms of crystal shapes, and interleaved with other alloying metals, and some non-metals in the alloying mix too, while we're at it.

Let's back up and get a grasp of ferrous alloys and their descendants.

The Iron Age began sometime around 1200 BC. Once it became known how to purify and shape iron in useful quantities, all other weapons metals became obsolete. The Bronze Age was done and combatants moved on. Bronze hung around for a long time (it is still with us, really) for several reasons: it was easy to shape, it was attractive and it didn't rust. As armor it worked fine. As the sword, axe or other tool, it did not compare to steel. Steel was difficult to make and shape, and it rusted. It rusted like mad. And, the early steel wasn't very steel-like, if you get what I mean. It was barely-hardened iron. But it was far superior, even then, to bronze as a weapon. In an otherwise fair match-up, the combatant armed with a steel sword would beat the one with a bronze sword pretty much every time.

And iron, the not-steel ferrous metal, was in common use until the end of the 19th century. Iron, as iron, comes in two forms: wrought iron and cast iron. In the smelting process, iron ends up with a large amount of carbon; too much, really. The resulting ingots cast into "pigs" are known as "pig iron." That poured into moulds is known as cast iron.

Cast iron, due to the excessive carbon content (3.5% or more) is very hard but brittle. It does well under a compression load but is weak under tension.

Wrought iron is iron that has been worked in the smelting process. It is rolled, hammered and otherwise shaped, and is thus called "wrought" or worked iron. It has a lower carbon content and holds up well under tension.

Early construction projects in the 19th century, ones that used large amounts of iron, used the two types of iron for different purposes. If making an iron base to hold great weight, they made it out of cast iron. But links, like the segments of the "chain" bridge in Budapest, were made of wrought iron, for its greater strength under a tension (pulling-apart) load.

What we now call steel could only be made in small batches. It required a lot more heat, at higher temperatures to "blow out" the impurities and the excess carbon and to fully mix alloying elements. This had to wait for the Bessemer process, patented by Henry Bessemer in 1855. The process was simple, really. Take a converter full of molten iron. Blow air (later, oxygen) through it to raise the temperature and over-heat the impurities, and also to speed the burning to keep the iron molten while the process occurs.

The impurities are oxidized and blown off as hot gases, or form slag on the top of the "melt" where they can be skimmed off.

This was not new. Armorers had known how to do this for centuries. However, it was one thing to fire up a forge with coal and forge a sword blade or a prince's chest armor plate, making five or ten pounds of steel. The Bessemer process produced tens of tons per melt, then hundreds. Then top-quality steel became available in the multi-ton lot, and quickly (the Bessemer process could run a batch of iron in half an hour, and produce batch after batch for as long as the equipment was kept in good working order) everything changed.

Think about it. Steel-hulled ships sailed the seas beginning in the latter half of the 19th century. Suspension bridges used steel rope to hold the weight of the deck, road-

The Chain Bridge, in Budapest. When iron was the miracle building material, engineers worked hard to use cast and wrought iron in the correct applications. Compared to those metals, the alloys we have today are miracle steels.

Tempering is a heat treatment process often used to improve hardness, strength, toughness, as well as decrease brittleness in fully hardened steel.

way and utilities. Skyscrapers with steel frameworks, and the walls, floors, ceilings and utilities all hung from the box-like skeleton. And then, at the dawn of the 20th century, automobiles. All made of steel.

Fair warning, we're going deep into the technical underbrush soon, and for some time. If you don't want the information that will give you a leg up on others in your Basic Materials class in engineering school, or discussing barrels and bolts in rifles, you might want to skim a bit. Or, pour a cold drink (non-adult would work best) hang on, and see what you can absorb.

At room temperature, iron forms a crystal known as Body-Centered Cubic, or BCC. In this form, named α-ferrite, it cannot absorb more than a small amount of carbon, 0.005%. It is soft and not very useful as a tool-making material. If we heat it up to steel-making temperatures (we're talking 1,600 degrees Fahrenheit here) and force carbon into it, once the carbon content gets above 0.02% or so the steel changes its symmetry and becomes a face-centered cubic

form, FCC. This is known as austenite, or γ-iron. It is also soft, but it has the wonderful property of accepting a lot more carbon.

We're in!

We now have a wide range of options, because the temperature difference and the carbon-absorption differences can be played to our advantages. For instance, if we take the aforementioned austenite, hold the carbon content to less than 0.8% and then cool it, we present the alloy with a problem. It cannot cool, keep its crystalline form and keeps its carbon. The result is that as the iron reverts to the ferrite state, back to BCC, it precipitates the carbon. The carbon forms into a state known as cementite. So, you have a mixture of ferrite and cementite, more or less evenly distributed through the mass. Think of evenly-distributed chocolate chips, in a loaf of bread.

If we hold the carbon content to exactly 0.8% and cool it, the resulting condition is called pearlite, where the laminations of α-ferrite and cementite form layers, sort of a nano-damascus steel.

Above 0.8%, the mass cools in aggregates of cementite and pearlite.

You can see, by messing around with carbon alone, just over, at or under a known amount, a smidge less than 1% carbon, we can create differing forms of steel. They will have measurable differences in hardness, strength and other properties we will go into in a bit.

Now, what if we force the steel to cool so quickly that it doesn't have time to screw around changing crystalline form and throwing the carbon overboard? What if we quench it?

Now we're cooking with gas.

Quenched steel creates a form known as martensite, When the steel is quenched, the atoms of steel are essentially locked into their BCC form, retaining the carbon. Well, at a carbon content below 0.2% it does. But above that carbon content, it shifts to an entirely new crystalline form: the body-centered tetragonal. Martens-

ite is stronger and harder than austenite. It is also, curiously enough, less dense. In the phase transition the mass actually expands. The atoms, locked in place as the mass expands, create tension on the bonds, increasing hardness and strength. However, if quenching is taken too far the structure can crack. You can create brittle steels in quenching and shatter the mass as it hardens. Or, once cooled it will shatter under any shock.

Recordings of the phases the iron or steel takes when the constituents are varied and the temperatures are known as phase diagrams. What a phase diagram reveals is a lot. For instance, if you have iron containing 1% of carbon at 1,600 degrees it will be a liquid. Lower the temperature below about 1,500 and it will form austenite. The rate at which you cool determines the amounts of pearlite, cementite, and so-on, created.

This leads us to the introduction of annealing and tempering.

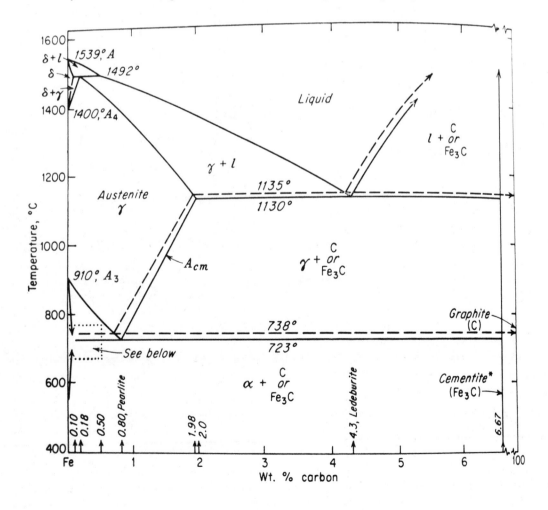

Metallurgists have spent decades, a century or more, developing phase diagrams as part of their degree and in research for their employers. Once you learn how to decipher this chart, you have the keys to the steel world.

ANNEALING AND TEMPERING

If you take your quenched and created martensite, and you slowly heat it enough to relax the tension created by the quench we just undertook, you can anneal it and make it softer without changing (too much) the martensitic structure. If you heat it too much or for too long, you can un-do the martensitic creation and end up right back where you started. The full, gory details of this work involve recovery, recrystallization and grain growth. They also consume an entire semester of your mechanical engineering degree or more.

The myriad of alloys of steel can be alternately massaged – by heating, quenching, annealing, re-crystallizing and so on – to form alloys with wildly different properties even though they contain the same amounts of ingredients. This leads us to the first depressing realization some of you will have: the alloying numbers you have practically worshiped are simply ingredient lists.

For example, let's take the big bugaboo of the mil-spec crowd, SAE 4150 steel. "Forty-one fifty" is the touchstone steel for AR rifle barrels. The number is a code created by the SAE (Society of Automotive Engineers) telling us it contains molybdenum and chromium (the "41"), carbon (the "5") and small amounts of silicon (the "0"). That is all it tells you.

Were I a charlatan, I could sell you a pretty shabby batch of steel, and truthfully and with a straight face call it 4150 steel. As long as it had the stated book amounts of those elements in it, within the specified limits, it would be what I said it was. So, let's take a step back.

No doubt many of you are familiar with what steels are called. The familiars are legion: 4140, stainless, nickel steel, moly-steel or chrom-moly. You see, to turn iron into steel you have to produce a certain amount of carbon, dissolved in the melted iron, and then manipulate it to keep crystal size and carbon inclusion under control.

Alloy steel is steel with elements other than iron and carbon in it. These elements can be introduced to control a host of variables. One such is the class of steels called stainless. They aren't really stainless, but their corrosion rate is impressively slow.

Other alloying elements increase strength, one being vanadium. When Henry Ford found that the French were using vanadium-alloyed steel and producing steel with twice the strength of American steel, he decided to build a plant to make his own steel. Thus the Rouge Plant was born, the Mesabi Range diggings expanded, and half a century later the Edmund Fitzgerald sank.

Other alloying ingredients can create changes in machinability, making an alloy easy to cut while maintaining its strength, create interesting changes in the heat-treatment an alloy can need or

Photo: ThyssenKrupp Steel

withstand, and on and on in almost endless variety.

Indeed, if you sign up for a degree in mechanical engineering, you can be certain of spending several semesters, perhaps more than a calendar year, learning the ins and out of alloying, materials, and a large part of that will be about steel.

Clever people like to say we live in a digital age, but we have been, and will for some time be living in the Age of Steel and Glass.

Skyscrapers are steel. They are now clad in glass, in an earlier age they were clad in stone. The Empire State Building isn't a stone building. It is steel with the stone hung on the façade. Stone buildings can only be about six or seven stories high before the base has to be so thick you start losing room in the ground-room floors.

4140 VS. 4150

Back to 4150 and the big argument: its "superiority" over 4140. As a quick summary, here's what's in them, and the relative amounts, by percentage:

The interior of an annealing furnace. By annealing the metal beforehand, cold working can take place without any risk of cracking. That's because annealing releases mechanical stresses produced during machining or grinding.

4140 VS. 4150	4140	4150
Chromium	0.8 to 1.0	0.8 to 1.0
Molybdenum	0.15 to 0.25	0.15 to 0.25
Carbon	0.38 to 0.43	0.48 to 0.53
Manganese	0.75 to 1.0	0.75 to 1.0
Phosphorus	0.040 max	0.040 max
Silicon	0.15 to 0.35	0.15 to 0.35

You can see that the only difference is the amount of carbon. The amounts are small and not very different. In fact, a high grade of 4140 could have 0.43% carbon, while the lowest grade of 4150 can have 0.48%. And on that you're going to condemn a barrel-maker?

If we may diverge for a moment, what is the difference in actual strength? 4140 can have a yield strength of 95,000 PSI (Imperial). That of 4150: 106,000 PSI (Imperial). So, eleven points stronger, at a yield level so far above the needs of your barrel that it is theoretical. What matters to the barrel-maker is the machinability, measured on a standard the AISI developed, the 1212. (1212 steel is a plain carbon steel, with no more than 1% of moly, and has been resulphorized and rephosphated. Translation: plain steel of the mildest grade.) There, 4140 has a machinability of 65, where 4150 has one of 55. Here, higher is better, as in easier on the machines. So, for a yield increase of 11.5%, the barrel-maker has to put up with a machinabilty "hit" of over 18%. That costs money in barrel fabrication.

Another common barrel alloy is 41V45. Here we have the addition of vanadium to the chromium and molybdenum, which makes for stronger steel. It also makes for a steel with different machining and hardening properties than, say, 4140 or 4150, so it requires different handling in manufacture. You trade one thing to get another.

Back to the alloying ingredients.

Chromium is obvious, it is added to reduce corrosion, right? Wrong. The chromium is added, in conjunction with the molybdenum, to improve strength, making the resulting alloys stronger and harder. Known as a class as chrom-moly, cr-moly, cromaloy they are so common as to be ubiquitous. They do have some drawbacks, however. They do not like being welded. To properly weld, you need to warm or heat the parts involved, and sometimes even heat after welding, to avoid cold-cracking from crystalline changes and shrinkage. One big advantage is the ability to surface-harden these alloys.

Molybdenum is used with chromium, as above, and on its own and it presented a problem in early steel making. Its melting point is in some instances a thousand degrees above that of iron. Getting it into iron to make steel wasn't easy. "Moly" improves hardenabilty, reduces temper embrittlement and other sources of embrittlement, and it is used in a special class of steels known as high-strength, low-alloy steels. These have a slosh of alloying components, made for construction work. They are lighter (up to 30% lighter) than carbon steels and have the same strength.

Manganese is added to increase toughness and abrasion-resistance, and reduce work-hardening.

Phosphorus increases the strength of ferrite, adding as much as 9,000 PSI to the yield strength. Of course, this assumes you are creating steel that has the ferrite form. If not, then phosphorus does not do much for your alloy. This is an interesting point to consider. You can have a super-strong, high-alloy steel, and if you mis-work it, heat, shape or otherwise abuse it, you end up with something no better than, or maybe even worse than, the cheaper stuff you could have used. Too much phosphorus potentially makes the mixture brittle.

Silicon, for construction and ordnance needs, is an impurity and is avoided. Where it is used is in the electrical field. There, silicon in steel increases its electrical resistance and improves the ability of magnetic fields to penetrate it. In college, I barely escaped my required electrical engineering classes (theoretical, not practical as in how to wire a house) with my life. So I will leave it to those who are curious to find an electrical engineer and ask him or her how and why this matters.

Now, the creation of alloys is not limited to just blending in a few pinches of this, or a dollop of that. Nosirree. The created mix can then be tortured by means of multiple heat-and-cool cycles, called quenches and anneals, until you have a result that performs the way the end-user desires.

You see, the mix of ingredients is just that, a list of ingredients. Saying "forty-one forty contains four-tenths of a percent of carbon" is like saying your Mom's apple pie "contains two pounds of apples." So what? As the author Robert Heinlein pointed out, it takes a cook to make a pie. Your mom bakes a pie and everyone loves it. If you don't have the practice, the same ingredients in your hands may produce an inedible mess. (Thank you, Bob.)

Here in the States, we don't have many, if any, ore mills producing steel. We have reclamation or recycling mills. An ore mill takes ore out of the ground and "blows" (by heat) the impurities out of it. They can then produce alloys, and many do, but the alloying they do is basic. If you need a couple of thousand tons of basic 1050 steel, you price it, and the combination of steel and shipping costs determines who you buy from. Mostly likely you'll buy it in large volume and with low alloying from an ore mill. If you need a hundred tons of 4140, you'll get it from a recycling mill, and one nearby.

The recycling mill does the same thing an ore mill does, but they "blow" the impurities (and in this instance the alloying mix of the scrap steel being recycled constitute the "impurities") out of the raw recycled steel, and then re-alloy it to the mix you need.

Taking alloy steel, which is, if you think about it, an "ore" that is 95-98% pure, and re-working it to service customers here in the States, is a lot cheaper than getting it from overseas. Of course that makes the margins on the steel mills in China, India and elsewhere even smaller. Too bad for them, operating costs and delivered price rules.

CASTING, FORGING AND MACHINING STEEL ALLOYS

You've got an alloy you like, how do you turn it into a part? Well, the traditional way is to take a lump of steel and use cutting tools to carve the part out of it. It wasn't long before forging was used to cover a lot of the preliminary steps. Let's step back and consider making a knife or a sword. You

Once the extrusions go into the CNC machine, they spend as much time as needed to come out as free-slot handguards. That is to say, they will be, after deburring, cleaning, anodizing and sealing.

Before and after machining, the receiver is inspected and gauged. Here a go/no-go hole gauge is used to make sure the hammer pin holes have been reamed to the correct diameter.

can take a big lump of iron or steel and file, grind and cut until it is the shape you want. That leaves a lot of filings on the floor. So instead you heat it up and whang on it with a hammer until it is more-or-less the shape you want. Then you final-cut it to the desired shape.

Interestingly, they found back in the olden days that the finished product of the second method was superior to the all-cut one. This comes about by one of two methods or a combination of them. One is that the metal being worked undergoes a strain-inducing process called work-hardening. Done to extreme, it results in brittle, weaker metal. But done just enough, it makes a stronger product. Also, the heating and hammering changes the crystal sizes, and the result is a stronger part. The hammering also worked some of the impurities out of the metal, but back then knowledge of steel was minimal, and a closely held secret at that.

Cast steel used to be held in low regard. It was used in a lot of much larger parts because casting steel was a relatively easy way to get a semi-finished part. All that changed with Bill Ruger, who adopted the lost-wax

casting process for firearms. The original cast-steel method is a process called sand-casting. There, a box of sand and binder is used to make an impression of the object. You use two boxes, one for each half of the part. Then, the two halves are clamped together, and molten metal was poured in. Once it was cooled, the sand could be broken away, and the part could then be sent for finish machining.

In the automotive industry, this process was used to make cast-iron engine blocks by the millions. When a lot of extra machining is saved, even if there's still a lot to be done, the process works fine.

In the lost-wax process, a wax model is dipped into a ceramic slurry in multiple passes. The slurry builds up a shell around the wax. The shells are assembled in a "tree" and once it is ready, the ceramic-coated tree is fired. The firing hardens the ceramic and also melts the wax out. Once the wax is gone and the ceramic is fully heated, molten metal is poured in.

When cooled, the resulting parts need a minimum of machining to be finished.

On your AR, the front sight A-post can be a forging, a casting or a billet-cut part. It is perhaps the only part on your rifle that could have arrived there via the casting process.

And all this talk of steel doesn't even get into the surface treatments that an alloy may be subjected to, in the final steps of it being turned into a useful part.

Steel can be roughly shaped in the first steps of its process by three methods: forging, casting, and rolled or billet.

Forging is simple: a piece of stock (usually a bar, but it can be a plate) is heated to a specific temperature. It is then placed in the jaws of a forge and the multi-ton forge slams the two halves of the dies together, rough-shaping the bar into the part. Forging is good in that it works the steel, it creates a grain structure to the crystal alignment, and it makes for a tougher part. The bad part is that forging is a specialized endeavor. It requires a dedicated setup, with machines that are big, heavy, noisy and expensive to operate. And, it depends on skilled operators, and the process produces parts that are difficult to fixture.

Fixturing is where the part is held for machining. The result of a forging process is a part with a very rough exterior surface. If you do not plan how to hold the part after forging, it may be impossible to actually make a part from said forgings.

Casting can be rough, like a mold made from sand, or it can be precise, like that of the lost-wax process. Because it does not produce a rough part that requires large amounts to be machined away, castings can be made from a much tougher alloy. It too requires a large capital investment and trained operators.

Rolled or billet is a process that will be familiar if you have watched any documentary about the industrial process. Here, hot but not molten steel is formed into big bars at the mill (multiple tons of steel, many feet long and even in diameter) and then the big old bar of steel is passed through sets of rollers. This happens while it is still hot, and it's re-heated if needed to keep it hot enough to be plastic.

The rolling does a lot of what forging does, but on a much larger piece. From the rollers, the steel billet (the original term, not the sizes used in making gun parts) can then be shaped even more. It can be rolled into plates, it can be turned into rolls of sheet steel, it can be extruded into railroad rails.

The most amazing process was one my brother used to do, at the plant he ran. That plant made seamless steel oil pipeline. They'd take a piece of steel the size of a 55-gallon drum, heat it to orange,

If designed for it from the start, even pistols can be billet-cut. Here we have two steps in the making. The piece on the right was cut from a slab of aluminum, and the one on the left is the result of time in the CNC machining center.

then punch a hole down its center. From there, they'd extrude it into the full 40-foot length of pipe, bring it to final dimensions, and then stack it to cool.

Your AR barrels will be forged or rolled. Your bolts and carriers can be rolled or cast. The process used will depend on a lot of variables much later in the process, such as the strength needed and the cost limits. Also, the amount and type of machining done later, as well as the surface finishes they may receive, can determine what the maker asks for form the mill.

LIGHT AND HANDY: ALUMINUM

Aluminum is the third most abundant element in or on the planet. (And in case you were wondering, first and second are oxygen and silicon.) Why then, is it not everywhere? Why can't you just haul chunks of aluminum (aside from the discarded soft-drink cans you find) out of the dirt in your back yard? Because it is so reactive that it has all been bound into mineral combinations with other elements long ago. And that reaction creates a bond so strong that it is nearly impossible for other reactions to free it. Basically, in nature, aluminum oxidizing and reacting to create various minerals is a one-way street. It is found in over 250 minerals, the primary ore-bearing type is known as bauxite.

Soft, durable, lightweight, malleable, aluminum has a lot of uses in a modern society. It takes, however, a modern society to produce it in any useful amounts. Bauxite so closely holds aluminum in its bosom that it takes a huge effort to separate the metal from the ore. OK, you've read about steel. To make iron from ore, you heat up the ore, blow air or oxygen through it, and skim off the slag. Then pour off the iron.

Compared to aluminum, you could train your pet retriever to make steel. The various processes (and there are a bunch of them) use combinations of, or all of the big three; heat, electricity and chemical reactions. Depending on the process in use, the price of making aluminum in electricity alone can be more than a quarter of the finished cost. So ferocious was the cost of making aluminum that Napoleon III was rumored to have an aluminum dinner set, and left the

platinum, gold and silver dinnerware for his guests. And as a result it was pretty easy to tell where you were in the pecking order of the Second Empire court. Platinum? In good. Gold? Need to work on your skills. Silver? Keep an eye over your shoulder, unless your courtier skills get a major upgrade, you are going to be gone with the arrival of the next batch of aggressive social-climbing rivals. As amusing as the tale is, no one really knows for sure, but it gives you an idea of how fabulously expensive it was to make metallic aluminum before the 20th century.

Aluminum, in its pure metallic state, is not useable as a metal to build things. It is too soft and too easily corroded. In a manner of speaking, we alloy steel to improve its mechanical properties. We alloy aluminum not just to improve its mechanical properties, but also to keep it from corroding so quickly it won't stand up to use.

A brief aside to give you an idea of how much metals can differ in this regard. Aluminum will corrode and disintegrate if you aren't careful. In fact, the alloy used in the AR-15 was changed early on when they found that the peculiar combination of perspiration and a humid jungle environment caused the alloy then in use to basically melt away. Steel corrodes, but it stands up to a lot of abuse before it gives way. Titanium, on the opposite end, corrodes not at all in the way we think. Oh, the surface oxidizes, but the oxide created is an impenetrable "skin" and the corrosion cannot proceed further. In fact, titanium oxidizes so quickly it is difficult to produce a surface of titanium that isn't oxidized to Ti-oxide color.

As with steel, we can alloy aluminum with a large number of other metals and elements. The two we will be most familiar with here are 6061 (aka "aircraft" aluminum) and 7075. But there are many others. One I recently found out about is 5083, an alloy with a lot more manganese, magnesium and a good dollop of chromium in it. Used in shipbuilding and some applications of naval aircraft, it welds like a dream and has very good corrosion resistance. It isn't heat-treatable, but it does not lose its strength as a result of welding.

But, we should spend our time looking at the common ones in the AR universe.

ALUMINUM ALLOY 6061

6061 is indeed an aircraft alloy, or at least was the most prevalent one back when aircraft manufacture shifted from wood and wire to aluminum. It is alloyed with magnesium and silicon, and it is a precipitation-hardening alloy. While it welds very well, it loses tensile strength at the area of the weld. So, a basic alloy, un heat-treated, would be a 6061, while something that has been heat-treated would be 6061-T6. (The "T6" reflecting the heat-treatment process, and just one of several.)

If you took a part that was formed and heat-treated, then welded on it, the areas around the weld would lose the strength added by the heat-treatment. In the area of the weld, the joined parts would be soft. That's a drawback, but only if you view the world solely through welding goggles.

6061 was developed in the mid-1930s and used in aircraft production. For some of you, the light bulb just went on. "Rivets." Yep, that's why aircraft then (and many now) have such a profusion of rivets. If you were to weld the skin of the aircraft fuselage to its ribcage, or spars, you'd lose tensile strength at the welds. But, if you drill holes through the plates, then rivet them on, you don't lose the strength. (You, of course, have to have good rivets, and well-trained riveters, but that is easy.)

If you're willing to put up with loss of tensile strength, or are willing to heat-treat after you weld, 6061 welds like there's no tomorrow. It's also very amenable to extrusion. Now, a quick up-to-speed on extrusions.

If you take a hot and malleable but not molten piece of metal, and you shove it through a shaped die, the metal flows through, yes, just like a tube of toothpaste. You can extrude a bar, and then machine it to whatever final shape you need. A neat trick in extrusion is to extrude a plate, then in multiple operations curve the plate until it is a pipe, and then allow the heated parts to re-join. Doing that just saved you a whole lot of time and cutter work, instead of boring out a bar to make a tube. 6061 extrudes very well, thank you.

ALUMINUM ALLOY 7075

The alloy you are more likely to have heard as an alloy number is 7075, specifically 7075-T6. Again, the "T6" part of it is the particular heat-treatment process given the aluminum alloy.

7075 is an aluminum alloy with a big helping of zinc in it. The total composition is zinc 5.6 to 6%, magnesium 2-2.5%, and copper 1.2-1.6%, with trace amounts of iron, silicon, titanium, manganese, chromium and others. Some of the trace amounts are there simply because it isn't worth the effort to completely eliminate them from the aluminum-bearing ore, and others are brought in from the various scrap sources. Recycled metals can't all be treated like steel scrap. There is no Bessemer process for recycled aluminum, whereby you can "blow" out the alloying ingredients as slag and produce pure aluminum.

In tensile strength, 7075-T6 rivals that of mild steel. With a tensile strength right around 75,000 PSI, it can be used in a lot of applications where the designer ensures stresses will be under that ceiling. If you need more, you have to jump up to steel, and accept the penalty hit in weight. Such is life.

FORGING AND HEAT-TREATING ALUMINUM

To make uppers and lowers of aluminum and to do it properly, the manufacturer has to do two things: forge the parts and then heat-treat them. So, let's go right into the life history of the upper you are holding in your hands. (I won't ask how you're both reading this and holding an upper.)

The upper arrives at the forge shop in truck-length bars, each four to six inches in diameter. It arrives as 7075-0 alloy, with the proper amounts of each metal in it, but no real heat-treating. All it has is the heat-treatment inadvertently done when the bars were created. In some instances, the mill will heat-soak the bars to relieve stress and remove (anneal) any inadvertent heat-treatment done by the process of heating aluminum and squeezing it out as bars.

The forge shop will then cut them to length. The specific diameter is something

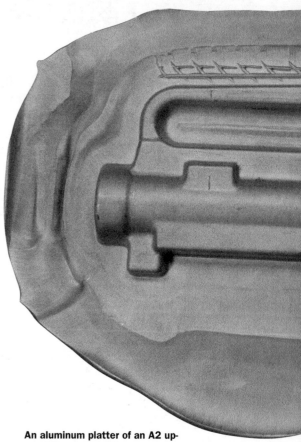

An aluminum platter of an A2 upper. This needs a lot more work before it becomes the upper you'll use in your Service Rifle upper build. But it is clearly an A2 upper.

TOP: The first hole down the magazine well is the access hole for the broach. The broach will ream the magazine well in one pass, an amazing operation to watch.
ABOVE: On the right, the forgings before drill and broach.
On the left, the lower receivers after broaching (and other machining operations).

handled in the order, and done by the mill. The lengths are done by the forge shop, because not all parts need the same lengths. The cut sections are then wheeled to the forge floor. There, a furnace feeds one or more forges. The furnace operator heats each bar to the correct temperature (and for aluminum it isn't all that high a temp), yanks them out when they are done and, in turn, feeds them to the forge. At the forge, the forge operator places the heated blank into the dies and trips the forge switch. The upper half slams down onto the lower half (each half has the 3-D mirror image of the part machined into its face) and the part is shaped. Depending on the particular machine, the alloy used and the part needed, the forge may come down once or several times.

The part, now called a "platter," is hauled to a different furnace. There, it is heat-soaked for the heat-treatment. For the T6 treatment, this involves first heating it up to just under 850 degrees Fahrenheit. It will sit there for a few hours (depending on the part, the specs the job calls for, and the experience of the furnace operators) and then it is shuffled off to a different furnace.

All these big, dirty, hot machines sit near each other so the parts can't cool any more than the short distance allows, and to keep the hot, dirty, noisy work away from the rest of the plant.

In the second furnace the parts will sit for a full day, "aging" at 250 degrees Fahrenheit.

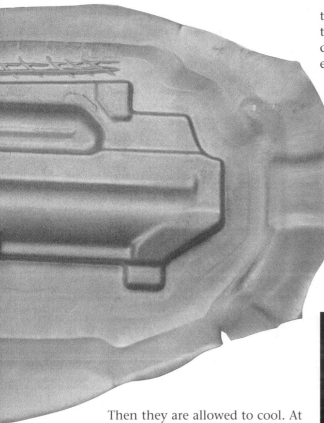

turer to both machine parts and anodize them. As you'll read about in the anodizing chapter, it involves vats of chemicals with electricity pumped into them. This is not something you do in-between your "real" work.

Once the parts come back, they are inspected, graded and then either assembled into rifles (if the machine shop is also the rifle manufacturer) or shipped off to the assembler. The specialized work of CNC machining requires a large capital investment, and to pay it off calls for constant production. It isn't unusual for a manufacturer who machines uppers (and lowers) to use them both in their own assembly, and to sell excess production to other assemblers.

Then they are allowed to cool. At this point your upper looks like an upper caught in an aluminum pancake.

The bin of platters are crated up and shipped off to the machine shop.

There, the first step (if the forge shop didn't already do it) is to use a cookie-cutter-like machine to cut the upper out of the disk of the platter. This is known as "blanking" and, if done well, produces no scrapped parts and a quick production rate. If done badly, it produces scrapped platters, slows production, and costs the machine shop money. Then, an index surface is carefully cut onto the blanked upper. This is what the CNC tombstone will clamp onto, to hold the parts while they are machined.

The CNC machine will whir away for minutes or hours and finally be done. The operator removes the finished uppers, replaces them with new blanks and closes the doors.

ANODIZING ALUMINUM

From here, the uppers get boxed up and sent off to the anodizing shop. Like forging, anodizing is a specialized operation, and it is almost unheard of for an AR manufac-

Steel vs. Aluminum

The two metals need to be processed at such differing temperatures that it would be rare for a forge shop to do both. Even if they did both, they would be doing them on different machines. Steel needs to be forged when it is cherry to salmon in temperature, or 1175 to 1550 degrees Fahrenheit. (Yes, they do use those descriptors as the color check. Honest.) Aluminum is a puddle at 1220 F, so clearly you won't be forging it at those temps. Aluminum is forged in the 600 to 800 degrees F range.

Also, the amount of force used by the forges is different. The multi-ton press used to hammer the cherry-red piece of steel into shape would splatter hot aluminum across the shop, were the operator to hold a hot piece of aluminum in there.

The force used, the space for the dies, and time spent hammering or swaging, differ between the two metals, and the whole forging process is so specialized that it is done by specialty shops. Your AR maker does not forge uppers and lowers. They order forgings form the forge shop, who orders in 7075, heats and forges it, and then blanks it or not according to the contract.

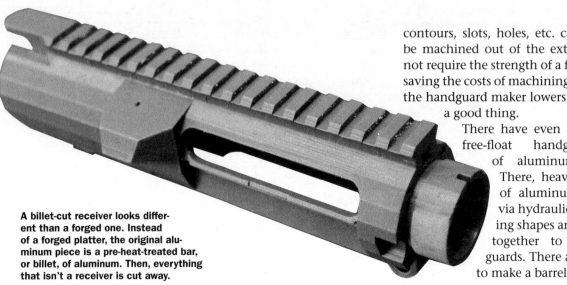

A billet-cut receiver looks different than a forged one. Instead of a forged platter, the original aluminum piece is a pre-heat-treated bar, or billet, of aluminum. Then, everything that isn't a receiver is cut away.

contours, slots, holes, etc. can more easily be machined out of the extrusion. It does not require the strength of a forging. And by saving the costs of machining from forgings, the handguard maker lowers costs, which is a good thing.

There have even been first-class free-float handguards made of aluminum stampings. There, heavy-gauge sheets of aluminum are pressed via hydraulics into interesting shapes and then welded together to create handguards. There are lots of ways to make a barrel float.

So, you may have ABC Corp, an AR manufacturer, also making uppers that they sell to DEF Co. that also assembles rifles, as well as selling uppers to GHI Industries, a wholesaler that sells to stores that sold you your bare upper.

That is pretty much the way a modern, industrial economy works, and firearms are no different. Now, your current-generation iPhone didn't get built that way, because Apple controlled the entire chain. But your non-Apple phone may well have been built that way. Apple in this is rare, as most industries do not have that level of vertical integration.

One question some will have is, why are my receivers made of 7075, and my free-float handguards made of 6061? The answers: cost and expected need of durability. The receivers are subjected to a lot more stress than the handguards. They have to withstand the heat of the gases, the cycling of the parts, and the recoil generated by shooting. 7075 is stronger than 6061, but also it is amenable to forging, which makes the receivers stronger still. Forgings need a lot of machining, but the external surfaces can be left rough, the forge die surface, and the rest machined.

Just for a moment, try to imagine machining a free-float handguard from a forging. You have an aluminum cylinder as long as your forearm, and you are going to machine out the middle of it? I think not. One of the useful attributes of 6061 is that is it amenable to extrusion.

A free-float handguard can be extruded as a hollow cylinder, and then the various rails,

BILLET?

OK, the mil-spec receivers are machined from forgings, but you will read of uppers and lowers that have been "machined from billet" or are "billet receivers." What does that mean?

Remember back in the section on steel, where I discussed hot-rolled steel? Where the steel is run between rollers to make a sort-of forged commodity, but one that is in a blank shape?

Well, they can make aluminum the same way. In this context, what they are doing is not starting with forgings to make uppers and lowers. Instead, they have big plates of 7075 aluminum which have already been heat-treated to the T6 standard.

The plates are cut into suitable sizes (automated band saws, water jets, the process is fast and does not involve human hands in the way) and then each chunk of aluminum is clamped into a CNC machining station. The fixture to do this (for all CNC machining) is called a "tombstone."

Each tombstone can hold many pieces, depending on the machine and the part size. The tombstones run on rollers into and out of the machine, and even from one machine to another.

You can recognize a billet upper and lower by the contours, which do not correspond to those of a forging. Some billet makers stay as close to mil-spec contours as they can, others feel free to do what they think is strongest, coolest or just eye-catching.

Billet is good. Done properly, billet is at

Plastic/polymers can be made in colors, molded into intricate shapes, and withstand uses and environments that metals cannot. But for all that, they still remain....plastics.

least as strong and perhaps even stronger than forgings. What it isn't, is mil-spec, so if you are building a type-specific or a period-correct AR, a billet anything might be off the table as far as being correct goes. Strong, yes, Do the job, certainly. But a correct [fill in the blank], no way.

CASTING ALUMINUM???

No aluminum part on an AR should be made from a casting. Back in the 1980s, there was a company that made cast lowers, but they were viewed with suspicion. Aluminum is so easy to machine that casting offers no advantage, unless your company is set up to cast and has no machining capacity. That is a non-existent subset these days, so unless you come across a cast lower you can acquire for free, don't bother.

And even then, don't depend on it for anything but the knowledge of building on it and using it until it breaks or otherwise lets you down.

Vertical Integration

This is a term of economics used to describe the control of materials and processes in a corporate structure. Let's compare two paper makers.

Company A buys timber from a forestry company, has a railroad ship it to their plant, makes paper, and then sells the paper to a wholesaler or retailer.

Company B owns their own forests. They cut the trees and have the timber shipped to their plant. There, it is made into paper and distributed to their own warehouses and retail stores.

Company B is said to be more vertically integrated than A. And, if they also happen to own the railroad, would be completely vertical. A power company that owns coal mines, a railroad and power plant is a similar setup.

Vertical integration is good in that it allows the company to shift costs (in the form of net profits) among the subsidiaries, to end up with a lower-cost product, a profit, and lower taxes.

It is bad in that it can easily lead to a monopoly situation, or a cartel, where a few vertically integrated companies can control a product and thus a market. For a good example of that, look at diamonds. Diamonds, compared to many other products, are as common as dirt. But the majority of diamond production is so closely held that the price is essentially what the producers say it is.

Compared to diamonds, the production of AR-15s is complete and utter chaos. That's why a top-grade AR-15 will cost you less than a medium-good engagement ring.

On top, a forged lower receiver meets all the specs for mil-spec except for not being select-fire. (This particular one is a NoDak spug M16A1 clone.) Below that is a billet-cut receiver, with 21st-century updates, like sling swivel sockets and ambi controls, from San Tan.

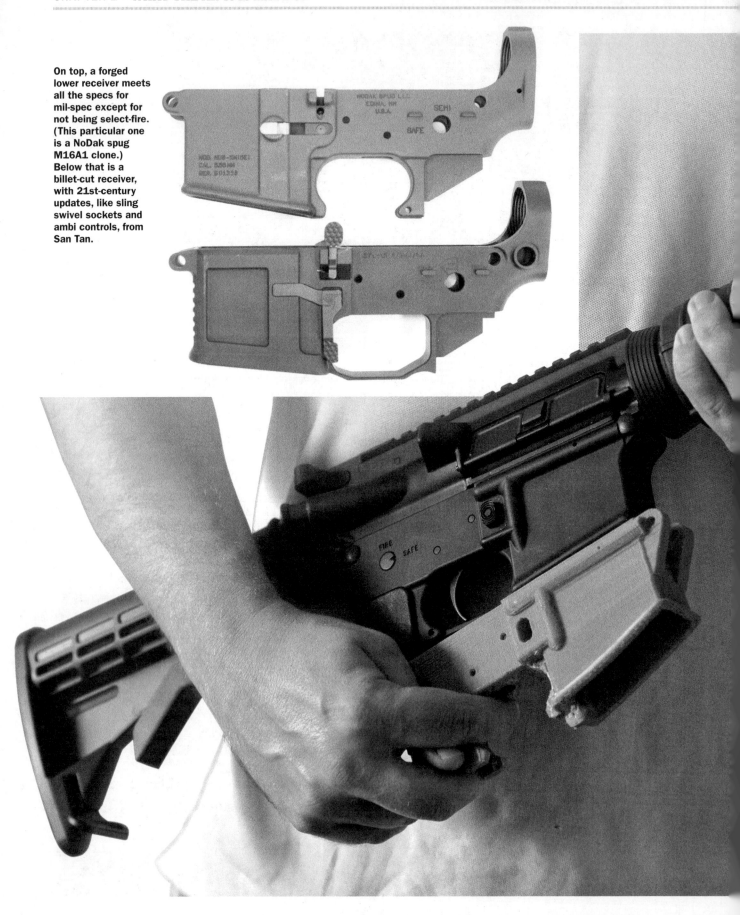

PLASTIC

Plastic. We all know what it is, right? Well, no we don't.

The older generation might still have a recollection of plastic as a fragile, cheap, and easy to mar and break. Younger readers are familiar with plastic as a common substance. Indeed, ubiquitous. Everywhere you go, there is plastic. Or polymer. Or resin, or fill in the blank because it is now a multi-faceted commodity. What happened? Chemists have done to synthetics what was done with steel a generation ago.

It is now possible to formulate a synthetic to withstand heat or acid or stress, and often even two or all three of those. It can be mixed with binders (think: rebar in concrete) and be made in many colors.

The big advantage of synthetics is that they can be molded. Once mixed or heated to a working state, the material can be squirted into molds, then removed once cured or cooled. Molding allows for shapes that could not be economically machined or otherwise crafted.

Synthetics are not perfect. Even those formulated to shrug off solvents, cleaning agents and the environment will eventually lose flexibility or color or strength.

The good news is that they are so low in cost that they are easily replaced.

The exemplar here is the PMag, made by Magpul. Once they worked out the bugs (there was a small hiccup some years ago, when they found that the warehouse-sized airing building wasn't big enough, and mag bodies were not curing properly), Magpul was able to make magazines so inexpensively that the aluminum-body magazine makers had to up their game.

We are now in a golden age of AR magazines, where you can buy as many as you want (offer not valid in some states, check your local laws) for ten dollars each. And when they give up or are damaged in training or use, they are so inexpensive that no one even thinks of stripping the parts out of them. Honest, that was what we did in the old days. If a mag busted, we'd strip out the follower, spring and baseplate, against future need. Now? Don't waste my time.

Buy what looks good, feels good, works or is just cool. Synthetics are the product of today, and until we have sucked the last barrel of oil out of the ground (most synthetics are petrochemical end products) they will be cheap, common and reliable. ∎

An AR-15 rifle with a lower receiver made of ABS (Acrylonitrile Butadiene Styrene) plastic.

CHAPTER 2
Barrels

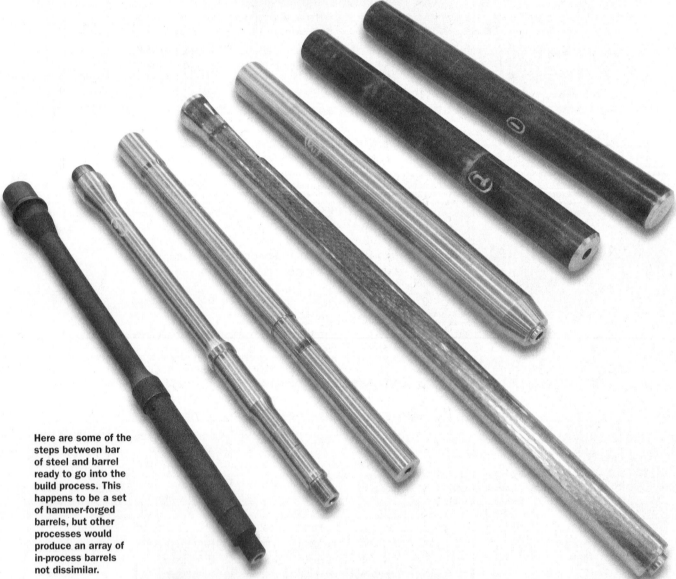

Here are some of the steps between bar of steel and barrel ready to go into the build process. This happens to be a set of hammer-forged barrels, but other processes would produce an array of in-process barrels not dissimilar.

A barrel is simple, really. You take a steel rod and drill a hole the length of it. Then, you create spiral grooves the length of that hole. Finally, you thread one end of it so you can attach it to the rifle receiver, ream a chamber and screw it into the receiver. *Voila*, a rifle barrel. Of course if you want a good rifle barrel, you have to attend to a few details. Let's get started.

STEEL

The steel has to be hard enough to produce a barrel that will stand up to use in the field. It can't bend from a small impact, it mustn't wear out quickly, it should not collect bullet residue (called fouling). If it is too expensive, the maker will go broke from not selling any. We covered steel in the steel chapter, so you should be up to

Drilled, reamed and polished-bore barrel blanks, ready to be fed into the barrel-making machinery.

speed on this aspect.

But, what steel? The choices here are four: stainless, carbon steel, carbon steel with chrome plating, and carbon steel with a Melonite surface treatment. We'll get into that choice once we cover barrel making.

BARREL CRAFTING

Now for the details, the nitty gritty.

First, the steel is ordered and checked, and a test barrel is made. The barrel-maker takes one bar of the shipment and makes a barrel. There may be enough steel on hand to make barrels for a year or two (and if so, this maker's accountant has a few choice words), but deliveries must be checked when they arrive. Otherwise, if you accept a bad batch of steel and don't get around to doing anything with it for a long time, the mill will tell you "too bad."

So you make a barrel. Let's walk with that barrel.

DRILLING

First, you deep-drill the steel rod. Typically, barrel steel comes long enough that a "blank" can be made as long as any needed barrel, even with the ends trimmed off, as with a 30-36" barrel blank. This also has the advantage of producing more than one barrel in special cases. So, into the drilling machine and the drill bit drills half-way through. Then the rod is reversed and the other half is driled.

Why? Even the best equipment can't stay on dead center, so the blank is drilled halfway from each end, and under-sized, so they meet in the middle.

The drilling machine is interesting. The drill bit is stationary and the rod is turned against the drill bit. The drill bit has a hole through it, and through that hole the machine pumps cutting lubricant. The lube cools the blank, flushes the chips out, and keeps the bit from chattering.

Once the hole is all the way through, the blank then gets reamed. The reamer cuts the hole the next step larger, straightens the connection between the two end-drilled holes, and smoothes the surface that was left a bit rough by the drill.

Depending on the equipment used, the production rate the shop wishes to keep, and the quality of the barrels they want to produce, the drilling and reaming can be done in three to ten steps.

Along the way, the blanks are inspected for straightness, bore surface smoothness and bore diameter. Whatever has to be corrected is corrected. If too many blanks need correction, the shop foreman will have a talk with that machine operator and find out what is going on.

The last step of this stage is called honing, and it is basically a polishing process.

Now the blank is ready to be rifled. There are five methods of creating a rifled bore: cut rifling, broaching, button, hammer-forge and EDM.

CUT RIFLING

This is the oldest method, and one still used by some barrel-makers. Imagine a large-diameter cylinder, four feet long, with spiral grooves cut into its exterior. This is what a barrel-maker in the black powder days would use as his guide. The cutting arm would track in the grooves, the cutting tip would follow, and the path would cut a groove in the barrel. That's the outside.

Inside there would be a single cutting tool, called a hook. The hook would scrape or cut a groove of perhaps a ten-thousandth to a thousandth of an inch on the inside of the drilled, reamed and honed barrel. The operator would draw the cutter down the bore and cut the groove. At the end he'd clean the hook, swab the bore, run the cutting arm back down the bore to the start, and adjust the hook for another pass. Once he had cut deeply enough, he'd switch to

Here you can see the guide slot for a cut-rifling machine. The slot determines the twist rate, not the cutting tool.

For all rifling, you use a hydraulic machine such as this one. The force needed to cut or swage steel is great, and you won't be doing it with man-hauled levers.

The button on the end of its rod, ready to begin its plunge down the bore of the barrel blank.

the next groove. Each groove took many passes to cut to full depth.

The last bit of work was to use the cutter on the full groove depth on each groove in turn, so they were certain to have been cut all to the same depth. The limiting factor here is the speed with which the operator can accurately adjust the hook to cut the next pass. Too shallow a cut and he's spending forever and a day on each barrel. Too deep a cut and he creates chatter and tool-marks, and perhaps even breaks the hook. He certainly dulls it faster.

This is fussy, detail-oriented, almost hand-work craftsmanship, and it can produce barrels of brilliant quality and accuracy. But it does so at the rate of X barrels per week.

To change twist, you change the cutter guide. The cutter itself doesn't create twist, the guide it follows does.

BROACHED

Let's take our hook cutter and multiply it. Instead of one hook, we have a hook for each groove. Four grooves, four hooks. Five, six, and so-on. And then, behind each hook we have another hook. Heck, let's make it half-a-dozen hooks, each in turn half a thousandth or so "taller" (larger in cutting diameter) than the one before it. And we angle them so their orientation is such that they create a spiral track. This creates a steel Christmas-tree looking tool called a broach. Well, a very, very, slender Christmas tree,

These are pistol-bore broaches. Those for rifles won't look much different, just longer.

since the distance from the bottom of the grooves to the top of the lands will be five-thousandths of an inch. If you can see that in a broach, you have far better eyesight than the rest of us.

What that means is that the first hook in the broach cuts a slot that is 0.219" in the 0.219" hole down the barrel. Each hook after that one in the broach cuts the groove a bit deeper, with the last one cutting the groove to 0.224" depth.

To do this we attach the broach to a powerful hydraulic machine, with the smallest-diameter hooks pointed towards the barrel blank it will soon enter. We flood the drilled, reamed and honed blank with cutting oil, and pull the broach through the barrel blank. In one pass, we create a rifled barrel.

Our production has just jumped from X barrels per week, to X barrels per hour. The limiting factor here is how many drilling, reaming and honing machines you have spitting out ready-to-rifle blanks to feed the voracious broaching machine.

This is not without costs. First of all, the broach itself is quite expensive. It has to be made by a specialty shop, to the utmost precision (a bad-quality broach doesn't just make crappy barrels, it ruins good blanks). It only lasts so long, and once it is worn too much it is scrap. As it wears it has to be periodically re-sharpened. Sharpening it changes the dimensions it cuts. Sharpen a broach too many times and your barrels will have wandered out of the allowed dimensions for that caliber.

Broaches are delicate. Yes, they are hardened steel, but drop one and it won't make barrels that are any good, any more.

And you need a new broach for each twist rate. The broach makes the twist, not the hydraulic machine.

BUTTON

Now let's take a different tack. Instead of removing metal by cutting it out, let's just squish it around until we have what we want. Here we displace metal. Instead of a tree-like broach, we make an egg-shaped tool called a "button." This button has the shape of the rifling, in reverse, on its exterior. We use the really strong hydraulic

press to push or pull the button through the blank. Since it will be swaging steel, the button has to be extraordinarily hard and smooth.

The high spots on the button push the steel out of the way, and it moves to fill the low spots on the button, thus creating the lands and grooves in the rifling.

Now, this requires a few things. First, the drilled, reamed and honed hole through the

bore has to be a slightly different diameter than it would be for a cut-rifle barrel. After all, we aren't removing any steel, so we have to account for what we move, and have a place to accept it, or we run into a problem. If the bore is reamed too large, we won't move enough steel to fill the gaps and we'll have shallow grooves and short lands.

If the bore is too small, the hydraulic machine may not be able to push or pull the button through. It will be moving too much metal, and that metal won't have a place to go. The machine stalls, or the button breaks, or the rod bends (if being pushed), or the button comes off (if being pulled) and makes a mess of things.

The button method, despite the need for a particular inner diameter, offers a number of advantages. First, it is fast. As quickly as the operator can pull the rifled blank out,

This is a hammer-forging barrel machine. Well, it's the end the barrels go into and come out of. The rest is another twenty feet behind what you can see.

insert a new smooth blank, hose it with lube and get the button aligned, he can punch the start button on the hydraulic ram to rifle another barrel blank. The button also smoothes the bore. The shaped steel is as smooth as the friction between the button and steel allows, and with the right lube and a properly honed smoothbore, the resulting rifled barrel is very smooth.

Since the button is swaging steel, wear on the button is not the same as wear on a broach. Broaches dull, and when they dull they cut less efficiently, and that leads to toolmarks and improper dimensions. The button wears through friction, and with precision measuring instruments the wear can be tracked and the button replaced when it gets to the allowed limit on dimensions.

Button-rifling a barrel blank also work-hardens the surface of the bore. How much it does so depends on the exact alloy and crystalline structure of the steel being worked.

The drawback to the button method is that it depends on proper steel alloys. Since you are swaging steel, you have to use alloys that react well to swaging. Also, you are limited in the shape of the lands you create. Since you are swaging steel, a shape that won't/can't be fully filled by the button is a poor choice. But, we have plenty of designs that work just fine with buttons, and just fine as rifled tubes, so that is a problem more theoretical than real.

HAMMER-FORGING

In this method, instead of cutting or swaging grooves, how about we hammer grooves? The hammer-forging method is really quite simple. You take a reamed and honed steel tube. You stuff a rod down the center, called a mandrel, which is shaped exactly like the rifling, only in reverse. Or, the rifling and the chamber. You then put the tube with mandrel in it into a hydraulic machine, and opposing hammers bang down on the tube with so much force they squeeze the steel down around the mandrel, forcing the interior into the shape of the mandrel's exterior.

As you can imagine, this is quite noisy. I first saw one in action in the Sako plant

in Riihimaki, Finland. Since then, I've seen them in a bunch of other places, and the basics are the same.

Treated with enough force, steel becomes plastic, if not quite fluid. So the mandrel, which is shaped exactly like the rifling you want the barrel-to-be to have, is the shape the steel is hammered down to.

The peculiarities of this method are interesting, First, the steel doesn't stick to

These are blanks ready to be hammered. They are precision-made, inside and out, and polished to the point that when the hammering is done, so is the rest of the barrel-forming work. Unless they want to lap them, of course.

the mandrel for the simple reason that it springs back a tiny amount, never coming to the exact dimension of the mandrel. So if you use this method, you have to know the amount of spring-back for the alloy you are using, and the thickness of the tube. Otherwise, the bore of your barrel will not be the dimensions you expect/intend.

Mandrels are fabulously expensive. They have to be made of special alloys and are very hard. Drop one and it is ruined. It has to be absolutely perfect in every dimension, because that is what the barrel will be. An error in fabricating a mandrel will be an error introduced into every barrel that mandrel makes. The expense is offset by the very low wear rate of mandrels.

The barrel that comes out will be longer than the blank that went in. So the barrel company has to be exact in the blank dimensions, both interior and exterior. The barrel will also be work-hardened as a result of the forging, and this too has to be accounted for in the completion. Use the wrong alloy or the wrong feed rate and you ruin blanks, and maybe even damage the machine.

Hammer-forged barrels come out of the machine with a delicate spiral pattern on the outside. For aesthetic reasons, many a company will lathe-turn or centerless grind the exterior to present the expected smooth surface. Removing steel from a hammer-forged barrel causes it to "spring" out a bit. Think about it; the barrel is essentially a compressed tube of steel. If you lathe-turn it or grind it, you remove some of the compression, and that barrel will expand a bit as a result. That makes the interior larger. So the barrel-maker may have to have calculate an offset, the amount they have to make the barrel a bit under-sized on the inside, so it will expand when turned and polished and end up at the right size.

Luckily, this isn't rocket science. A barrel-maker can produce test barrels and see what they get, then adjust to make it perfect.

EDM

You probably have heard of EDM, electrical-discharge machining. Those who know it, bear with me.

Take an electrode and place it near an object made of a conducting material. Pump a very large electrical charge into the electrode, and thus complete the circuit with the object. When the electrode is moved close enough to the object, electricity will jump the gap. The electrical flow will erode the object, and the charge will stop jumping when the erosion reaches the maximum distance it can jump.

It does this without heating the part, and without damaging its heat-treatment or the adhesion of parts attached to it.

If you shape the electrode and move it in concert with the erosion rate, you can EDM a hole or slot through a part, without otherwise changing it. This is the process

Here we have barrels out of the hammering machine. They will require lathe-turning to profile them, and to thread the chamber end for the barrel extension, but a lot of the difficult, expensive work has already been done.

developed by Larry Kelly, who founded Mag-na-Port. He developed it for machining rocket nozzles for NASA. He used it on firearms to put in ports to divert gases and reduce recoil.

For EDM rifling, instead of a port-shaped electrode, construct a non-conducting rod with electrodes on the outside, sort of like bolt heads. Now press this through the reamed and honed bore, using the electrode "caps" to erode the grooves for your rifling.

Voila, a rifled barrel.

FINISHING THE BARREL

At this point you have a rifled tube. Now what? The barrel-maker might, if they do nothing but make rifled tubes (aka barrel blanks), ship them to their customers –

manufacturers or custom gunsmiths. The barrel-making division of a manufacturer (some make their own barrels, others buy barrels from barrel-makers) sends the barrel blanks off to the finishing line that will profile, thread, chamber and install them in the company's product.

Some barrel-makers lap the barrels after they have been rifled. This process is a bit more involved, and requires experience and a delicate touch. The method is to stick a rod down the bore to a certain depth (each barrel-maker has their own details), and then pour molten lead into the bore. The lead cools and grips the rod. As it cools, it shrinks a small amount away from the surface of the bore. The lead part – the "slug" – is pulled partway out of the bore and lapping compound is smeared onto the exposed portion. Then, the slug

The best work, and the most accurate, is done when the chamber is hammered along with the bore. This absolutely ensures axial alignment of the two.

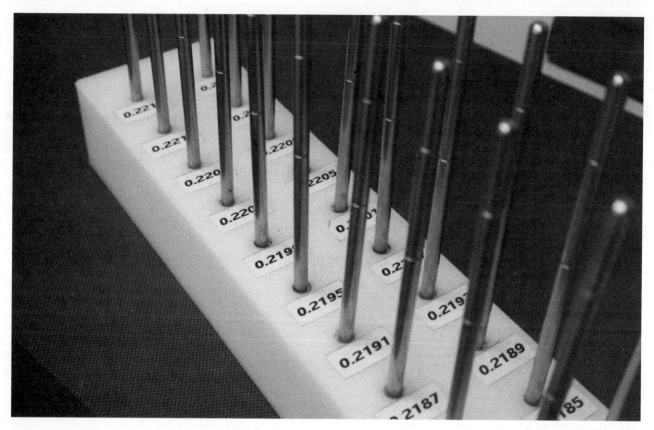

A good barrel-maker leaves nothing to chance. This set of gauges checks the diameter of the deep-drilled barrel blank. The operator or supervisor will use this set on a random barrel blank to ensure things are within the dimensions required.

is simply (as if this process could be called "simple") cycled back and forth. The lapping compound polishes the surface of the bore, grinding down the toolmarks left by the manufacturing steps up to that point.

A custom barrel installed in an expensive rifle meant for accuracy will often have a lapped barrel. Some barrel-makers lap every barrel they make, as it is part of their process and their reputation for premium barrels.

It should be obvious that, if you are going to lap a barrel (this is analogous to sanding a part before painting), you must account for the metal removed when you are boring and rifling the barrel blank. If you do not, you may end up with a bore that is oversized. An exaggeration would be to bore a barrel to 0.219" land and .224" groove diameter, and then lap it to 0.220" and 0.225" respectively. No-one laps a full thousandth off the surface, but making a bore to the perfect dimension and then lapping a bit more is counter-productive.

WHAT KIND?

Stainless or carbon? And plated or something else? The decision tree has one first branch: must you go mil-spec or not? If you do, there is only one choice, and that is a chrome-lined barrel with a twist of 1/7 (unless you are building retro, then it is a twist of 1/12).

And there the choice is not of need, desire or use, but to be technically correct.

For everything else, the choices are stainless, plain old carbon steel, or something new, a carbon steel given a Melonite treatment. Stainless was for a long time the "best" choice because it was "more accurate" and of course, stainless. The long-range shooters have found that stainless might be a bit less accurate than plain old carbon steel, and maybe a bit less rugged. But, the differences matter only to those who fight for the last few points in a match.

The last, a Melonite treatment, is a modern case-hardening process that makes the surface harder and also more corrosion-resistant. It is so hard that you cannot make changes to such a barrel, at least not internally. If it happens to be a bit under headspace or the leade is too short, you cannot ream it to correct it. So, if you are starting with such a barrel as the basis of a build, you'll want to check those dimensions before you do anything else. Only if it has remained un-molested can you return it for an exchange.

And yes, the Melonite treatment is essentially the Glock Tenifer process. Both are trademarks (I didn't bother with the symbol) and both, along with other similar processes, use a cyanide treatment to harden the surface. They differ in the application method (gaseous or liquid) and the temperatures used.

Were I in the position of contesting for the top score at Camp Perry, I'd go with whatever the barrel-maker suggests, and go to the same maker that the other top scorers go to.

For a competition rifle, I'd go with either a stainless or a Melanited barrel, and get it ready to be plugged in, completely profiled, fluted (if that was what I wanted/needed) and chambered, with a matching bolt.

Only if I was a varminter would I opt for a plain carbon-steel barrel, and that would be only because I'd be building two or three identical uppers for my varmint rifle, so I could swap them when the one I was using got too hot. But if the cost of going stainless wasn't that big, I'd go stainless there, also.

YOU CHOSE WRONG?

If you spend any time with any mil-spec maven, you will be told "only 4150 is the correct steel for barrels. Anything else is a waste." Really? I had an opportunity to look over the original blueprints for the AR-15, when it was still an Armalite product. That's right, the real-deal, paper products that were the state of the art, circa 1958. And the steel specified for the barrel? 4140, the same steel that was in use for the M1 Garand, M14, and most other rifles of the time. Eugene Stoner was a machinist, and he chose 4140. So let's not hear about how "4140 is a poor barrel steel, and if you bought it, you wasted your money." That's not what Stoner was thinking, then.

TWIST RATE & DESIGN

Steven Hawking, in "A Brief History of Time," recounted a conversation he had had with one of the staff of his publisher. Basically, they told him that for each formula he included in his book, he could count on sales being halved. With regrets, he included one equation, even though it promised to decrease sales.

I'd like to think that readers of this book, and those interested in the AR-15, would be made of sterner stuff than the readers who peruse the NYT Times best-seller list, looking for the latest potboiler or historical fantasy. But, I do feel compelled, in all fairness, to tell you, "there be equations ahead."

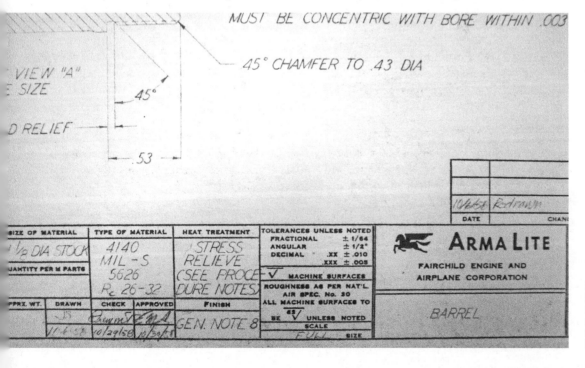

Back in 1958, Eugene Stoner thought 4140 was plenty good enough for his new rifle, the AR-15. It still is.

Rifles have twisted grooves in the bore that spin-stabilize a bullet. Handguns also do, but shotguns do not. Well, most don't, but some shotguns, known as "rifled-bore shotguns" or "rifle-barrel shotguns," do. But they are still, curiously, shotguns.

No one knows how rifling got invented, or who first noticed that muskets with rifled bores shot more accurately than muskets without them. Rifling matters come down to two considerations – twist rate, and land and groove design.

Let's do the design first.

CLASSIC, ENFIELD

What we see as "normal" or classic rifling, Enfield rifling, wasn't always the case. Back when the British were adopting their first magazine-fed rifle (what became the Lee-Enfield), they were still in the throes of the black powder paradigm. No surprise there, the French didn't let on that they had invented useful smokeless powder until the end of the 1880s. The Lee was adopted in 1888, as the Lee-Metford. The cartridge was the .303 Inch, loaded with black powder and a hardened-lead round-nose bullet. (Not surprisingly, British efforts to develop a smokeless powder cartridge took longer than expected, so the rifle was adopted using some of the old technology.)

Hey, in 1888, even using black powder, a ten-shot repeating rifle was hot stuff.

The new British smokeless powder, called Cordite, was ferociously hot and abrasive in burning. Barrels were toasted in short order. Depending on use, a rifleman could shoot-out a barrel in a few thousand rounds. The British Empire was vast and wealthy, but that was not an acceptable cost. The problem? The Metford rifling was too shallow, composed of rounded segments (can anyone say "Glock polygonal rifling?") and eroded quickly. Well, the real problem was the powder, but having found something that worked, the British prudently looked to a barrel rifling design that would stand up to what they had, better, before the spend a couple of decades developing a new powder. (And they never really did. As long as they had the SMLE, it used cordite.)

Enfield rifling, with a cross-section that looks like a gear, was better able to withstand the erosion of the cordite. In 1895 (when the Lee-Metford became the Lee-Enfield), they didn't have the options of a harder steel, or of chrome-plating the bore. Both of those came later as options, and the chrome-lined bore was never adopted by the British, at least not for the SMLE.

The Enfield rifling design is easy to fabricate, withstands a lot of wear and abuse, and is easy to adjust in bore and groove depth, as well as twist rate. Let's use it as the standard, while we explain what those variables are and what they do.

GROOVE DIAMETER

This is the depth of the hole through the barrel after it has been rifled, as measured from the bottom of one rifling groove to the bottom of an opposing groove. We'll assume for the moment an even number of grooves. In-between those grooves are "lands," the raised portion of the rifling which was the bore when it was just a smooth tube.

BORE DIAMETER

That is the original, reamed before rifled diameter of the hole down the barrel. You measure the bore from the top of a land to the top of the opposing land. Let's take as an example the normal .30-06. If the bullet is meant to be .3080" in diameter, then the grooves will be .3080" in total depth. If the lands are each .0040" tall from the grooves, that makes the bore diameter .3000" (.3080", minus the lands on both sides, two at .0040", subtracted gets us .3000").

In a curious reversal of what would seem to be important, the bore diameter, the one we all obsess over, is actually the byproduct of the barrel-making process. The barrel is created by first drilling the steel bar, the barrel-to-be, to the bore diameter. Grossly simplified, it is drilled to .3000" and then the rifling is cut, each groove .0040" deep. So we obsess over groove, but it is the bore diameter that is the beginning, and the dimension from which the rest of the barrel interior comes from.

It is also the descriptor that is often used in European caliber designations. Since the rifle is first bored to a smooth tube, and then rifled, it is obvious (or should be) that we can make the grooves as shallow or as deep as we want. But the original, the bore, will always be what it was made as.

THE BULLET'S FLIGHT

The Bullet's Flight by Franklin Mann is a great book, now much more than a century old, and still useful and important. Mann tested a lot of things, but one that impressed me was the start of the journey. As the bullet leaves the case, it slides forward, propelled by the burning gases. It travels however far forward it takes in order to contact the rifling, a distance called the leade (pronounced "leed"). In Weatherby rifles this is known as freebore.

At the origins of the rifling, the bullet stalls. You see, the powder has not completely burned yet. And the bullet when it hits the rifling stalls because it takes a certain amount of force to engrave the bullet. That is the process of cutting the grooves in the bullet, by the lands, as the bullet engages the rifling. This force, or energy, has to be taken from the velocity of the bullet because there is no other place to steal it from. As I understand it, some very large artillery or naval guns had the grooves for the rifling already machined into the shell. These were done to bands of copper or brass, hoops around the shell called "driving bands." Well, rifle bullets don't have those.

Once the bullet begins to be engraved, it also begins to rotate. Inertia being what it is, the bullet may slip a bit, and a careful observation of a recovered bullet can sometimes show that slippage. The bullet stalling causes a small spike in the pressure. Or sometimes a not-so-small spike. It depends on the bullet toughness, the chamber pressure at that moment, the burn rate of the powder, the distance the bullet "jumps" to the rifling, and sometimes I think even the phase of the moon.

Now, if you think the twist rate of rifling isn't cause for much argument, then you haven't heard an animated discussion of rifling design. And the numbers of lands and grooves? That one could start a fist-fight. The norm, if we can assign that word to any, would be four lands and grooves. That was the number the U.S. Army adopted for the '03 Springfield, and thus all "normal" thirty-caliber rifles made in America since 1903 have had four lands and grooves.

During WWII, we were so short of rifles that the bolt-action Springfield was kept in production, and even had production expanded, to arm as many troops as possible with rifles. To speed up barrel production, the armories tested, and the Ordnance Department approved, two-groove barrels. They proved to be every bit as accurate, for battlefield use, as the four-groove barrels. Post-war there was considerable interest in obtaining surplus two-groove barrels for use in cast-bullet loads.

The number of grooves in more-or-less normal rifling designs is from two to eight. The normal for ARs is six.

RIFLING CROSS-SECTION

The purpose of riling is to grab the bullet and spin it up. Is there a shape that creates less friction, requires less engraving force, or resists wear better? Ask ten gunsmiths and you'll get ten answers. Ask ten accuracy nuts and you'll get eleven answers. The Enfield rifling design works well and stands up well to

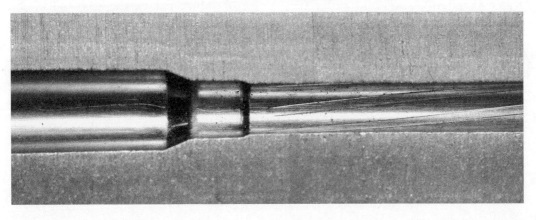

The rifling begins forward of the chamber. The gap the bullet has to jump is called the leade, and it is there to control pressure.

use, but there are others. We'll discuss the big two, as the rest will be proprietary, uncommon, untested or too strange to consider.

5R RIFLING

"5R" rifling differs from Enfield in two regards. First of all, it has five lands and grooves instead of four or six. This puts a land opposite a groove, said to reduce stress on the bullet. Also, on the Enfield rifling the lands have side walls that are square to the bore. In 5R, the lands have side walls that are at less than a ninety-degree angle, and this also is said to reduce stress on the bullet. Another benefit is that, with the corners of the groves not being square, there is less fouling buildup there.

5R rifling is used on premium barrels. I suspect that while the advantages of 5R are there, they are small compared to the OCD barrel-makers' attempts to make perfect barrels. Match winners use 5R barrels because the top-end barrel-makers make barrels with 5R rifling.

In any case, 5R is not mil-spec. And it will usually be more expensive than Enfield-pattern rifling, if only because it comes from a premium barrel-maker.

POLYGONAL RIFLING

Here, instead of a gear-like cross-section, we have lands that are created by rounded intrusions into the bore. The famous one would be HK rifling. It can also be created by making (do this as a 3D mental exercise) a six-sided hole down a cylinder, and then twisting the cylinder. Not so much rifling, as a twisted hexagonal or octagonal bore.

Advantages? Even less stress on the bullet than 5R, and no corners for fouling to collect in. Also, the fabrication of barrels using polygonal rifling makes hammer-forging barrels much easier. There are no corners to form, and thus less hammering is required.

Rifling designs past these are really exotic, rarely found in ARs, and beyond the scope of this book.

TWIST RATE

The landmark study of rifling twist rates was done by Sir Alfred Greenhill, Professor of Mathematics at the Royal Military Academy, which was where Victorian army officers who were to be assigned artillery and engineering careers received their education. He taught from 1876 until retirement in 1908. This formula, the Greenhill formula, calculates the twist rate needed to stabilize a bullet.

Before we dive into it fully, you have to have at least a basic grasp of how this happens. A mass, rotating about its center (any other rotation is useless to us, although mathematically interesting at times) generates angular momentum. That is, it wants (if any inanimate object can be said to want) to continue to so-rotate, and furthermore, it resists external forces and will self-stabilize back to its orientation when the force is removed. You've all had the science lab demo in junior high, where the gyroscope, spinning on the bench top, stays upright (until the spin rate drops too low) and moves aside when you push it, but stays upright and spinning? That's a rifle bullet in flight.

So, Greenhill developed his formula, which is:

$$T = \frac{CxD^2}{L} X \sqrt{\frac{S_g}{10.9}}$$

Where;
T is the twist
C is a constant, in this case, 150
D is the bullet diameter in inches, which is then squared
L is the bullet length, in inches

And then, as the extra, we have:
Sg, the specific gravity of the bullet. For lead-core, copper-jacket bullets, the Sg is 10.9, thus making the second half the square root of one.

The constant Greenhill used, 150, gives us a twist rate in inches, when the other dimensions are also given in inches. The constant works up to velocities of about 2,800 fps, and above that a constant of 180 gives a better result.

Why the differing constant? Simple: rpms, or revolutions (or rotations) per minute. Or in our case, rpcs, as bullet travel never lasts a minute. As the rpms of the bullet increase, gyroscopic stability also increases. Calculating gyroscopic stability, as a mathematical subject, is divided into at least two fields, the static and the dynamic. The dynamic stability equations are upper-level maths. The static, also called the overturning moment coefficient derivative, is less-brain melting, but still far beyond this book. So we'll leave the upper maths to those in the classroom, and consider our real-world needs.

Rpm can be calculated pretty easily. The equation:

$$V \times \frac{12}{T} \times 60 = rpm$$

So, your basic .30-06 with a 150-grain bullet at 2,600 fps produces an rpm of 187,200. Load that same bullet in a .300 Winchester Magnum and boot it out the muzzle at 3,100 fps, and the rpm becomes 223,200. Greenhill had to compensate for the increased rpm.

Professor Sir Alfred made his calculations for artillery. That meant large-diameter, heavy projectiles, with relatively stubby ogives and flat bases. But, it worked, and it worked well enough for my brother, a century and a half later, calculating firing solutions, to hit targets miles from his artillery battery location. The projectiles were stable.

In use, all you have to do is plug the relevant dimensions into your pocket calculator and it spits out the twist rate. Let's give a go, shall we? Let's start with a problem from a generation before Greenhill develops his formula. What is the twist rate for a .50 Hawken rifle, one in use in the West before cartridge firearms came about?

We ignore the specific gravity because it may not be relevant right now. Half-inch bullet length (it is a sphere, after all) squared, times 150, divided by half an inch bullet diameter gives us 75, the twist rate in inches. Hmmm, that's a bit slow, compared to the 48 inches or so that was common. But, over-stabilized is not a problem when hurling spheres at just barely above supersonic velocities.

Let's see if the specific gravity is the problem. The Sg of lead is 11.43. So, the square root of 11.34 divided by 10.9 is….1.02. Two

percent difference, not a concern. Which leads us to believe that at the "slow" twist rate of the muzzleloaders, the bullets were by today's standards over-stabilized.

Let's jump to a slightly more-modern situation. When the U.S. Army adopted the Krag in 1892, and the .30 Army cartridge it was chambered in, the bullet used was a 220-grain FMJ, .308" diameter. Let's call the bullet 1.300 inches long. So, we plug in the numbers, keep the Sg at 10.9 so the second half of the equation disappears, and we get 10.9 inches. The Krag, and all rifles the Army adopted after that, had a twist rate of one-in-ten. That is, a ten-inch twist, close enough for government work, to coin a phrase.

And now, let's jump right to our question – the original M16 bullet and twist rate. A 55-grain FMJ has a length of .728" to .755". So, let's use the longer of the extremes, just to be safe. Plug in the numbers and we get 9.9 inches. Interesting, so the standard government twist rate, as determined by the tests for the M16, is a bit on the slow side.

But wait, some of you have noticed what was missing – the constant. The M-193 bullet left muzzles at 3,100 fps or more. That means the Greenhill Constant should be 180, not 150. Let's re-calculate. Now, we get a twist of 11.98 inches. Spot-on.

But we can do more.

One of the beauties of symbolic logic, in this case, mathematics, is that as long as you follow the rules, you can move the parts around to structure the equation any way you want. That's the process by which Einstein came up with his breakthrough:

$$E = MC^2$$

He simply kept cranking the changes that mathematics permitted into the equations he knew to be correct, until he came up with one that took his breath away. Once he devised it, it was up to mathematicians and physicists around the world to prove him wrong. No voting, no "consensus," just here it is, prove me wrong or sit down and pour yourself a big, steaming mug of "shut the heck up." And I don't mean to discount his work, by phrasing it as "he just kept cranking" because that's what mathematicians do, they just keep trying all the variations.

So, we use that aspect of the symbolic logic we call mathematics, and instead of making the twist rate the results of the equation, and a constant, we turn it into one of the variables. Instead, we use the constant as the variable. That is, we want the equation to read so the end result is always 150. (Or, in the case of a cartridge over 2,800 fps, 180.)

To do this, we shift things around. Originally, we have:

$$T = \frac{CxD^2}{L}$$

So we multiply both sides by length, and thus negate the length on the right side of the equation.

$$LxT = CxD^2$$

Next, we divide both sides by the square of the diameter, negating diameter squared on the right:

$$\frac{LxT}{D^2} = C$$

We flip it, so our result is on the left, and we have:

$$C = \frac{LxT}{D^2}$$

That is, the Greenhill constant is the result of the bullet length, times the twist rate being used or considered, and that sum divided by the square of the bullet diameter. I'm going to be bold here, and name yet another technical aspect of firearms after myself, and do the following.

I'm going to divide the regular Greenhill constant by the results of the above formula, and call the resulting ratio the Sweeney Stability Ratio, or SSR, technical symbol of $\mathcal{M}$, or capital mu, the Greek letter used for coefficient of friction.

$$M = \frac{C_g}{C_c}$$

Where Cg is the Greenhill Constant, and Cc is the calculated constant, by our above equation.

Why? Just because the thought of the friction between the desired/appropriate spin rate, and the actual one existing in the barrel, is amusing.

So, if the twist rate of a barrel for a given bullet is correct, as calculated by means of the Greenhill formula, then mu will be one. If the twist rate is too slow and stability is decreased, then the ratio, or mu, $\mathcal{M}$, will be less than one. If the twist rate is faster than the Greenhill formula calculates, the ratio, or mu, will be greater than one.

In researching this (after having done the algebraic work), I found that there had been other work expanding on Greenhill's formula. A Don Miller elaborated on the Greenhill formula, but while his formula adds in variables, it still produces a twist rate. Berger comes closer, with a plug-in software formula that uses Miller's formula, and produces a result with the same desired result as the Sweeney mu.

I recently came across a paper by Elya and Michael Courtney that suggests the ballistic coefficient of a bullet changes as its stability factor changes. This could lead to a desired twist rate for a given bullet, leading to a much higher BC, but there are drawbacks to that consideration, and it is beyond the scope of this book.

Let's take a look and see what we get by calculating mu.

As we established above, if we calculate the desired twist rate of the 55-grain FM-Jbt, as found in the M-193 bullet, we get a predicted twist rate of 11.96 inches. Turned into a mu ratio, the M-193 out of a 1/12-twist barrel produces a figure of 1.003.

If we take that bullet and push it down a 1/9-twist barrel, we have a mu of 1.33. And out of a 1/7-twist barrel, the mu is 1.71. And in all three instances the bullet will be stable and accurate. We are not considering the effects of rpm on bullet structure itself. A lightly constructed, varmint-type bullet will be stable out of a 1/7 barrel, right up until centripetal forces tear it apart. I have seen that happen with my own eyes, it is not an urban myth.

So, having established that we have not yet encountered an upper boundary for stoutly constructed bullets, let's see if we can establish a lower boundary. We have two classic cases in the history of the AR-15/M16. One is the original twist rate of one turn in fourteen inches. There, the 55 FMJ was barely stable, and any degraded variable caused a loss of accuracy so bad that the Army would not have it. So, we can establish that as our boundary. Dense Arctic air, worn barrels, pretty much anything but a new rifle in shirt-sleeve weather, caused accuracy to go away. So, the calculated mu in this instance is the original, and classic, dividing line.

Second, the use of a 62-grain SS-109/M855 bullet in a 1/12-twist barrel. Practice has established that this is less than marginal, and it is a case of the created stability of the bullet as being insufficient to produce accuracy. M855 ammunition fired through a 1/12-twist barrel will produce keyholed impacts on a target at 25 yards. So, we are clearly below a threshold for mu of stability with this combination.

A 55 FMJ out of a 1/14-twist barrel produces a mu of 0.8547.

An M855 out of a 1/12-twist barrel produces a mu of 0.8272.

We can thus determine that we are on the threshold of stability with a mu of 0.85 or 0.86 or less. (The engineering-schooled among you will assert that we have only proven the case for .224" diameter bullets. Good for you. We'll not overlook that.)

We can then use this to extrapolate, and compare to experience.

The hot 5.56 load for many uses and users is the Mk 262 Mod 1, which features a 7- grain bullet and is typically used in a 1/7-twist barrel. Will it be stable in a 1/9, the more common twist rate found on many ARs? The math tells us that the mu for that combination is 0.979. That is much, much closer to our ideal of 1.0 than it is to the threshold of 0.86 that we have empirically established. And experience has shown that most rifles with a 1/9 twist will shoot the Mk 262 Mod 1 at least as well as the user can. Those that can't, we can lay the blame not on bullet stability, but on it being a barrel made with a cost figure in mind, that is, a crappy barrel. Or poor handloading skills or habits. Or something, but not twist rate and stability.

If we then work the equation in other instances, we can calculate the stability of heavier-than-77-grain bullets, commonly used in long-range rifle competition. NRA high Power shooters single-load bullets of up to 90 grains in weight. What is the stability of these bullets, in a 1/7 barrel?

First, remember that these are not faster than 2,800 fps, so the Greenhill Constant drops to 150. (At least, I hope, out of .223 case, they are not trying to exceed 2,800 fps. If they are, I want to leave the range before firing commences.)

The 80-grain bullet is over an inch long, as much as 1.080". So, the mu for it out of a 1/7 barrel will be 0.996. Which is close enough to the mu for a 55-grain FMJ out of a 1/12 barrel, and pretty darned close to our desired mu of 1.00. Hmmm. The 90-grain bullet, at 1.198" in length, gives us a mu of 0.897, which is still in the stable range, as we have calculated.

In talking with the high-end High Power shooters, I find that the 80-grain bullets, pushed as fast as people dare, is the bullet for long range. It is touchy, however, as you are pushing everything to the redline. The 90s are not so popular, simply due to the limited case capacity of the .223. You just can't push the 90s fast enough to take advantage of their greater ballistic coefficient.

With the re-worked Greenhill formula, we can calculate stability for any number of bullets, with differing twist rates, and see the result.

MORE GYRATIONS

Gyroscopic stability is not a free thing. We have to spin the bullets up, and we need a velocity to do that. So we have to use high pressure cartridges to get results. And high-pressure cartridges in rifles lead to certain expectations: long-range use, accuracy and power. However, there are certain unavoidable factors that come with gyroscopic stability. The two biggies are precession and nutation.

PRECESSION

Precession is the wobble around the axis of rotation. Again, back to junior high and the gyro spinning on your desk. Notice that the gyro wobbles, however minutely, about the axis of the shaft? Did the physics teacher turn the gyro on its side and place the base on a post? If he/she had, you'd see the gyro slowly rotate around the post, and not fall off. Precession, in the technical lingo, is the combined effect of the gravitational torque (gravity trying to pull it off the post) and its own angular momentum. Precession acts on a ninety-degree angle from the force added to the gyroscopic movement. So, as gravity tries to pull the gyro off the post, angular momentum keeps it there, and the result is a force that causes it to rotate about the top of the post.

Back to vertical: as the gyroscope slowed down, it began to wobble more and more. That is the precession rotating it, as gravity slowly tips it over. The angular momentum decreases as the gyro slows down, leading to the greater and greater wobble. The three variables of a gyroscope – spin, torque, precession – all orient to each other according to the right-hand rule. That is, if you were to grip the shaft (or an electrical line, for example) with your right hand, and your fingers point in the direction of rotation, then your thumb will indicate the direction of the third force.

Say, did you know the earth precesses? Yep, that's right. Right now, the North pole points pretty much at the North star, Polaris. But the earth's rotation causes gyroscopic stability, and since it is tipped in its axis, the axis will precess. The period of one rotation of precession is about 26,000 years, so don't expect to need to change your nighttime orienteering plans just yet.

But, a bullet rotates, and anything that acts to divert it off of its path creates a force acting ninety degrees to that force.

OK, let's do some more thought experiments. Your bullet is traveling through the air. It is spinning. What are the chances that it is so perfect a bullet that the center of its rotation, its axis, is exactly the same as that of its center of mass? No matter how perfect, they will not be exact. That minute difference creates a gyroscopic mis-match. For a right-hand twist barrel, the result is to put the axis a minute angle up and to the right. Left-hand twist barrels, up and to the left. The result is gyroscopic drift. How does this matter? Simple, the longer and heavier

the bullet, the greater the force. The faster the velocity (and thus rpm) the higher the gyroscopic force. And the longer it travels, the more it adds up.

Where this matters is more the province of snipers than AR shooters. But, the more ARs move into the long-range precision shooting arena, the more we'll have to pay attention.

Also, please note that this is entirely different than wind drift. This would happen in still air, but not in a vacuum.

How much can it matter? At a thousand yards, it can range from a couple of inches to nearly two feet. While not definitive, it seems that the effects of sectional density overmatch gyroscopic stability, and the bigger and longer your bullet, the less gyroscopic drift has as an effect. Drag has to be a part of that as well, but again, we are dangerously close to wandering out of the subject area.

NUTATION

Nutation, simply put, is a small, back-and-forth change in the angle of the precession of a rotating body. Wobble in the drift, if you will.

In bullets, this is wobble in the precession, which has pretty much nothing to do with bullets, accuracy or terminal performance.

So, what does all this tell us? Simple: aside from a few well-known bad combinations, the twist rate of your barrel, something shooters obsess over, is not a big deal. If you stick with a good quality barrel, and feed your rifle good quality ammo, accuracy problems are more likely a "you" problem or a scope problem.

BULLET MATERIAL

Jump back to the original Greenhill formula and remember that he had a correction for specific gravity in his equation. Specific gravity is the density of the materials used. In a lead-core copper-jacketed bullet, the Sg is so close to the figure he uses, of 10.9, that we can simply ignore it. However, new bullets pose a new problem. All-copper bullets are much less dense than lead-core bullets. Copper, as a metal, has a specific gravity of 8.89. Hmmm, that seems like a lot. So, let's calculate the effect this would have on Greenhill's formula. Sg of copper, divided by the standard figure of 10.9, and then take the square root. The division results in 0.8155, and the square root of that is 0.902.

That means we need to increase the twist by 10%, to come back to the same figure for mu. Most bullets are stable enough that we needn't increase the twist at all, except for one thing: the decreased density of an all-copper bullet means it is longer than one of the same weight with a lead core. And the length is the reason we need to increase twist, not the decreased density. (Although they do work in concert.)

The lesson here is that, if you are planning to use all-copper bullets in your AR, you should move up to the next-faster twist rate. If you use all-copper varmint bullets in your varmint rifle, go from 1/12 to 1/9. And for everything else, go up to 1/7.

WHICH TWIST, THEN?

For those shooting heavy bullets, you can't go wrong with a 1/7 twist rate. Those using the 80- and 90-grain bullets for long-range shooting, even go to barrels with a 1/6.5 twist, but the calculated mu would not require this. (Hey, if they think it gains them a few more points, it probably does.)

For most everyone else, even those who want to use the 75- and 77-grain match bullets, a 1/9 twist will work just fine. You can go with a 1/7 if you wish, but you aren't gaining anything, so if a smoking hot deal on an appropriate 1/9 barrel comes your way, jump on it.

For varmint shooters, who will never in the time they pull the trigger on that rifle ever be using a bullet heavier than 55 grains (and here we're talking just of .223/5.56 rifles), a 1/12 barrel is what you want.

FLUTING

No, not Doug Flutie, but fluting, cutting lengthwise or spiral grooves on the outside of a barrel. Supposedly, a fluted barrel, because of the greater surface area, will cool faster. At the rates we shoot, I'm not sure how much of an advantage that really is.

Another advantage; stiffness. This one is a bit hard to grasp for some people. A fluted barrel is stiffer than a non-fluted barrel, right? Well, kinda. If we compare the fluted barrel to two other barrels, we can see. Assume we have a barrel that is the same external diameter as the fluted one, but not fluted. It is heavier, and it will be stiffer. Then, we have another unfluted barrel, but a slimmer one. It weighs the same as the fluted barrel. The fluted barrel will be stiffer.

So, the fluted barrel gets us a compromise that actually gains us something: it is lighter than the bull barrel, but stiffer than the pencil barrel. Forget about the cooling rate. So, you get most of the accuracy performance conferred by the bull barrel diameter, and still don't have to haul the weight.

That's advantage enough for me. Plus, fluted barrels, at least for most shooters, and in the current design vogue, are cool.

They cost more not just because it takes time and machine tooling to cut the flutes, but also the fluting has to be done properly. With a correct machine setup, you can flute a barrel and not decrease its accuracy. If you do it wrong, you create stresses in the barrel from the machine work and decrease accuracy.

SUMMARY

There we have it, the complete rundown, and the why of barrel selection.

How long will your barrel last?

The answer is the all purpose "it depends." It depends on how you use it, and your idea of "accuracy," if you clean it and how, and on how good a shot you are. Again, let's use an example.

Let's assume that you have, through some method (even luck) laid hands on a rifle capable of delivering 0.5 MOA accuracy. Further, that you, on a good day, are a 3 MOA shooter. You give it care and the proper cleaning, and you will have an accurate rifle for a long time. It will be accurate until it has worn to the point of firing noticeably larger than 3 MOA groups. Before then, it will always be more accurate than you are.

A second shooter, one who on a good day can actually shoot 0.5 MOA groups, will find that the barrel has become inaccurate a lot sooner. Basically, when it becomes a 1

The starting point? Twenty-six inches of stainless, beautiful barrel. The things we do for knowledge.

MOA performer.

A plinker will find a rifle to be accurate for a lot longer (and more of them to be accurate) than an NRA High Master would.

"Accurate rifles" are a lot like "fast cars" – they are race-dependant.

AR rifle barrels wear in three places and for two reasons.

They wear at the throat, the portion just in front of the chamber, they wear at the gas port, and they wear at the muzzle.

The throat and gas port wear is from

the bullet slides over it, it uncovers the port gradually. The first opening causes a jet of gases to squirt from the bore into the gas channel. The squirt happens at a right angle in the barrel steel, and that corner gets eroded. The muzzle? The gases don't have any effect there.

The throat and muzzle get worn from improper cleaning. Using a jointed steel rod without a support allows the rod to flex and rub against the bore. It does so at the throat, and at the muzzle as the rod drops when the brush or patch clears the crown.

To reduce shooting wear, do not overheat the barrel. That means don't shoot the rifle hot. Since one of the aspects of the AR is that you can shoot it a lot, and quickly, that means deferring gratification.

That's life.

To properly clean the bore, either use an upper receiver guide to keep the rod straight, and use a single-piece coated rod. Or, pull the cleaning brushes and patches through the bore from chamber to muzzle.

To see if a barrel is "shot out," clean it thoroughly and properly, put in a good, high-powered scope, and then shoot it for groups. If it shoots well, then it is still accurate with that ammunition. If not, it isn't. You can inspect it with other methods. An erosion gauge will tell you how much of the throat has been scoured away by the hot gases, but that only gives you a measurement of steel, not an accuracy read. A bore scope will tell you if the gas port is eroded, but again, that is just a visual indication, not an accuracy check. And the muzzle? There are gauges, no one uses them, and I don't think anyone cares.

To circle back, how long should a barrel last? The government puts the service life of an M4 carbine at 7,500 rounds. Of course, that is in the hands of soldiers, sailors, airmen and marines, who are not always able to baby their equipment. It also assumes a good dollop of full-auto fire, and all this in a hostile environment.

I've gotten 15,000 rounds or more before I saw a drop in accuracy in some barrels. They were not babied, but "acceptable accuracy" was head shots in competition targets at 100 yards.

One example I recently saw was a Sheriff's Deputy who arrived with his no-name A2

shooting. Each shot produces blistering hot gases at high pressures, gases laden with particulates. Those gases funnel out of the case and are at their hottest and most abrasive just in front of, and for the next couple of inches of the bore. The gas port wears as

rifle. He had been using it as a patrol rifle in his squad car for more than twenty years. He'd shot the annual qualification course, the certification course, regular training courses, and even a few practical rifle matches with it. At the patrol rifle class, he was finding it difficult to determine if his rifle was still zeroed, the groups kept wandering and changing sizes.

Out of curiosity, I inserted an erosion gauge. Nothing else seemed wrong, and we were mulling several very esoteric possibilities. The gauge has a mark. Past that point, the throat is too eroded for government use. Most rifles checked stop the rod a couple of inches away from the mark.

On this rifle, the erosion gauge went more than halfway down the bore. Instead of being eroded away by a couple of inches, the rifling on the bore was worn away for a foot.

He brought the rifle and a replacement barrel to the class the next day, and we swapped them out for him.

Gas ports can erode enough to harm accuracy. But the accuracy loss is dependent on (yes) the accuracy expected, but also in the bullets used.

A rifle with a severely worn gas port may still show acceptable accuracy with the tough little 55-grain FMJs out of .223 or 5.56 M-913 ammunition. But feed it something better, like a 75- or 77-grain match, or the Mk 262 Mod 0 or 1, and accuracy goes all to heck. The thinner jackets of those bullets are more-readily torn by the jagged gas port, and they can't fly straight once torn.

So, your plinker M4gery with its Melonited barrel is going to stay accurate longer than you custom-built Mk 12 with it stainless tube. Partly because the Melonite makes the barrel tougher. Partly because the M4gery is only ever going to see 55-grain FMJs, and partly because the 75- and 77-grain match bullets in the Mk 12 are more sensitive to an eroded gas port.

How long will it last? No telling, until you shoot it, use it up, and then install another one. However long it lasts, you will get a lot of practice out of it. Look at it this way: a replacement barrel for your M4gery will cost you approximately $150. If it only lasts as long as the government expects,

you will have, at current ammo prices, put about $800 worth of ammunition through it. If you fed your Mk 12 only Mk 262 Mod 0 or Mod 1 ammunition, you will have put something like $5,000 worth of ammo downrange in the same time.

New barrels are cheap, compared to ammo.

BARRELS AND VELOCITY

OK, we all know that longer barrels create more velocity, and shorter barrels less. But what does "shorter" cost you? The old rule of thumb was "X feet per second, per

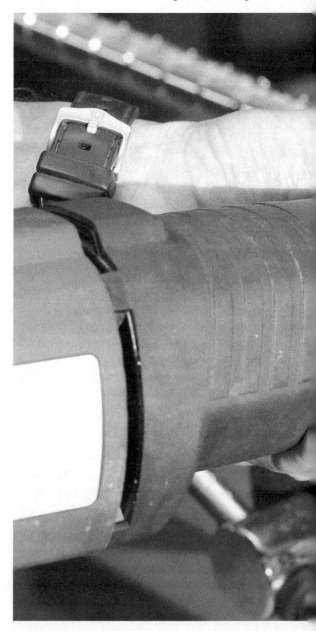

inch." And X could be pretty much any figure someone cared to dream up.

Readily-obtained, inexpensive chronographs put a little bit of light on the subject, but only a little. Yes, you could chronograph ammo out of two rifles with different-length barrels, but the difference was not just because of the lengths. Even barrels in the same production lot will offer different velocities. The difference is small, but measurable. After all, if you are chronoing a 5.56 load that hurls bullets at 3,100 fps, a one percent difference in velocity is 31 fps. Don't kid yourself, people obsess over 31 fps.

A long time ago (not in a galaxy far, far away) I built two absolutely identical IPSC Open guns. They were built on steel 1911s, using a pair of Bar-Sto barrels I received from Bar-Sto at the same time. With ammunition I had loaded myself, one posted velocities 100 fps faster than the other. That was a shift of 7.2 percent.

So, it is not beyond reason that two rifles with identical-length barrels could post 100 fps difference. Heck, a 7.2% difference would be a loss of 223 fps, enough to make anyone crazy.

If we want to know that actual difference in velocity, according to length, we have to

A Sawz-All, a vise, and the grim determination that this sacrifice will generate useful data, are what's needed to do this kind of work. That, and a bit of care. One slip, and I'm sawz-ing my leg, and that would be bad.

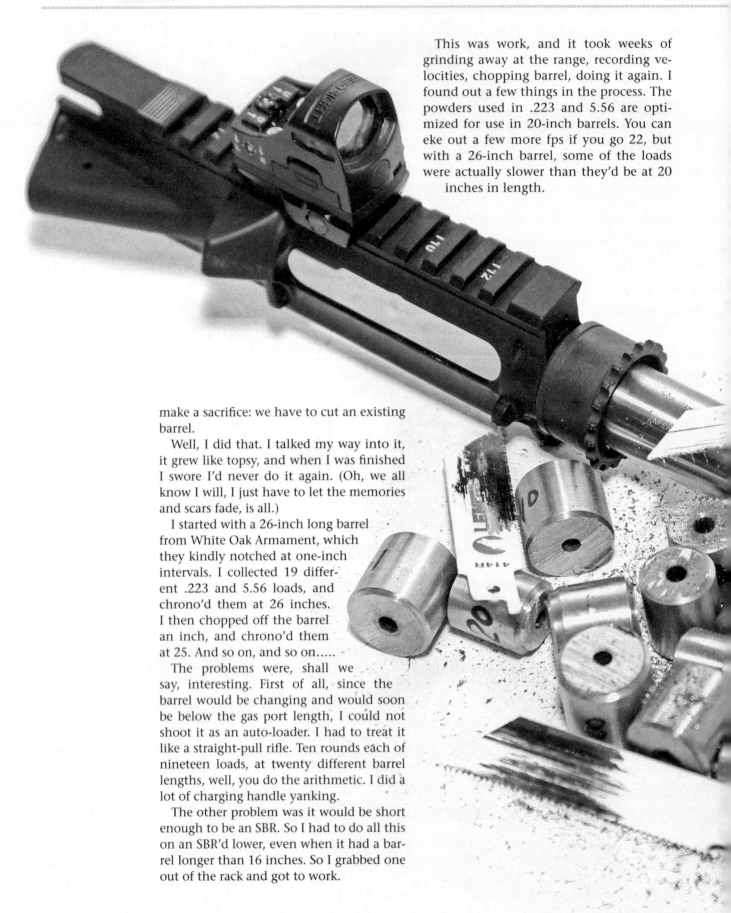

This was work, and it took weeks of grinding away at the range, recording velocities, chopping barrel, doing it again. I found out a few things in the process. The powders used in .223 and 5.56 are optimized for use in 20-inch barrels. You can eke out a few more fps if you go 22, but with a 26-inch barrel, some of the loads were actually slower than they'd be at 20 inches in length.

make a sacrifice: we have to cut an existing barrel.

Well, I did that. I talked my way into it, it grew like topsy, and when I was finished I swore I'd never do it again. (Oh, we all know I will, I just have to let the memories and scars fade, is all.)

I started with a 26-inch long barrel from White Oak Armament, which they kindly notched at one-inch intervals. I collected 19 different .223 and 5.56 loads, and chrono'd them at 26 inches. I then chopped off the barrel an inch, and chrono'd them at 25. And so on, and so on......

The problems were, shall we say, interesting. First of all, since the barrel would be changing and would soon be below the gas port length, I could not shoot it as an auto-loader. I had to treat it like a straight-pull rifle. Ten rounds each of nineteen loads, at twenty different barrel lengths, well, you do the arithmetic. I did a lot of charging handle yanking.

The other problem was it would be short enough to be an SBR. So I had to do all this on an SBR'd lower, even when it had a barrel longer than 16 inches. So I grabbed one out of the rack and got to work.

Here we are at the end, with a super-stubby barrel and lots of blast and flash.

Also, when the velocity starts to drop off, down under 10 or 11 inches, it really drops.

Rather than produce the entire chart (who is going to build a rifle with a 17" barrel, really?) I'm charting the velocities for four barrel lengths: 20", 16", 11" and 7".

This is what's left, along with a big pile of brass, when you do this sort of experiment.

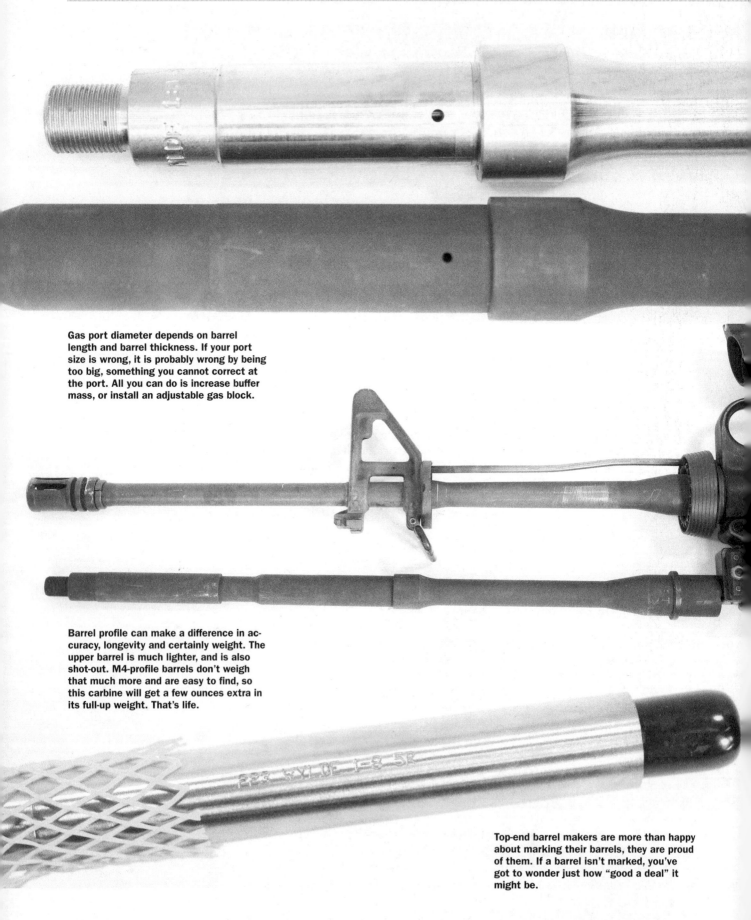

Gas port diameter depends on barrel length and barrel thickness. If your port size is wrong, it is probably wrong by being too big, something you cannot correct at the port. All you can do is increase buffer mass, or install an adjustable gas block.

Barrel profile can make a difference in accuracy, longevity and certainly weight. The upper barrel is much lighter, and is also shot-out. M4-profile barrels don't weigh that much more and are easy to find, so this carbine will get a few ounces extra in its full-up weight. That's life.

Top-end barrel makers are more than happy about marking their barrels, they are proud of them. If a barrel isn't marked, you've got to wonder just how "good a deal" it might be.

The piston in this SBR eases the gas flow problems of short barrels, and the Keymod handguard is a definite improvement over the quad rails of old.

AMMUNITION	20" V	16" V	11" V	7" V
HORNADY 223 35-GR NT	3677	3364	3120	2480
W-W 223 S-TIP LF 35-GR	3606	3422	3035	2516
BLACK HILLS 223 40-GR V-MAX	3279	3239	2778	2293
FEDERAL PR. 223 55 NOSLER	2955	2836	2542	2037
WOLF 223 55 FMJ	3116	2901	2579	2116
W-W 223 55 FMJ	3089	3029	2657	2196
W-W 556 55 FMJ	3110	2966	2603	2091
FEDERAL 556/XM193 55 FMJ	3243	3129	2812	2284
CORBON 223 55 BLITZKING	2998	3000	2705	2222
W-W 556 M855 62-GR FMJ	3108	2930	2654	2201
W-W 223 PDX1 60-GR HP	2871	2832	2471	2078
B. HILLS 556 62 BARNES TSX	3082	2960	2612	2220
HPR 223 62-GR OTF	2930	2784	2491	2096
W-W 223 69-GR HPBT	2669	2554	2244	1729
HPR 223 75 BTHP	2608	2429	2165	1829
ASYM 223 77-GR OTM	2700	2618	2354	2009
BLACK HILLS 77-GR OTM	2836	2669	2406	2016
FEDERAL PR. 77 BTHP	2591	2458	2204	1838
GORILLA 77-GR SMK	2633	2567	2236	1771

You can see the grim results of the 7" barrel length. There are heavyweight bullets that don't go past two grand in velocity. And 55-grain FMJs that don't do much better than what the 5.7x28 does out of the PS-90 carbine.

Now, not all 11" barrels will produce these velocities. They may vary by as much as 50-75 fps. Which means your SBR could be doing 50-75 fps more. Or less. The XM-193, at just over 2,800 fps, isn't so bad, really. It will still be able to yaw and break apart, out to 150 yards or so, which is well past the distances most of us might ever be called on for.

But at the 2,284 fps it produced out of the 7" barrel, it can't be counted on to yaw at any distance past "hard off the muzzle." It will still yaw, if the engagement distance is 5 feet, but that's not because it yaws from density instability. It yaws because it is still actually yawing in air. And the 2,284 fps probably isn't enough to break the bullet at the cannelure, so you have a high-speed knitting needle. Good luck with that. ■

CHAPTER 3
Barrel Installation

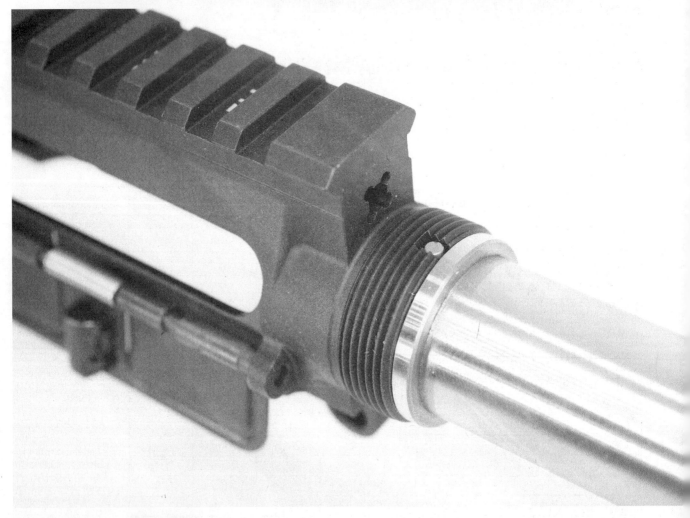

You want a fit of barrel extension to upper receiver that requires some effort. If it slides in easily, you are not getting the full potential of the expensive, premium barrel you just bought.

My attitude towards barrel installation has evolved. In the beginning, once the parts were checked for fit (that is, hand-assemble, hand-tighten, and see that everything lines up) I'd tighten and loosen twice, then do a final tighten to get the barrel nut to line up. Done.

Well, that process still works, and given good parts and careful assembly you can build a rifle that will deliver under 2 MOA every time. That was tack-driving accuracy for an AR, back in the 1980s when I was learning how this all worked. Today, it is considered an American birthright to own an AR that is on its worst day a 1 MOA rifle, and sub-MOA rifles are apparently as common as apples on the tree. As if.

Now, while I'm more than happy to build a basic rifle, say a truck gun or an inside-of-300-meters rifle or carbine for training, if there's going to be any accuracy consideration, I'll do it differently. Maybe.

BASIC INSTALLATION

The trick is to make sure everything fits by hand-assembling the parts. The manufacturers have done a good job of this, and you can pretty much plug a ready-to-go barrel (sight installed, barrel nut and delta ring already in place) into an upper and be set. The tricky part is getting the barrel nut torqued enough but not too much, and correctly timed.

From hand-tight to fully-torqued, you do not want to wrench a barrel nut much more than one full notch. If you get it tight and find that the gas tube can't clear the nut notches, you have to remove it and either dress down the receiver face or install a barrel shim, depending on which is the shorter re-set: less turn or more.

This is a simple process, covered in other volumes that I (and many others) have written, so I won't go into the gory details here.

Ideally, you'll find that the barrel extension diameter is large enough and the internal diameter of the receiver extension is so tight that you have to press the barrel into place to start. If it wobbles, you will not have anything more than a casually-

accurate rifle. To build a top-end-accuracy rifle this way is a waste of time. I will go out on a limb here, and suggest that if you are going to the effort of building a really accurate AR, and have borne the expense of a premium barrel, you should not be cavalier about fit. In fact, you might even just buy 2-3-4 uppers of the type you want, and go with the one that is the proper, tight fit. Keep the others as parts for future, less-demanding builds, sell them to gun club members at cost, or return them for a refund, but do not try to "improve" the fit of a barrel to a receiver.

The work needed to make a loose barrel fit is not worth it.

Start with a snug or tighter barrel-to-receiver fit. Again, hand-assemble everything to make sure it fits. The next step is to apply a light coat of oil to all the parts and torque the barrel nut into place. This is your alignment check. If the barrel nut torques up and everything aligns properly, move on the to next step. If not, you have to make them fit.

A clean workbench is a sign of ... who knows. Some say an OCD personality, some say a slow worker, some say a genius. Regardless, you need the correct tools to install a barrel. They are not complex, nor difficult to use, but they are necessary.

FITTING

For a precision AR, I will gladly spend some time dressing the face of the receiver. This involves either the receiver face reamer or a lapping tool (both available from Brownells). With them, you are simply lowering the high spot or spots, or adjusting the face of the receiver if it was finished at an angle. Since you will be removing metal, and this adjusts the location of the barrel nut once it torques up, you have to re-check barrel nut alignment after receiver facing.

For a barrel nut alignment on a standard build, I will opt for a shim. For a precision build, I'd rather dress the receiver face, as I'm keeping the bearing surfaces as original, supported metal, and not shimmed. That's just me, you can shim if you want.

Once I have the receiver face squared, I use my selection of barrel nuts to find the one that times up perfectly. I have a box of spares, taken off of barrels that were shot-out, or from projects that used handguards with proprietary barrel nuts. If you do not have this supply, having one or two extras on hand can solve a problem with timing. If you want to take this approach, Brownells has them for a bit less than ten dollars each, retail. If you are building an upper using a barrel that starts at $300-$500, adding the "excess" cost of a couple of spare barrel nuts, at less than ten dol-

Factory assemblers use bins of parts and simply grab the next one they need from the bins. You will be building yours with just the parts needed, and not an excess of them. So take things one step at a time, make sure you have what you need and that you understand each step.

lars each, is an inexpensive backup plan.

The receiver is squared, the barrel is a tight fit, the barrel nut times up when torqued to the proper figure. Now what? Take it all apart.

Break out three things you have not needed until now: degreaser, Loctite, and two brushes – one for the Loctite and one for your lubricant. Keep paper towels handy, along with some cotton swabs.

With the receiver and barrel apart, degrease all the bearing surfaces. You want the inside of the receiver and the outside of the barrel extension to be dry. You want the threads dry, both on the receiver and in the barrel nut.

Now use the brush to apply your lube (which brand doesn't really matter, as long as it doesn't wick too much) to the threads of the receiver and the threads of the barrel nut. Then, apply your Loctite to the inside of the receiver where the barrel extension will reside, and on the barrel extension.

Why are we doing this? So you will be able to get the barrel and receiver apart once you have finally shot-out the barrel. If the receiver is not something you are worried about salvaging once the barrel is toasted, then don't bother with all this.

Assuming you wish to retrieve the receiver at some future point, once you have the parts brushed appropriately, slide the barrel into the receiver. Do not simply slam it in, but ease it in, watching the flow of excess Loctite. Wipe up the Loctite that oozes out, and keep it off of the receiver face or the barrel ring that abuts the receiver face. Even a thin layer there will change the torqued position of the barrel nut. You can't avoid it completely, but you can minimize it, and reduce the extra torque you'll need.

Once you have the barrel solidly set into the receiver, take one last look to wipe up excess Loctite, and then spin on the barrel nut. Torque it in place. Take the receiver out of whatever fixture you were using, and use the cotton swabs to mop up the excess Loctite inside the receiver.

Any excess Loctite that you do not mop up will find its way to someplace you don't want it and cause problems.

Let the assembly set for a day or two before you do anything else with it. You

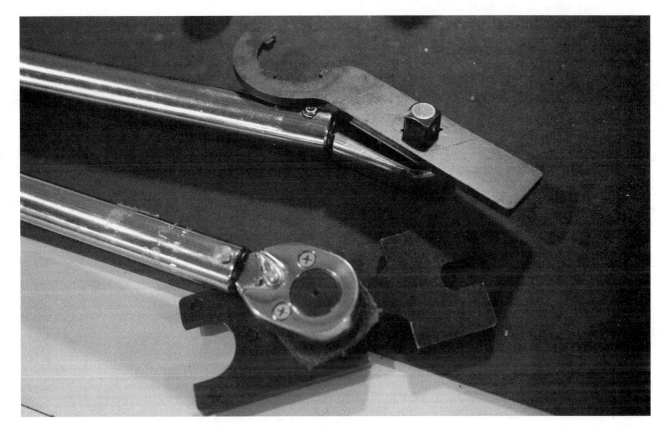

want the Locitite to cure completely before you proceed with any more work.

Which Loctite? Which lubricant? It doesn't matter, within limits. The purpose of the Loctite is not so much to "glue" the parts together, although it does that. What it does is fill the very small gaps between the barrel and receiver. This greatly reduces the space into which the barrel can move and cause misalignment between receiver and barrel.

What is important is that the Loctite not wick. If it does, it will aggressively move from where you want it, to where it wants to be. Similarly with the lubricant, as you do not want it wicking over and getting in-between the barrel extension and receiver. Also, you do not want a fast-acting Loctite, as you will be working things together for more than a few seconds. Even several minutes.

One definitely off-the-list Loctite formula is one of my favorites for other purposes, the dark green Shaft and Bearing Lock. This is a formula that sets in the absence of oxygen, and it does so quickly. I found this out while spinning a comp, or muzzle brake, onto a 1911 barrel. The phone rang,

I stopped turning, picked it up to answer, and reached back to turn, only to find the comp immovable. I ended up using a propane torch to break the Loctite (it breaks down at 356 degrees Fahrenheit), cleaning up the threads and surfaces, and starting again.

After that, whenever I apply Loctite, I do not stop what I am doing unless the fire alarm goes off.

USEFULNESS?

How much does this help? Not a lot. If you are building a precision AR and you have a promised sub-MOA barrel, if you are using sub-MOA ammunition, and if you have good enough technique that you can actually take advantage of those, you may see a quarter-MOA improvement.

Obviously, if you are using an M4-style or A2-profile barrel, and you are feeding the carbine whatever you can find is the cheapest useable ammo, a quarter-MOA improvement in accuracy isn't even noticeable. The effort will be a waste of time, unless you are writing it off as AR-building practice.

In which case, knock yourself out. ∎

For precise results, using a torque wrench (and learning how to use it properly) is important. You can do a good assembly job just by feel, but to eke that last bit of accuracy out of a barrel, use a torque wrench.

CHAPTER 4
Bolts

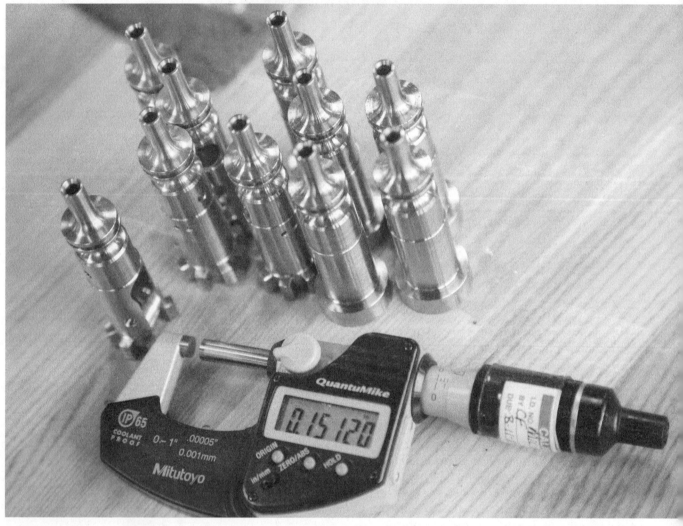

On the right, bolts partially machined, with the lugs not yet broached. On the left, lugs that have been broached or otherwise machined. In front, the digital calipers used to check them.

Everyone knows what steel bolts are made of, right? Some of us can practically recite it in our sleep: Carpenter 158.

You will search in vain in the SAE alloy lists for Carpenter 158. Why? Because it is a trademarked steel. What is in it? Carpenter and the government know. But as with the alloying we saw in the chapter on steel, that is simply a list of ingredients. What process Carpenter uses, and what heat-treatment routine it goes through, is known only inside the walls of Carpenter.

If you want to make bolts for the government, you have to order steel from Carpenter to do it. And when you submit your bolts to the government, there had better be an invoice in there, proving you received a supply of the appropriate-sized steel from Carpenter.

Which is not bad, except for one thing: Carpenter 158 is a product of the 1950s. There are a lot of things made in the 1950s that are still the best, but we have made great strides in steel fabrication, alloying, heat-treatment and finishing since the Eisenhower administration.

Your mil-spec bolt had the bar stock of the C-158 fed into a CNC lathe. There, it had the outside profile turned. If done on a multi-axis machine (and most would be, it is far quicker, more consistent and cost-effective to do as much on one machine as possible), it would also have the various holes drilled and the extractor slot cut.

Then the bolts would be taken to a broaching machine. There, a multi-toothed tool cuts the locking lugs in a single pass. Think of it as a barrel-rifling machine turned inside-out. Last, it is placed in one last machine to be bored from the rear for the firing pin tunnel.

The next step is to be heat-treated and shot-peened. The heat-treatment process is perhaps the most delicate step in the entire rifle-making process. The various cross-sections of the AR bolt are quite thin. Any

These are bolts in process. They have had most, if not all, of their machining done, and will be measured, inspected and sent off for proofing.

One of the original drawings from Armalite of the bolt. Yep, right there, Carpenter 158, with hardness specs. What is Carpenter 158? You have to work at Carpenter to know.

mis-step in time, temperature or other conditions of the heat-treatment can leave a bolt (or an entire batch of bolts) too soft or brittle.

The alloy known as Carpenter 158 is one that responds well to case-hardening. That is, it is hardened on the surface, to a known and closely-controlled depth, but the core remains relatively soft. This hardness resists wear and provides load strength, while the softer core provides support and shock strength. If, however, the surface hardness goes too deep or is too hard, the bolt will break under a load.

For those who have to know (not that there is any way for any of us to test this) the surface hardness as originally laid down was 60 to 62 on the Rockwell C scale. The core was to remain at Rockwell 37C. Oh, and were C-158 listed on the ASE steel nomenclature lists, it would probably come in as a grade of 3310. Basically, pretty darned good steel.

PEENING

Shot-peening is a step that relieves stress. The heat-treatment makes the surface of the bolt hard, but not the entire bolt. Shot-peening is done with steel shot of a particular size and hardness, blown at the bolt at a given speed. The peening of the surface further hardens it, while evenly distributing or relieving stresses caused by the heat-treatment process.

The last step is to surface-grind certain surfaces: the rotating band you see in the middle of the body of the bolt, and the tail where it runs into the carrier bore. These have to be precisely on-center, and smooth and circular.

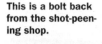

This is a bolt back from the shot-peening shop.

PROOFING

Up next is the abuse. A government contract calls for each and every one of the bolts to be fired with a proof load. The proof cartridge is a cartridge loaded to 130% of maximum chamber pressure. (The ammunition you shoot may run at an average pressure of only 90% of maximum, maybe even less.) The bolt-testing is usually done in a special fixture, and not in an assembled rifle.

Once proof-tested, each bolt is then given a magnetic particle inspection. This involves creating a magnetic field in the bolt, coating it with a dye solution containing steel particles, and observing the slathered bolt under lighting of a particular wavelength. Any cracks in the bolt will create disturbances in the magnetic field, and the particles will follow those disturbances. A trained operator can see the bad, or uncharacteristic, patterns, and find the crack.

The government has particular and exacting standards on the tests. If a certain number of bolts in a given production lot fail the proof test or show cracks in the MPI test, then the entire lot will be rejected. This can mean destruction, and it can mean "we won't buy it, but be careful who you do sell it to," depending on how the contract is written. My suspicion is scrappage.

The passed lot will already have been marked with the makers code and the "MPI" acronym, since the bolt will be too hard to mark otherwise. That's why I think most failed lots (and there would be few, it is expensive to make bolts and the makers are very careful) are scrapped.

Not all bolts are so-marked. The government requires it, but not everyone else does. In fact, most don't. Also, not all bolt makers proof-test and MPI every single bolt they make in a production run. The mil-spec approved process dates from (you

This bolt has gone the full route – manufacture, testing and proofing – and soon will be assembled into a rifle.

guessed it) the 1950s, when the only way to be absolutely sure all parts passed was to test all parts.

Today, statistical modeling and experience can tell us a lot.

Let's take an example. A bolt maker gets an order for 5,000 bolts. These are not government contract bolts. So, they are free to use modern business methods and alloys, not 1950s methods and alloys. They acquire the steel, all from a single pour, from one mill. They test the steel and find it to be exactly as described. They then feed it into their machines and, in a non-stop process, go through the entire bolt-making procedure. They proof-test and MPI the first hundred bolts and all pass. No rejects. The next hundred, they test twenty-five. No rejects. By the time they get to the last batch of 100, they take one sample, test it, and guess what? Not rejected.

At no point did any bolt fail. What are the chances that one of those non-tested bolts in this production run will be faulty? If you said "no chance," you failed statistics class. If you said "so small as to not be worthy of calculating," then you get a passing grade.

Which leads us to the next step in this information process.

URBAN MYTHS

"STEEL OTHER THAN C-158 IS CHEAP STEEL"

Steel is steel. It can be alloyed, it can be heat-treated, and it is a subject that has produced a tsunami of master's degrees and PhDs in mechanical engineering and metallurgy. There are entire handbooks printed to let you determine the physical characteristics of steels. Let's say you want an alloy that can stand up to a hot, abrasive and corrosive environment. (Oh, I don't know, nuclear reactors, or the interior of suppressors.) You can find them.

The greatest strength? No problem. Low cost, easily-machined and more than strong enough? A materials handbook, next to your tablet with materials prices, and you're done in five minutes.

There are better steels than C-158. If that is the case, why hasn't the government ad-

opted them?

Two reasons: One, it would cost more to prove something is better, than to simply pick a better steel from a list and swap out all the bolts in inventory. No, I'm not kidding. The second one is an admittedly glib, but nonetheless true, statement I made many years ago: "The U.S. Army has been trying to replace the M16 since before they

adopted it." Why upgrade something that will be replaced, once the current search for a replacement produces results?

No, the Army is not the exemplar here, of a group that always has the best tools for the job. And an AR with a bolt made of steel not C-158 is not one that has a cheap bolt. Well, not necessarily, some might be.

"GAS RINGS LEAK IF LINED UP"

Despite all the efforts to produce and issue the best bolts possible, ca. 1957, the Army is still (as of 2008) instructing troops to make sure they stagger the gas rings on their bolts. The number of reasons this is pointless are legion. Let's cover a few.

It is a long, complex and expensive process to make bolts. Even when only partially-machined, they are protected, nestled in egg carton-like holders, to keep them from banging into each other.

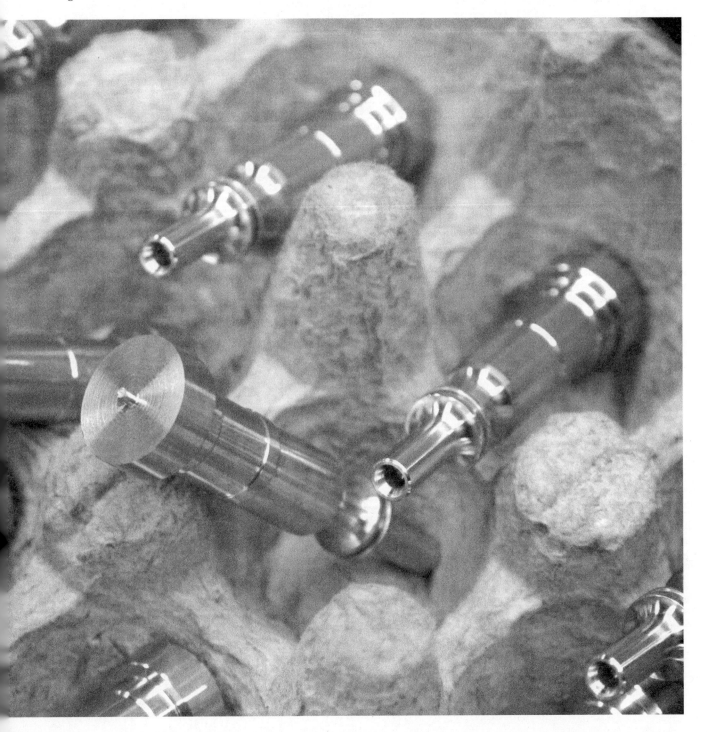

You test gas rings by standing the carrier bolt assembly, when clean, on its head. If the assembly collapses (the one on the left), then the rings are too worn and must be replaced.

The rings move when the bolt cycles. Try this: line up the gaps in your rings. Install the bolt into the carrier, and put the cam in pin. Now hand-cycle the bolt a bunch of times (as many or few as your patience will stand). Now pull the bolt out. The gas rings are no longer lined up. Each time the bolt cycles, each ring is subjected to the frictional forces of moving back and forth. Since the rings are and carrier bore are not perfectly circular, the rubbing will be unevenly distributed.

The rings are overkill. You need three because that's what the rifle was built to use. But, and this comes as a surprise to a lot of shooters, your rifle will probably work just fine with only two. Or even one. I have a rifle that will cycle 100% (but it won't always lock open when empty) with no gas rings. Change them when the bolt/carrier assembly fails the test, but do not think for a moment that your rifle, with three properly-installed gas rings, even when worn, won't cycle. Odds are, it will, for many more rounds. Still, when parts wear, you replace them. So replace your gas rings, just don't care, not one whit, if the gaps are aligned.

"BOLTS LAST 7,500 ROUNDS'

That's the figure the government puts on them. But then, that is the average service life of rifles and M4s owned by the government. That includes rifles lost in training. "Ooops, the rifle went overboard in 1,200 feet of sea. The bolt had 127 recorded rounds on it. That'll pull down the average." It includes rifles run over, blown up, and dropped out of helicopters in combat zones. Don't forget the large dollop of full-auto fire that they receive, in harsh environments.

Now, if you maintain your rifle that you use as a prairie dog popper, and keep it clean, don't let it overheat (too much) and don't do full-auto fire, will your bolt last more than 7,500 rounds? Probably, almost certainly. I have a rifle that is on its third barrel, and the round count is now over 20,000 rounds on the original bolt.

If you want to change bolts when you change barrels, go right ahead. It isn't a bad idea, it is just one that costs money.

I just checked, and the cost of a black nitride bolt from Brownells, complete with extractor, spring, pin and gas rings, was less than fifty dollars. (Of course I ordered a few. Do you think I'm slow or something?)

For that, stock up. If you want something with a bit more panache, or a "better" name in ARs, you can have your choice of AR-15 bolts for less than $100.

BETTER BOLTS

There are better bolts. Some makers who are not making rifles for the government have changed to other alloys. It could be availability or cost. It could be less hassle in heat-treatment. It could be easier machinability, and it could even be that the resulting bolts are stronger, tougher and last longer. The thing you have to remember with a mil-spec, MPI-marked bolt is this: it passes the government tests. It is no better than it has to be, which is plenty good enough, but it is not better than it has to be.

There are also improved designs. Again, the AR-15 is 1950s technology, and computer modeling has allowed us to improve many other designs since those days.

Improved designs required R&D, testing and exhaustive tests to destruction. Which is why they will cost more than non-mil-spec or mil-spec bolts. But if you want the best, they are what you have to pay.

One alloy in common use in bolts is ASE 9310. This is a nickel-chrome-manganese alloy with a sprinkle of other alloying ingredients mixed in. It has between 0.08 and 0.13% carbon in it. It is an oil-quenched steel, and the result is a tough, hard part that is readily machined.

Bolts can be improved in ways other than fiddling with the alloy. Lewis Machine has an improved bolt design where the lugs are shaped in such a way that they are more resistant to cracking and shearing. By shaping them so the forces acting on them are directed more into the bolt body, they in effect are larger, as they have more steel taking the load.

Of course the improved steel, the updated heat-treatment, and the corrosion-

The bolt on the left is marked as having been magnetic particle inspected. The one on the right is not marked. Which will fail first? Nobody knows, and just because it isn't marked doesn't mean it is junk.

resistant coating adds to the price. Where you'll spend less than $50 for a Brownells bolt (and probably be happy for the life of the barrel it works with, or longer), you'll spend over $200 for the LMT bolt. That's life, and this is America.

BOLT ASSEMBLY

Bolts need extractors, ejectors and gas rings.

The extractor is a simple and often overlooked part. It was originally under-tensioned, and we have spent decades increasing the tension until we have it right, which is almost too much. To be properly tensioned, a bolt should have three parts under its extractor: the little synthetic insert inside of the spring, the spring and an O or D shaped ring around the spring.

The little insert inside the spring should be black. If it is any other color, replace it. If it is missing, install a new one.

More tension is better, and the way to tell if you have too much is simple: at the range (Do Not Do This At Home) lock the bolt back. Drop a round into the chamber. With the safety on Safe, grab the charging handle, hang onto it, release the bolt, and ease the bolt forward. If, when it arrives at the chambered cartridge, the extractor has too much tension to snap over the rim, you have too much.

Even when eased forward by hand, the extractor needs to be able to snap over the rim. If it won't, replace the overly-strong spring with a standard one. Keep the little insert and the D or O ring.

Ejector springs are easy. There's only the one size and strength, ever, and it is the correct one. Install what comes from Brownells, if you are assembling a bare bolt.

Gas rings? You need three. The classic test is with a clean, lubed bolt/carrier assembly. Snap the bolt forward. Now stand it on the bolt face, on a table or bench. If the weight of the carrier causes the assembly to collapse, you need new rings. The rings are probably good enough to work, but new rings will keep it from collapsing, and they are cheap. Install new ones. Replace them in sets of three, don't use old rings. ∎

Extractors are small, precise and hard-working parts. They must be made to incredibly tight dimensions, or they won't work. Well, or they won't work well, that is what we all worry about.

CHAPTER 5
Carriers

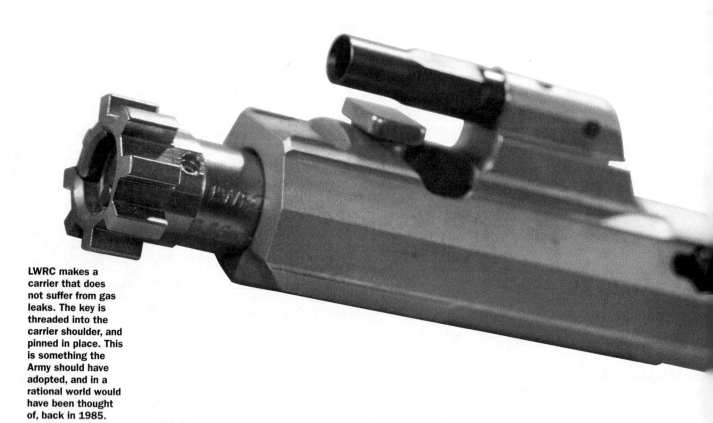

LWRC makes a carrier that does not suffer from gas leaks. The key is threaded into the carrier shoulder, and pinned in place. This is something the Army should have adopted, and in a rational world would have been thought of, back in 1985.

The carrier is the part the bolt rides in. It serves four purposes. It holds the bolt on-center, so it can strip a round out, and rotate to lock and unlock. It contains the cam path, which rotates the bolt at the appropriate times, and it adds mass to the bolt. The mass makes the rifle more forgiving in the start of its cycle, and able to deal with differing levels of gas flow. It slows the cycle speed of the bolt so the magazine has time to lift the cartridge stack for the next round to properly feed. The last thing it does is route the gases from the gas tube to the back of the bolt, and the expanding gases are what drive the cycle.

The correct or better or best carrier is not the heaviest, nor the lightest. It is the one that cycles the rifle properly. In other words, the rifle will tell you when you have the right-weight carrier in there.

The best carrier is one that causes a properly extractored and ejector-sprung bolt to eject the empties out to three or four o'clock. That is, if the direction you are shooting at is deemed to be noon, then the empties will fly out at a right angle, or slightly behind that angle.

Carriers of the standard sort come in three flavors. The original is the heaviest, and the bottom shelf is the same length as the top shelf. The bottom shelf is there to trip the full-auto sear, and outside of an M16/M4 it doesn't do anything but add weight. For a long time we all wondered, and some were quite wary of using them. The ATF finally clarified the issue by not caring if we used them or not. Since then, many manufacturers ship them with their assembled rifles, simply because as the heaviest and original it works the best.

The other two are the Colt-modified carriers: the "AR" version, with the shelf trimmed back a bit, and the "what the heck?" version, where the entire bottom of the carrier has been shaved off. In an otherwise well set-up rifle or carbine, they don't make a difference. If your rifle or carbine is right on the margin of working properly, a non-M16 carrier might cause problems.

What about the special lightweight carriers? Avoid them unless you have an adjustable gas block on your rifle, and you are using the rifle for competition or varmint shooting. The idea of the lightweight carrier is to avoid having the bottom-out bounce of the cycling mass as a recoil component. By making the carrier lighter, there is less weight to hammer the back end of the tube, and you. This is only a partial solution to the recoil problem, and leads to feeding problems. You see, the impact of the carrier

The surface on which the gas key rests has been machined or ground to be flat and provide a good seal against gas leaks. You can help by using a gasket liquid when you install your key.

in the tube (or the fully-compressed spring, if that happens to be the limiting dimension) is a more vigorous return. The carrier literally bounces off the inside end of the tube faster than if the spring stops it, and then pushes it forward. The lighter spring can then arrive at the back of the magazine before the magazine has lifted the cartridge stack. This causes mis-feeds.

Usually, the cartridge stack lifts nose-up. The heavier and wider back end doesn't lift as fast, and the bolt careens into the side of the case. This is called a "bolt over base" failure, and it means your rifle is cycling too fast. Or, rarely, that your magazine spring is tired and can't lift fast enough.

The problem is also that there is also less weight to handle the gas flow and the impulse to drive the mechanism. That's where the adjustable gas block comes in. (Covered in the competition chapter in detail.) By throttling back the volume of gas that arrives in the carrier, the adjustable block allows you to tune the system. Less weight shuttling back and forth means less felt recoil. Adjusting the gas flow so the carrier and buffer do not bottom out at the back end makes recoil even softer.
You are, how-

Piston systems solve some problems but bring others with them. This rod will prevent hot gases from reaching the upper receiver, but when it pushes the carrier it will do so with an axial offset. Carrier tilt.

ever, giving up operating margin. If your rifle gets too dirty, or you use ammo not like what you tuned it for, your rifle might become unreliable.

No, scratch that. Not "might," but will. You see, the "overtravel" of the bolt, the distance (and thus time) it moves behind the back of the case rims, is not large. There is not a lot of margin for error (or gunk) in that short space, and if you fall under the required distance/time, you get malfunctions again. And there, the malfunctions appear as bolt over base failures. Yep, the same failure whether you have too much or too little.

So, unless you are building a rifle for competition or varmint shooting, and are then willing to be fussy about ammo and maintenance, do not use a lightweight carrier.

CARRIER PROBLEMS

Carries are a low-stress item made of durable steel, and short of blowing a case I'm not sure how you would go

about wearing out a carrier. There are, however, two things that can effect reliability and service life. One you can check and fix, the other you can't.

The steel that your carrier is made of is 8620. This is a low-carbon steel that takes very well to case-hardening. The resultant part is one that is very hard on the surface, but not hard through. As a result, it shows great wearability, and can shrug off incidental bangs and knocks with no effect. Drop a regular carrier onto a concrete surface (oops, in cleaning) and you might cause a small ding on the edge of the carrier. The concrete might have a chunk knocked out of it. If the carrier was hard all the way though, dropping it the same way might crack it.

This also leads to the phenomena we see when you blow a case. The bottom of the carrier, the stripper rail that rides

over the cartridge stack of the magazine, gets broken loose from the carrier. But rather than blowing off, it usually ends up bent down at an angle, as a "tongue." The soft interior bends, even though the hard surface cracks at the bottoms of the furrows.

The fixable problem is the carrier key. This is the spigot that draws gas from the gas tube down into the carrier. If there is leakage, the rifle might short-stroke and you will have malfunctions. The cure here is to remove the old key, clean the parts

and dress the mating surfaces until they are smooth, even and clean. Then use Loctite and a MOACKS (the Mother Of All Carrier Key Stakers) to crimp the metal of the key over the heads of the cap screws holding the key in place.

Some complain that this is ugly. So what, who cares? And who looks inside your rifle, anyway? Some complain that once Loctited and staked it can't be removed. When will you ever remove it? That's right, when it is worn out.

Keys wear out. Keys can be replaced. When you do replace a key, do you care if you have to destroy it to remove it? And the screws should not be re-used, so do you care if they are destroyed also? No and no.

One company, Yankee Hill, insists that their carrier keys not be staked. They are quite insistent on the matter, so if you use their carrier, be aware that staking it will void the warranty.

The service life aspect you cannot fix is the gas ring issue. The rings ride on the bolt, and inside of the carrier bore. They are exactly like the piston rings in your car.

They seal the gas bore of the carrier until the cycle causes them to move and uncover the vent holes, to blow excess gas out of the system. No seal, no stroke. When the carrier is manufactured, the bore of the carrier has

Carriers require precision machining and are made out of tough steel. Unless you blow a case, they are subject to such low stresses that you will never wear one out.

been machined, reamed, honed and then hard-chrome plated. If all of the tool marks have not been removed, the chromed bore will act like a tubular file and wear down your gas rings in short order. We have seen rifles that in less than 500 rounds had gas ring wear so bad that the assembled bolt/carrier failed the stand-up test.

The only solution to this is to replace rings when they wear, or replace the carrier.

The bore cannot be polished smooth if it has machine tool marks left in it.

REPLACEMENT CARRIERS OF THE GOOD SORT

Carriers were originally (pre-M16A1) hard chrome plated. That was dropped for "don't be shiny in a combat zone" reasons in Vietnam. Today, since we have a whole

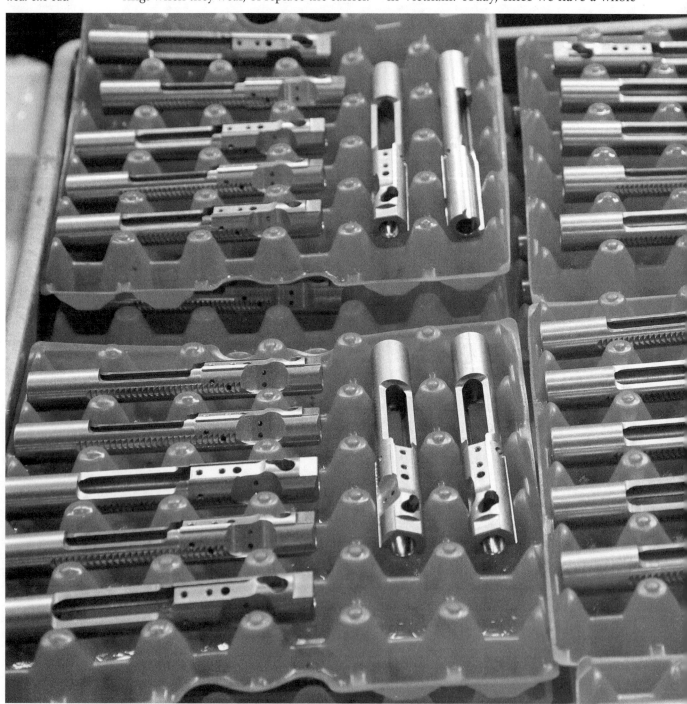

lot more uses and needs for rifles than combat zones, you can buy carriers with various platings or non-corroding alloys. Keeping a carrier clean when it has been given a nickel-boron plating is a lot easier than one that is parkerized.

Don't pass on a good carrier just because it is shiny.

Also, the issue of keeping the gas key tight has been solved. LWRC has a carrier with

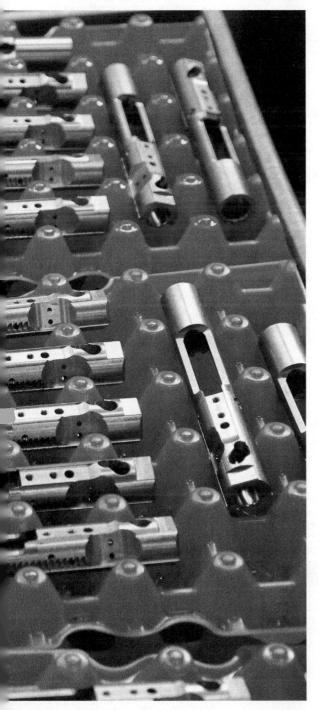

the shoulder of the gas key machined as an integral part of the carrier. The spigot is screwed into the shoulder and cross-pinned to keep it in place. It will not leak gas, and in the event of wear the spigot portion can be removed and replaced.

PISTON OR NO PISTON?

I spent some time trying to figure out just which chapter to put this into. Barrel? Carrier? One of the build chapters? I finally decided to put it in with carriers for one simple reason: all piston designs replace the carrier. Well, one of the first didn't, the Adams Arms. It used a replacement key, but other shooters had problems with that approach. (I never have, in years of shooting mine.) And so Adams first improved it, and then re-designed the carrier to have an integral thrust shoulder.

Piston systems are touted as the solution to all problems. Actually, they aren't, but they do have some use. How useful they are depends on your needs. So, consider a few questions:

Do you plan on shooting a lot of full auto?

Are you building an SBR?

Will you do a lot of suppressed shooting?

Will your ammo vary from premium to drek?

Are you seeking the absolute best accuracy?

Do you expect using a piston to not bring problems?

FULL AUTO?

Full auto is hard on rifles and carbines. Yes, the AR-15/M16 (the first versions were marked AR-15, before it got typed as the M16) were designed and built to be full auto. But it is hard on them anyway. The big deal is heat. Not just the heat of the barrel, but the heat pumped back into the action by the gases running the carrier. I've tested, and measured the temps of semi-auto rifles, and the heat that gets back to the action is pretty much negligible. Not nothing, but not something that will make the rifle quit.

Full auto is a lot harder, and the heat does not have as much time to dissipate,

When you go to a piston system (as these gas blocks are made for) you have to change carriers.

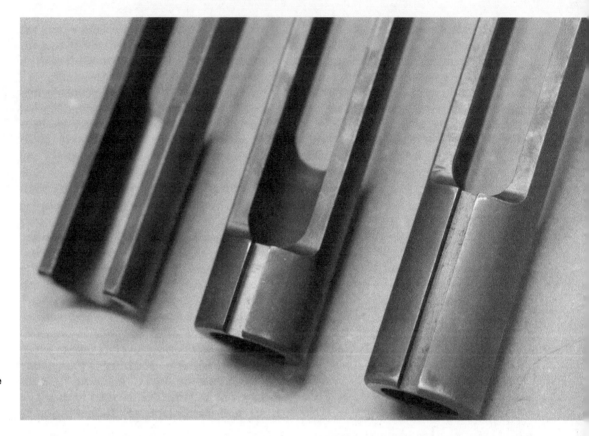

The three types of carrier rear shelf. On the right, the original shelf, M16 for the auto sear. In the middle, the Colt AR-15 "we want you to not get in trouble" design. And on the left, the Colt "we really, really want to keep you out of trouble" design. The ATF doesn't care anymore, if they ever did.

resulting in a hotter receiver. Piston advocates will tell you "piston rifles run cooler," which is not true. Heat is heat, piston designs just dump it in different places. The front sight or gas block gets hot on any AR, but when it has a piston system that area gets hotter, faster. You're just moving the heat that would have been in the receiver to the gas block and piston.

Carrier keys are made to precise dimensions because they have to seal gas until the carrier has moved. If there is no seal, gas leaks and your rifle malfunctions.

It doesn't cause as many problems there, as in the receiver, but the heat still exists.

SBR?

Short-barreled rifles, in the direct-gas impingement system, can be very touchy. The time the gas has to work before it bleeds off is small. The gas impulse on an SBR has a much smaller allowable range than on a carbine or rifle. The various piston systems, because they use the gas flow to drive a rod, are a bit more forgiving. A piston system can be overgassed, with extra bled off from the block, and still properly run an SBR. On a DI-SBR, the gas can't bleed off until it has flowed all the way back to the carrier. Even so, a piston system is only better than a DI system in an SBR, it isn't a well-engineered one, unless the designer has worked with SBRs in mind.

The original designs were meant to convert existing rifles and carbines. We now have been seeing second- and third-generation piston systems, which better-handle the problems of an SBR.

A piston system is a viable option on an SBR. On others it brings its own problems along with the benefits.

SUPPRESSED?

Adding a suppressor to an AR causes problems because of excess gas. Not that the "back pressure" is increased, but the dwell time. Dwell time is the length of time the gas is working, once the bullet passes the gas port and until it leaves the muzzle. The gas port size is calculated using the length of barrel from the chamber to the gas port, and the length of barrel from the gas port to the muzzle.

Adding a suppressor delays the release of gases, thus increasing the dwell time. It is as if you added a couple of extra inches to the barrel length, but kept the gas port the same size for the shorter dwell time.

Piston systems help here by having multiple settings. You can set the gas flow for normal, un-suppressed. You can set it for reduced flow, with a suppressor installed. And some have even more settings than that.

PREMIUM TO DREK?

If you only ever feed your rifle one type of ammo, you can have a perfectly drilled gas port and be happy. The gas port size on an M4 (a real-deal M4) barrel is drilled to a specific dimension because the military expects that rifle to see only a few types of ammo. And those particular loads have been developed with that specific gas port diameter in mind.

Now you go and feed your rifle imported ammo. Varmint loads. Heavy-bullet match loads. Reloaded ammo that you have loaded up for reasons of economy, performance, whatever.

Will all that ammo deliver gas pressure to your gas port and the correct continued pressures during the dwell time? Who knows?

A piston system, with an adjustable setting or settings, allows you to dial in the gas flow you need for the ammo you are using.

ABSOLUTE ACCURACY?

Piston systems cause problems with one of the absolute hallmarks of the AR system – a free-floated barrel. The AR can de-

liver stunning accuracy because the barrel is untouched by anything. Well, anything but the gas tube, in many builds and designs.

So, you go and clamp or pin a block to it, and hang a spring-loaded rod on that, which is attached at one or more points in the handguard or receiver. What will that do to accuracy?

For someone interested in "minute of felon" accuracy, or wanting a run-n-gun 3-gun rifle or just a plinker, no problem. For the match shooter who is sweating every wind call, who wants to claw not just every point but every x-count out of a match, big problem.

So, for varminters and long-range, precision shooters, pistons are a no-go.

PROBLEMS?

Pistons bring their own problems. Besides the potential accuracy issues, there is the matter of axial tilt. When the gas system on a regular AR pressurizes, the carrier is thrust directly back on its centerline. When the piston comes back and hits or pushes on the carrier, it does so up where the gas key was or would have been. This is an off-center thrust, and it creates what is called "carrier tilt."

The effect is that the rear end of the carrier dips down slightly. It can be nothing, and it can lead to carrier tilt chatter marks on the back of the receiver or on the buffer tube. If the chatter is just wrong, it can hammer the leading edge of the buffer tube, chew up bits of aluminum, and generally make a mess of things.

The piston makers or piston conversion makers deal with this by adding metal to the back bottom of the carrier, "anti tilt pads" they are called. The buffer tube makers address this by extending the front bottom lip of the tube, so as to put metal underneath, and closer to, the carrier. This minimizes tilt chatter opportunities, and puts replaceable aluminum (the buffer tube) under the carrier.

Piston systems can be good, depending on what you need. But they are a perfect example of what Robert Heinlein termed TANSTAAFL. There Ain't No Such Thing As A Free Lunch. ■

CHAPTER 6

Buffers and Springs and Ports, Oh My

In the pantheon of awful, this one wasn't so bad, but it still caused the carbine it was in to malfunction now and then. Once it was replaced with a proper buffer, the carbine worked just fine. One piece of steel is not right, and why the maker thought this was better, we have no idea.

There is a current vogue in some circles of using the heaviest buffers to be had in all applications. Don't fall for this. The buffer is that weight that rides in the buffer tube, or as Colt calls it, the receiver extension. The original was far too light for actual use, weighing a mere 1.9 ounces. Once the rifle was finalized for production and use, the rifle buffer ended up weighing 5.0 ounces. (This was done by Colt, in part to deal with the change in powders that the whiz kids and the Army cooked up. That the heavier buffer weight actually solved the problem was a near-miracle. And it was quickly negated with further changes to the rifle.)

The carbine buffer, for a long time, was a short and light affair, and it tipped the scales at 2.9 to 3.0 ounces. It had to be short in order to work in the shorter carbine buffer tube and not bind up the action. It could be lighter because the carbines used a different-dimension gas tube port, and thus delivered just the right amount of gas for proper function.

In a carbine with a 16" barrel, back when suppressors were almost as rare as machine guns, that was enough. But, then SBRs began to become popular, and the military began using SBRs even more often. (The M4, with a 14.5" barrel, is an SBR, barely, and only because the law says so. Mechanically, I wouldn't call it one.) An actual SBR, a carbine with a shorter barrel, like one with an 11.5" barrel, needs more mass to keep the cycling parts under control. If you add a suppressor, things get even more obnoxious.

So, the industry developed the H, H2 and H3 buffers.

The buffer is designed to act like a dead-blow hammer. The weights inside are free to move a small amount. When the buffer drives forward, pushed by the spring, the weights inside, due to inertia, slap to the rear of the tube. The bolt closes, the carrier stops, and the weights then slap forward.

Why? Originally, the M16 was designed as a select-fire rifle. When the carrier comes to rest, it strikes the rear face of the barrel extension. In engineering parlance, a steel-on-steel impact is very elastic. If you drop a steel ball bearing onto a steel plate, it will bounce higher than pretty much any other material hitting that plate.

The carrier bounces off of the barrel extension. In full-auto fire, if the hammer happens to release and come forward at the very time the carrier is bouncing back,

the hammer can't hit the firing pin. This causes a "live chambered round misfire" and it is most annoying. Especially if you were counting on getting the extra shots in a combat situation.

So, the loose weights inside the buffer slap into the inside front of the buffer tube, just as the carrier would be bouncing, and kill the bounce.

Those weights were originally made of steel. To increase the mass, manufacturers went with tungsten, and as a result, the three heavier buffers have one, two or all three of the steel weights replaced with ones made of tungsten. The H is 3.8 ounces, the H2 is 4.7 ounces, and the H3 is 5.6 ounces, heavier than that of the rifle carbine.

A special buffer is the 9mm carbine one. Since the 9mm is a blowback and uses only mass to control the cycling, that buffer weighs 5.5 ounces in the Colt carbine.

WHICH ONE?

You might think "well, the rifle buffer is the full weight, can't I just use that? Not if you have a carbine with a telestock. The

Yet another craptastic buffer. This one is a three-part assembly, and the tube even had a seam in it. And the seam split.

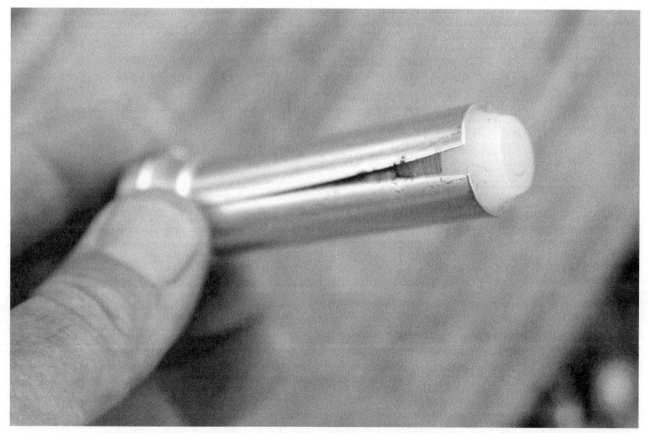

If your gas port is over-sized like this one, you can tame the system with a heavier buffer. It isn't ideal, but you can't shrink holes in steel, so your options are limited.

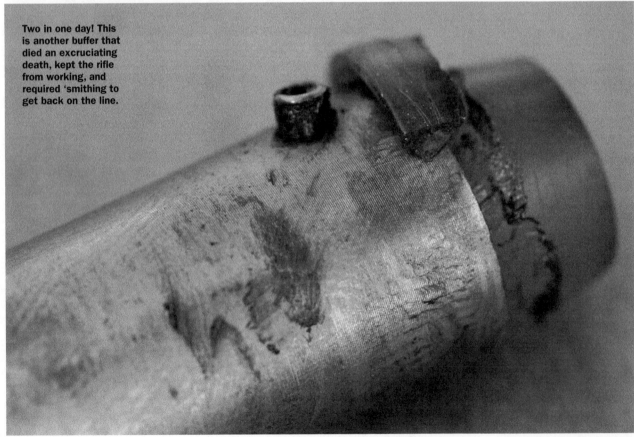

Two in one day! This is another buffer that died an excruciating death, kept the rifle from working, and required 'smithing to get back on the line.

carbine buffer tube is too short inside, and the rifle buffer too long, and the combo won't let the action cycle far enough to run properly.

Well, then, just use the heaviest one, since heavier is better, right? Again, no. The weight you need depends on the ammunition you are using and the size of the gas port on your AR. A lot of low-end, commodity ARs have the gas port drilled a drill size too large. They are over-gassed because the manufacturer knows that a lot of shooters will use the cheapest ammo they can find. Cheapo ammo likely means underpowered ammo, and if you put under-powered ammo into a carbine with a too-heavy buffer, you may be inducing malfunctions instead of eliminating them.

We'll assume you have a standard carrier in your rifle or carbine. If not, go back a chapter and read up on what you should be using. With a standard carrier and using good-quality, brass-cased American ammo, your ejection pattern should be:

- Full-sized rifle: 3-4 o'clock
- 16" carbine: 4-5 o'clock
- SBR with a slickside upper (no forward assist): 5 o'clock
- SBR with ejector lump: 2-3 o'clock

Why the difference with the SBR and the "lump"? Because the brass is bouncing off of the lump and being ricocheted forward.

As the bolt cycles, the ejector is constantly pushing on the base of the case. As the case comes out of the chamber, it is already tilting to go out of the ejection port. How fast the bolt is traveling back determines what angle the brass is thrown. For Uhtred, son of Uhtred, destiny is all; but for us, bolt velocity is all. The faster the bolt travels back, the sharper the angle it is ejected to the side or behind.

A bad sign in rifles is when the brass is thrown ahead of you. That means the bolt velocity is so great that the brass hasn't time to clear the ejection port before the bolt has pulled it back to the back edge, and the brass bounces off of the rim, going forward.

You want to use the heaviest buffer that provides the correct angle of brass ejection. If that means the one the rifle came with, you aren't improving things by going to a heavier one.

However, if you have a commodity M4gery and the maker drilled the gas port too big to "ensure" it functions reliably, you may well find that going to a heavier buffer reduces felt recoil. It also will mean

JP Enterprises makes this excellent competition-only low-mass carrier. They'll be the first ones to tell you not to use it in a Duty or Self Defense build.

Check your buffer. Low-cost parts can break, as this one did, and it tied up the gun. It took three of us to get the rifle apart, extract the buffer, and get the rifle up and running again.

the brass is hurled in the correct direction, without being dented, bent, mangled or otherwise made difficult to reload.

BUFFERS TO AVOID

We've been over this in earlier volumes, but it bears repeating, especially since we still see the fabulously crap-tastic plastic buffers from time to time. First on the "replace it right now" hit parade are the molded plastic buffers with lead shot inside of them. They may weigh the same, they may act like dead-blow hammers, but they cause malfunctions. I suspect that the plastic drags on the inside of the tube more than the aluminum of real buffers does, and that causes problems.

Second up are those that do not rattle when you shake them. A buffer with a solid piece of steel in it is just asking for trouble. No, you won't be encountering the full-auto malfunctions, but they are still problematic.

Last are any buffers that are obviously made up of multiple pieces. The buffer

body is designed to be made of a single piece of aluminum, with the synthetic bumper pinned to the back. I've seen cheapo buffers with the head screwed onto the tube, the tube with a seam up the side, and even one that was just a single piece of aluminum with the bumper pinned onto the back end. (How that was cheaper to make, I have no idea.)

COMPETITION BUFFERS

Just as there are lightweight carriers for competition, there are also lightweight buffers. They generally are the same shape as the standard rifle buffers, but they do not have the internal steel weights. You use them in conjunction with the lightweight carriers and for the same applications. Don't use them unless you have an adjustable gas block and you're tuning the system to have the softest possible felt recoil, regardless of the risk of malfunction.

The manufacturers will tell you right up front not to use them in duty or defensive firearms.

Top, a carbine buffer. Middle, a low-mass competition carrier. Bottom, the original design, and one not to be used even in a retro build.

Buffers are marked if their weights differ from the normal, expected weight. Heavier can be useful, but it is not always better.

SPRINGS

Do not use extra-strength buffer springs. The spring as-made is the correct one. If there is a problem with your rifle, using a heavier spring is not the way to "solve" it. We have seen springs that were a few coils over, but the record? Well. The correct spring length for a carbine spring is 37 to 39 coils, and a relaxed length of 10-1/16 to 11-1/4 inches. The rifle spring should be 41 to 43 coils, and 11-5/8 to 13-1/2 inches. The record in a class was was a carbine that was malfunctioning (no surprise) that had a spring in it of 50 coils. That's way too many.

If you're having problems with your rifle or carbine, pull out the spring and buffer. Look at the buffer markings, if any, and count the spring coils.

GAS PORT DIMENSIONS

You'll find a lot of angst in some circles over "what is the proper gas port diameter?"

The unfortunate and unavoidable irony? There's nothing you can do to change the gas port diameter except to make it larger. There's no way to put steel back. The gas port is what the gas port is, and all your efforts afterwards will be bent towards dealing with the gas flow it produces.

Now, you may find a custom barrel maker willing to accommodate you on gas port size. If so, expect a bit of resistance and an upcharge. Resistance because they have a lot of experience on what works and what doesn't. They will be understandably reluctant to go and make it something they aren't happy with, because they don't want you coming back with a problem, or bad-mouthing them because your rifle doesn't work.

And there will be an upcharge simply because it is a bunch of extra steps. Someone has to take the fixture that drills gas ports, replace the usual drill, install the one you want, and then make sure the original, correct-diameter drill is replaced for the rest of the barrels being drilled. When something is working properly, without stumbles or errors, a good production manager is loathe to change anything. Anything.

Your request is a change. So, they will charge for it, and likely will hold off drilling your barrel until it comes time to replace the usual drill anyway. They'll drill yours in-between parts swaps and dimensional checks, and you will wait. And be charged.

If you find that your gas port has been drilled too large, you can/will have to make changes in the system elsewhere. You can use a heavier buffer (that's one proper use for the H series buffers) or find a way to throttle down the gas flow. ■

CHAPTER 7

Triggers

For non-service-rifle competition, an adjustable trigger like this one can garner you the extra points needed to win.

This is a touchy subject (no pun intended). The trigger mechanism is what you use to fire a cartridge. Since the whole point of a rifle is to be an accurate bullet launcher (distinct from a shotgun, which hurls a cloud of shot), then anything that interferes with accurate shooting is bad.

However, a trigger that is too easy to set off can be a distinct hazard. Running around with a rifle that has a trigger pull measured in a few ounces would be a bad thing, as almost any inadvertent bump would set it off.

Benchrest shooters use triggers that have pull weights measured in ounces. But, they are using relatively heavy rifles, sitting at concrete benches, and trying to fire the smallest possible groups. Their rifles do not even have safeties, as they do not load their single-shot rifles until they plan to fire.

When the Army adopted the M16, they were planning on an environment that was almost the opposite. In combat, rifles are bumped, dropped and fallen on, equipment bangs into them, and through all of this they must not fire. One aspect of the AR-15/M16 design makes this a particular problem: it has a single-stage trigger.

The AR trigger is a simple lever: the nose of the trigger rests in the notch of the hammer. The force needed to fire the rifle is the force needed to lever the nose of the trigger down out of the notch, against the compressive force of the hammer spring.

Other designs add levers or arrange the forces so the trigger is not being pushed directly towards its axis. The advantage of other designs is that they allow for adjustability, or decreased force to initiate. The advantage of the AR design is simplicity. With three moving parts, each with its own dedicated spring, the hammer, trigger and disconnector of the design are easy to fabricate. They are also easy to track, that is, keep the relevant dimensions within acceptable limits.

The trigger manufacturer need only to keep the trigger face a known distance from, and at a known angle to, the pivot hole in the trigger. The other dimensions can be pretty much what they are when the trigger falls out of the forge dies or casting mold.

Similarly, the hammer notch needs to be a precise distance from, and angle to, the hammer pivot hole.

The disconnector? It is stamped out of a heavy-gauge sheet of steel. Usually a process called fine-blanking, but sometimes not.

The trigger pull is a result of the frictional forces of the trigger sliding against the hammer hook. The springs involved don't have a lot to do with it. Once the hammer spring is strong enough to guarantee that it will set off the primer 100% of the time, and the trigger spring is strong enough to ensure it snaps up into the path of the hammer so as to avoid an inadvertent full-auto setup, you are up past the "rifleman's trigger" weight of 3.5 pounds. Well past. The spring weights and the engagement surfaces (the amount

Timney makes excellent replacement triggers, but some of them are definitely not mil-spec or Service Rifle designs. Good for them.

of overlap between the hammer hook and trigger tip) also have to take into account the variances of the receiver holes. The trigger and hammer pivot on pins that are set into the lower receiver through holes.

So, the full assembly has to remain safe even when the "tolerance stack" of the parts has worked in all directions to the maximum allowed. Or, when wear in the holes has made them a bit sloppy. Some who have high-volume or extremely expensive (read: transferable) M16/M4 rifles obsess about pinhole wear. To prevent it, they invest in pins that have external locking straps, from KNS, to eliminate pin rotation and reduce pinhole wear. I've shot perhaps a hundred thousand rounds out of a rack of ARs and can see no wear yet. I'm not worried.

The mil-spec-allowed trigger pulls for the various models are: M16A2, M16A4, M4 is between 5.5 and 9.5 pounds. For the M16A3 and the M4A1, it is 5.5 to 8.5 pounds. That's right, the best mil-spec trigger pull you can have is 5.5 pounds, and they can go up to nearly twice that. Why? Any lower than 5.5 and the risk of tolerance stack becomes too great. Also, military rifles are subject to a lot of bouncing, jarring, dropping and other handling problems. So the armed forces want triggers that won't go off accidentally, even if the rifle is dropped when the safety is off.

Now, not all military triggers are like that. For use in marksmanship-oriented applications, the end-users can expect triggers that will be as clean and crisp as possible, and perhaps (perhaps) a bit lighter than 5.5 pounds. But they will not be like the "target" trigger on your uncle's hunting rifle. They can't be. Even the SpecOps people who will be using them, and perhaps the DMR users, need a rifle that won't go off when it is bumped and falls to the ground.

BETTER TRIGGERS

Before we went with the M16, we were using a better trigger design and had been for decades. The M1 Garand and the M14 used what is called a two-stage trigger. Here, the trigger surface and the hammer hook do not work as a simple lever. The trigger surface slides off the hammer

hook, and when it has traveled most of its distance there is a spring-loaded second stage. So, the initial pull can be very light, since there is a spring-loaded backup (if you will) to keep it from bouncing off.

The two steps can each be a couple of pounds, very light, but combined they add up to 4 pounds or more.

The feel of the two designs is markedly different.

In a single-stage trigger, you press the trigger and it seems to not move. Once you reach enough pressure to move it, it moves all of a sudden and completely. If the two surfaces are rough enough, or the trigger pull needed is great enough, you can feel it move grittily through its path.

On a two-stage trigger, you start pressing, and once you get past the first stage, say 2 pounds, the trigger moves. Then it stops. It stays there until you reach the rest of the force needed and then it moves again, and the rifle fires. You might read about "taking up the slack." This is that.

These demo blocks are perfect for testing trigger pulls side-by-side, and picking the one that feels the best to you. But, they're not easy to find.

If you take up the slack and then release, the trigger moves back to its original location, and you have "lost" the 2 pounds. This is not a "set" trigger where you can set the mechanism to then fire when you press a second time.

IMPROVING THE SINGLE STAGE

One way to improve the single-stage trigger is to polish and coat the engagement surfaces to reduce friction. You still have the spring forces, but the parts slide over each

This M16 is over 50 years old, has been shot a bazillion times, and the hammer and trigger pin holes are still fine. If you want to use non-rotating pins, go ahead, but it isn't a problem.

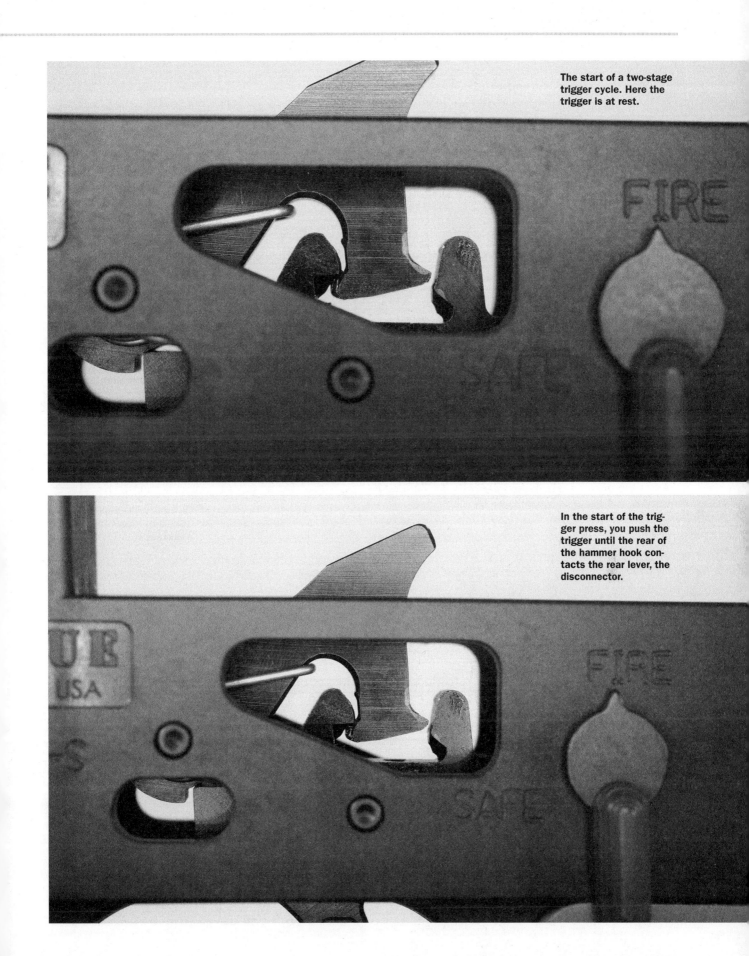

The start of a two-stage trigger cycle. Here the trigger is at rest.

In the start of the trigger press, you push the trigger until the rear of the hammer hook contacts the rear lever, the disconnector.

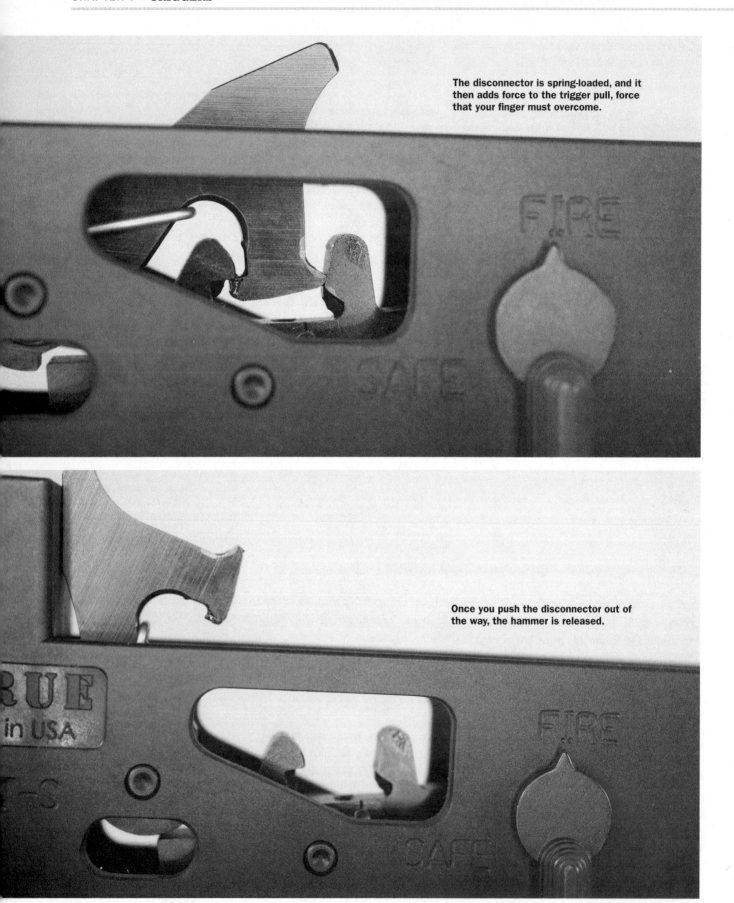

The disconnector is spring-loaded, and it then adds force to the trigger pull, force that your finger must overcome.

Once you push the disconnector out of the way, the hammer is released.

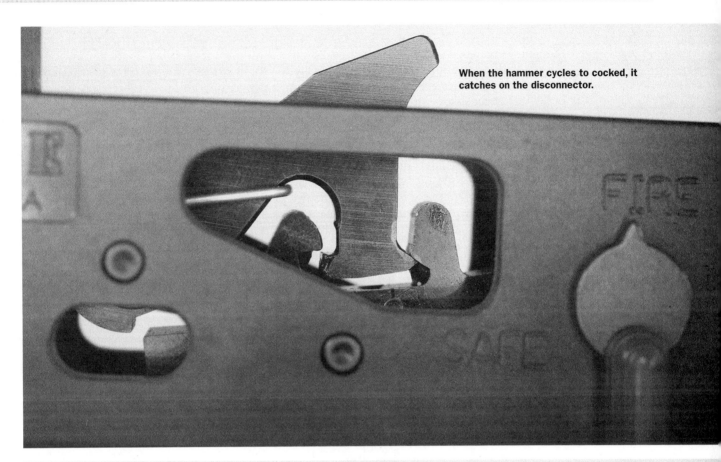

When the hammer cycles to cocked, it catches on the disconnector.

When you release the trigger, it slips off of the disconnector and gets caught by the trigger sear, starting the cycle over again.

other with friction that is so reduced that the net effect is a much lighter trigger pull.

The various improved military or coated single stage triggers, such as those from ALG Defense, operate this way.

Another way is to use a "packet" trigger. Here the design is manufactured with much tighter tolerances. By keeping the trigger and hammer surfaces more tightly controlled, the engagement surfaces can be shorter. The springs needed can be less. But, what to do about the receiver hole locations? Simple: enclose the hammer, trigger and other parts in a shell, and then let the shell "float" for a few thousandths inside the receiver. The packet has hollow tubes across this span. The hammer and trigger rotate on the outside of these tubes, and the receiver pins that hold the packet inside pass down the hollow centers of the tubes.

The exact location of the receiver holes is of little matter. The trigger and hammer remain in place, rotating around the tubes, which are fixed to the shell of the packet, and their relationship will not change. The packet can rattle on the receiver pins for all that matters, because the sear engagement will never change because of that rattle.

Chip McCormick came up with the idea and product first, and now everyone makes one type or another.

The same packet can hold a two-stage trigger as well.

IMPROVING THE TWO-STAGE

It doesn't really need improvement, as the design is inherently prone to clean, crisp trigger pulls.

DRAWBACKS

One drawback to the improved trigger pull either approach represents is not with the rifle itself. Properly installed they will be safe and improve your rifle shooting. Where the hazard lies is this: what handgun do you use? If you carry a polymer-framed striker-fired pistol, you probably have a trigger pull that is 5.5 pounds, or heavier.

So, you do lots and lots and lots of practice with your handgun, with its 5.5- to 6-pound trigger pull. Then you pull your rifle out of the bag, load up, and try to shoot with its 3.5-pound trigger pull. How many times does it go off just a bit early, as your handgun-trained trigger finger is pulling through the first four pounds of the expected 5.5-pound process?

We've seen it happen in police classes, when an officer has a duty sidearm with a 5- or 6- or 7-pound trigger pull, and a rifle with a two-stage trigger and a clean, crisp 3.5-pound pull.

It isn't safe or unsafe one way or the other, it simply is a mis-match in expectations, and one you should consider if you are going to change the trigger in your rifle or carbine.

HORSE FOR COURSES

This is a British expression, and it simply means you select the appropriate tool for the job. If you will be working on duty and are issued a striker-fired pistol with a spongy trigger pull of 5 to 6 pounds, you'd better have a patrol rifle that is the same. If, on the other hand, you are a SWAT trooper and your issue rifle has a clean, crisp 3.5-pound trigger pull, you would do well to see that your handgun is the same.

A 3-gun or multi-gun competitor, or a varmint shooter? Go with whatever you want, that feels good and doesn't interfere with the proper manipulation of your handgun trigger. The top competition shooters often use (at least in divisions other than Revolver or Production) triggers that are under 3 pounds. And to be clear, they are not beating your scores because of the light trigger they use. They use a light trigger to try and edge out the other top shooters. Were you to trade guns with them, the Grand Master you shoot against would still handily beat you.

Clean is good, light is icing on the cake, and too light will get you in trouble.

Oh, and then there are the matches where the rules require a certain weight. If you go to shoot a Service Rifle match, your trigger had better hold 4.5 pounds, or you will have to get it corrected. Or shoot in some other equipment Division.

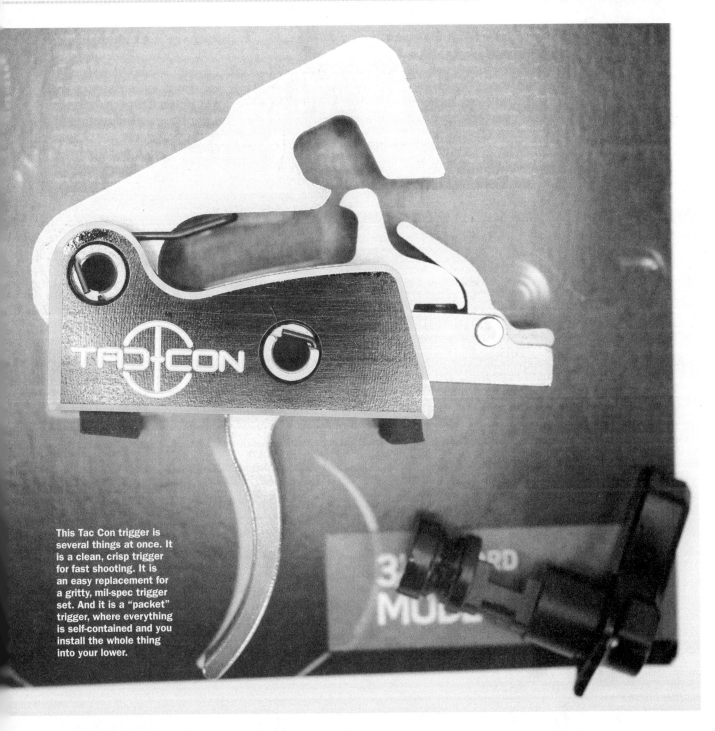

This Tac Con trigger is several things at once. It is a clean, crisp trigger for fast shooting. It is an easy replacement for a gritty, mil-spec trigger set. And it is a "packet" trigger, where everything is self-contained and you install the whole thing into your lower.

WHICH TO USE?

The easiest way to get a better trigger pull is to simply invest in a packet trigger and drop it in. You don't have to worry about correct assembly, whether the receiver pinholes are in the right place, or if the springs have enough oomph.

You could even have a single lower, and an array of upper assemblies and packet triggers. Going to shoot the Service Rifle match? Install the Service Rifle packet trigger, slap on the Service upper and head out (with the correct ammo, one hopes).

Going varmint shooting? Swap out the packet for a much lighter one and install the varmint upper. Off to the multi-gun match? Leave the varmint trigger packet in, put the appropriate multi-gun upper on, and get to the match. ∎

CHAPTER 8

How Tight, What Color and What Rail?

This is a camo pattern that is the anodizing of the receivers. It is not easy to apply, and it is not mil-spec, so you get it because you want it. And it is worth it.

HOW TIGHT?

If your AR has an upper-to-lower fit that is so tight you have to use a hammer to tap the takedown pins in and out, it is too tight. The problem isn't the wear, but the tapping. If you tap too hard (because it is tight, and "doggone, I've got to get this open to clean it"), you can break the thin skin of the takedown pin retaining plunger tube wall. What causes the fit to be too tight? And, can we fix it?

The fit of the upper to the lower is controlled by two variables, neither of which is under your control. The first is the distance from the center axis of the takedown pin holes in the upper and lower, and their respective "decks." The deck is the flat surface where the upper and lower meet. The distance, or height, of the deck is controlled in the upper and lower by the plus-or-minus dimensions of the blueprints, and the machine that is programmed to cut them, or the machine operator following the prints. (For the digital among us, that would be the paper equivalent of the CAD/Cam file.) The proper dimensions are known precisely

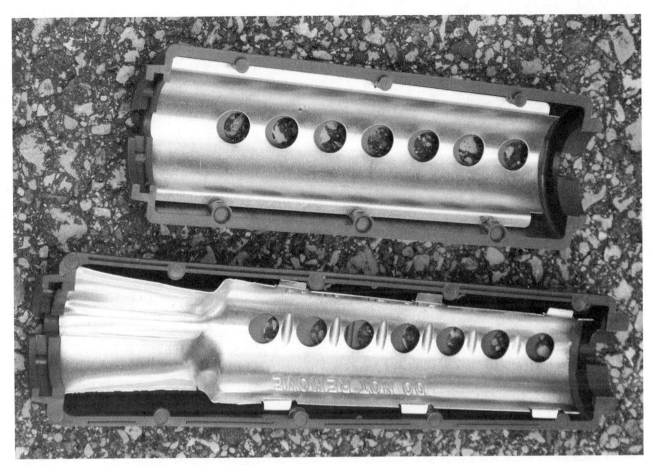

only to those manufacturers who have access to the TDP, the Technical Data Package. That is a very small group.

Everyone else who is making AR uppers and lowers has had to "reverse engineer" the dimensions. The would-be maker buys five, ten or twenty receivers and measures the exact location of all the relevant dimensions. They then take the average, and give the correct location and allowed wanderings, the "plus or minus" dimensions of each their best guess, and start making parts.

Let's construct an example: let's assume we're in the business of making cubes, as a competitor to the authorized manufacturer of cubes. One product in particular is the most popular, let's call them one-inch cubes. But, we don't know that they are one-inch cubes to an exact measurement, so we buy a fistful and measure them. We find that they actually measure more-or-less an inch. The ones we have vary from 1.001" to 0.999" in size. OK, that gives us our spread, we can assign the cubes the measurement of "one inch, plus or minus

one-thousandth of an inch." But, we don't know things that may or may not be critical. Can they be plus-or-minus randomly in each dimension? Or is there a critical set that must be held to a tighter set of dimensions? How parallel must the faces be, that is, can a cube be 1.001" at one corner, and 0.999" at its opposite corner on a face, and still be "in spec"?

And the cube, Mk2, with a half-inch hole through it? It is one more feature, but it brings with it at least three new dimensions that must be held to standards. How much can the hole diameter vary? How centered in the face of the cube must the hole be, and how far of an angle off of dead-center-through can it wander before it is no longer acceptable?

These are trivial examples of the problems of reverse engineering an AR upper and lower set can present. So, it is understandable if the deck distance of an upper and lower, made by manufacturers who reverse engineered their parts in distant parts of the country, are a bit tight. Or shockingly loose. After all, if one manufacturer has

The heat shields inside the handguard protect your hands by reflecting the heat back to the barrel. The M4 handguards have two shields, with an air space between them.

While we were in a real war, and in the places where we're actually shooting bad guys, a painted M16 or M4 was no big deal. Back here in the States, painting your issue rifle will get you in big trouble.

determined that the deck height can vary plus-or-minus .001", and another feels that .005" is fine, what happens when you get an upper and lower, one from each, that have the maximum spreads of each maker? You get a sloppy or too-tight fit, that's what.

The second variable that can cause a tight fit (but not so much a sloppy one) is the curve at the rear of the upper, and its matching curve in the lower. Where it is, where it starts on the lower and upper, the radius of the curve, and how well they match, all matter. A tight mis-match makes the overall fit tight. A loose mis-match might not make the overall fit loose (the deck heights might match up, and create a snug fit), but a loose mis-match in the curve will blow gas, and this can lead to gas puff in the face.

WHAT TO DO?

You cannot easily make a tight fit less tight. And it is more work than it is worth to try and tighten up a loose fit. The US-AMU did this, and perhaps still does. They take an upper-lower set that is wobbly, measure the gap, cut shim stock to fit the top of the deck, then epoxy it in place to fill the gap. Even when I first read this, I was stunned. What the heck? Can the military procurement system be so screwed up that they have to resort to such measures for a tight fit? I mean, does the Army not have warehouses full of rifles? Rather than spend that much time on one rifle, the entire fleet of assigned competition lowers could have matched, properly fitting uppers, simply by walking the aisles of racked rifles, trying uppers until they fit, then swapping uppers.

That is what you should do, except for the walking aisles of rifles. If you want a properly-fitting upper and lower, take the lower to the gun shop and check the fits of uppers until you find one you can build on. Yes, this is a plug for the actual, brick-and-mortar gun shop, opposed to online shopping, and darn right. Phone ahead to make sure they have bare uppers. Ask if you can check the fit. If not, dial the next one on your list. Or, buy a matched set. If you are building a rifle for a specific purpose, then order a matched set. Brownells will do this, and the makers of uppers and lowers will, also. After all, if they are machining

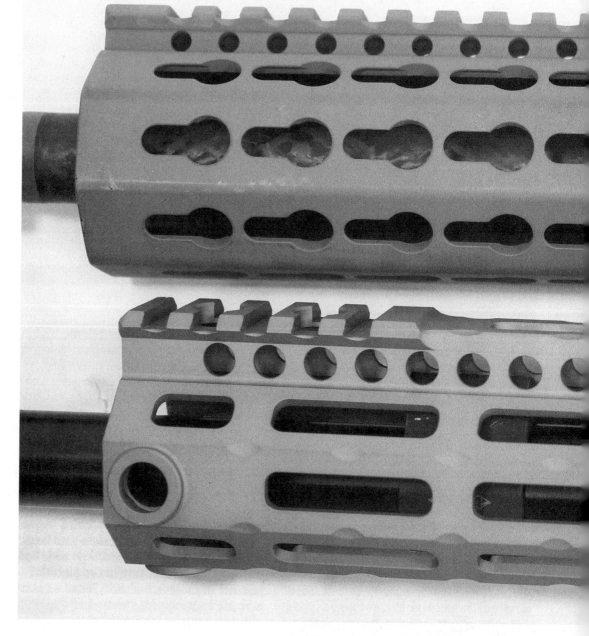

The new rail isn't a rail. It is a non-rail that uses accessories with attachment hardware built in. On top, Keymod, and on the bottom, M-Lok. It looks like M-Lok is winning, but there may be something even better in the future.

both, they can easily make sure the two are a snug and proper fit.

If you are buying an already-assembled rifle, with the idea of re-building it to what you want (and it had better be a real bargain, for this) then check the fit. If you are going to re-build it anyway, do you really care about the changeable features it has? A tight fit is more important than the barrel length (which you'll remove and trade or sell) or the handguards (ditto on those) so check for fit. Move down the rack and buy the snug one.

WHAT IS SNUG?

This is simple: when assembled, the upper and lower do not have any felt wobble. You needn't break into a sweat, trying to make them move, but if hand strength alone doesn't make them move, they are tight enough. And with that fit, the takedown pins should be snug, but still loose enough that you can move them with finger pressure, or a slight boost from the end of a pen, pencil or bullet tip. If you are practically breaking a fingernail prying

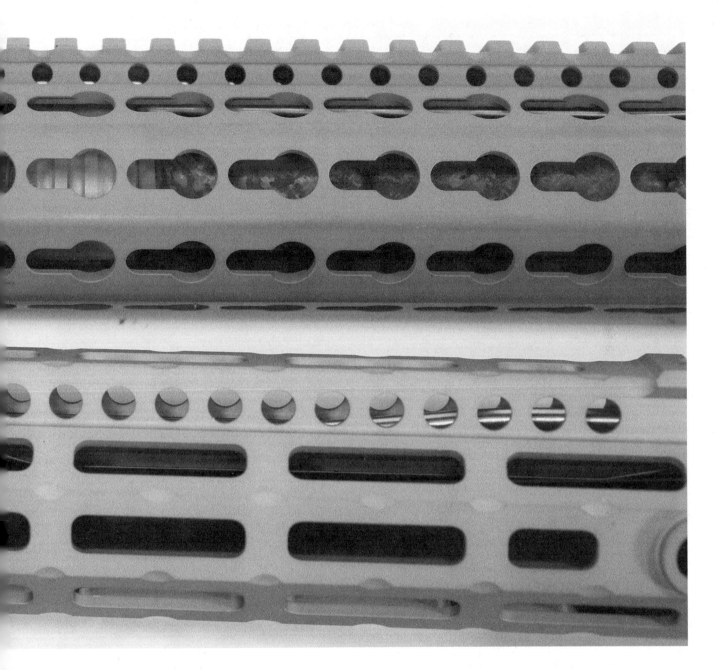

the pin up once it has been budged, that's close to too tight. It might wear in to be a bit looser, and it might not, before you are done with it.

WHAT COLOR?

What color is your AR? For the longest time, it was formal: black. However, that is not always the case, as the earliest ones went through a couple of shades of gray before coming black. As mentioned before (and elsewhere, and repeatedly), the finish-ing process that makes aluminum tough enough to serve our purposes is anodizing.

This is an electrochemical process that "passivates" the surface. The oxidation lo-cations on the surface are aggressively oxi-dated, and the process drives that change deeper into the surface than would happen naturally. The end result is a tough skin on the surface that cannot be further oxidized. However, the process is not done once the parts come out of the anodizing tanks.

The crystallized surface is also slightly porous, and the surface also "grows" as a

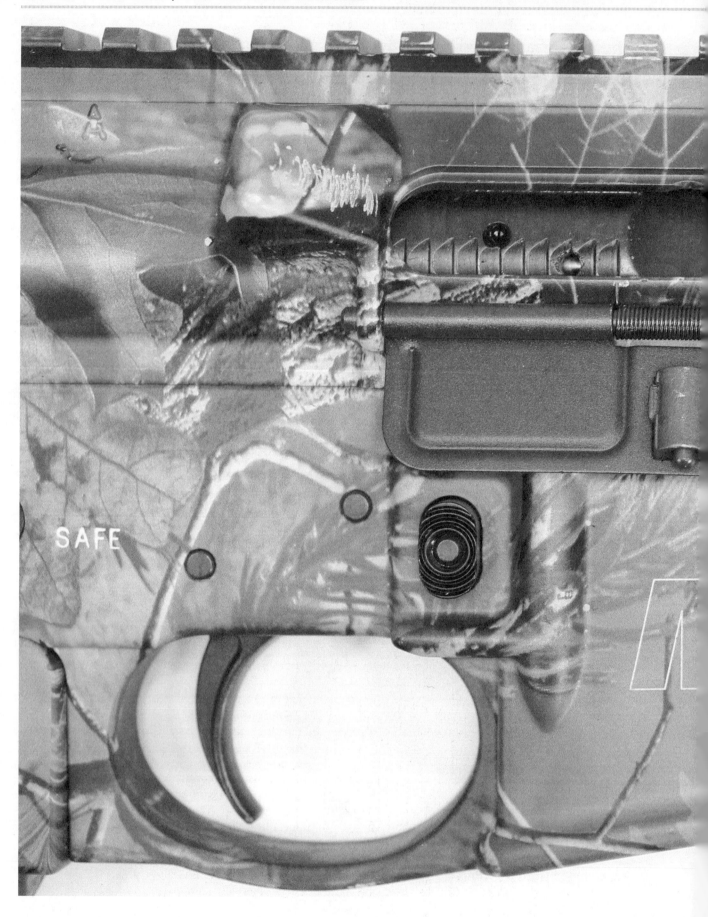

result of the anodizing. That's part of the reverse engineering, by the way. OK, take a pin hole of .2500" in diameter. How much does it grow, from anodizing? One-thousandth of an inch? That means your hole shrinks, and by twice that (simple geometry). The hole you so carefully reamed to .2500" is now more or less .248" in diameter. If your takedown pins are lathe-turned to .250", you have a problem. Especially if the person who wrote up the specifications didn't understand their use, and the blueprints read .250" plus-or-minus .001" Your random takedown pin, snatched out of the bin, could actually measure .251", and you're going to force it into a hole that is .248" large? I don't think so.

This is further complicated by the simple fact of manufacturing: metal cutting and metal chemical treatments are rarely done by the same company. An AR receiver machining company will often truck the day's parts to the anodizer, who can be across the street, across the state or in the next state. If you do that, you'd better have a good han-

We can thank deer hunters and duck shooters for this. The complex camo patterns that only dipping can produce come to us from them. Without them, we'd have black and spray paint.

dle on just how much their process "grows" your aluminum, so you can make sure you remain in spec. And if you change anodizers? You'd better find out their growth, before you start sending truckloads of uppers and lowers to them.

The tough skin is dyed a deep black, and then sealed with an application of nickel acetate.

The DoD will, sooner or later, adopt a new color for small arms. Until then, the issue M16/M4 will be black.

Anodizing can be done to different thicknesses, and by using difference chemical processes. These are, in generally ascending order of toughness, Type I, Type II and Type III, the last also known as "hard coat" anodizing. The toughest, the Type III anodizing, can be dyed black. Type III cannot be dyed other colors, so the "lesser" types have to be done to aluminum that will be dyed the

bright colors you see in some aluminum products. This matters only in the most extreme uses.

Make no mistake, the competition AR you see done up in bright anodized red, blue or something else is "less tough" than the mil-spec black only when subjected to the most extreme conditions. Conditions so extreme that it is the rifle

that is the limiting factor, not the person holding it.

PAINT AND OTHERS

The simplest way to get your AR some color other than black is to paint it. Called "rattle can camo" by many, it simply involves an afternoon at the gun club, a selection of appropriate spray paint colors, and whatever you want to use as your pattern-making material. I've done this a few times, and there are a few important things to keep in mind.

Cover your optics. It won't do you any good to get overspray on the lenses of your scopes or on the screen of a red-dot, so use tape to cover those up. Also, any important markings, like the scope adjustment direction, shouldn't be painted over. I know, it seems silly to point this out, but you'd be surprised at how many I've seen.

Degrease the surfaces. Paint doesn't stick to lubed surfaces. I know, "Well, duh." But, unless the surface is bone-dry, the paint will flake. Wiping the surface with a clean, dry towel won't remove the oil that will prevent adhesion. Almost anything will do, if applied liberally enough. Rubbing alcohol, carburetor cleaner (does anyone know what a carb is, any more, besides the dietary ones?), any paint degreasing prep solution will do. Apply it a couple of times, let the surfaces dry in-between applications, then start painting.

Colors matter. You may lust after the old-school Rhodesian camo pattern. You may thing the desert camo "chocolate ship" pattern is cool as all get-out. But, will they fit your area? If you are sitting there in your mossy-oak-whatever camo clothes, perfectly hidden from the coyotes, will they spot your rifle? If you are in the high plateau or the desert scrub of a lot of the southwest, that woodland-pattern rifle is going to stand out like a sore thumb. Just like your perfectly camo-painted clone of a spec-ops carbine for use in Iraq or Afghanistan is going to stand out in the woods of the Midwest.

You can paint the individual parts if you want, or paint the entire, assembled rifle, it doesn't really matter.

Some shooters make sure every part is given the new color. Others can't be bothered, and make sure what matters to them gets the new color. Clearly, the owner of the rifle on the right either can't be bothered or didn't have time to finish before coming to this class.

Another thing to keep in mind with painting is this: you can always practice on found objects, or pieces of cardboard. If you take a piece of cardboard and seal it with a coat of anything paint, even old house paint, it will then hold paint and colors. Give it a base coat of flat black, for verisimilitude.

Remember the rule of addition: what you paint first is seen the least, and what comes last is seen the most. And patterns overlaid subtract from the cost then painted. Next, added layers do not have to be complete coats. You can paint in bands or spots or areas, and only apply the extra color or colors there.

You want your base coat for a lot of patterns to be the original anodized black. Then the colors come over it, and you are left with stripes, patterns or mesh of black in the other colors.

A popular pattern is to give a rifle and its parts a base coat that matches the area. Tan in desert, light-medium green in woodland and then lay a mesh over the rifle. By painting in bands or spots, you would then apply a pattern of the new color dots or squares over the base color.

And if it doesn't work out, remember you have been painting metal. (Well, some plastic, too.) You can always use a paint stripper to remove the old paint and try again. Heck, that could even be a pattern. Apply a painted camo job, then partially strip it, to give it a worn, distressed look, then touch it up so it looks like it has spent a couple of years rattling around in Iraq or Afghanistan. You could make it so ugly your gun club buddies would be jealous.

COMMERCIAL FIRMS

You can have your camo or solid colors done by companies that do that. You can use one of the Cerakote companies, or send your rifle off to Robar to do it in their colors and patterns. Look over the offerings, select colors and patterns, and contact them for time and cost. But, keep one thing in mind: changes show.

I knew this, of course, but then I had to make changes. I have a rifle that Robar did in one of their lighter camo color patterns, just because. Then I had to have a differ-

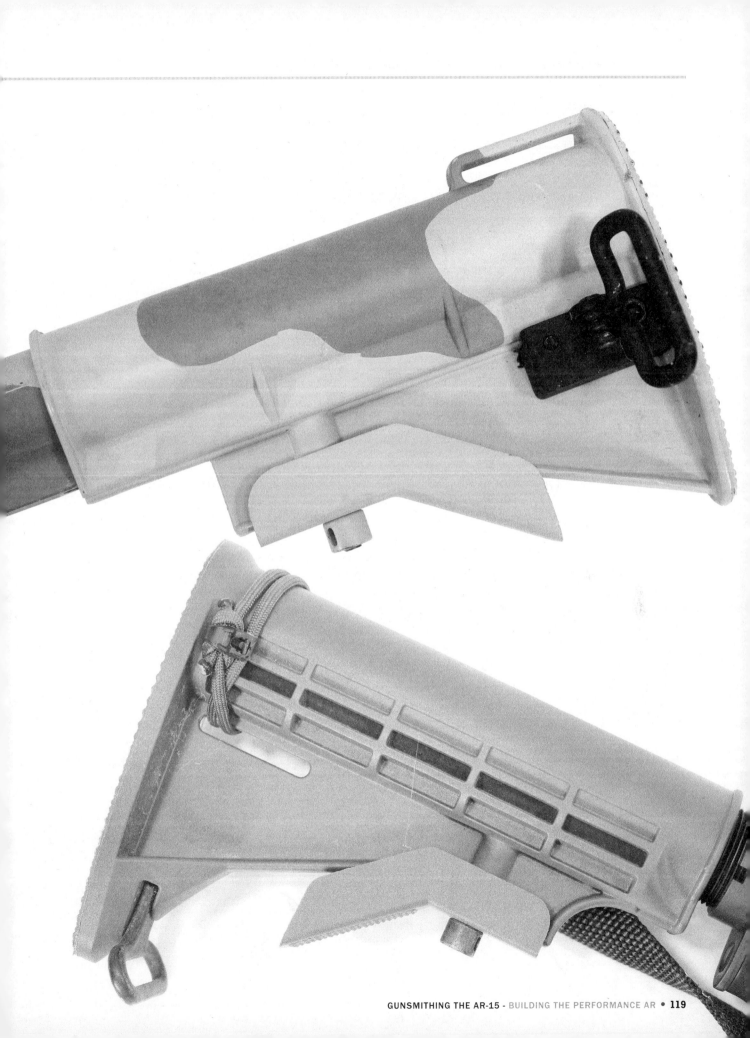

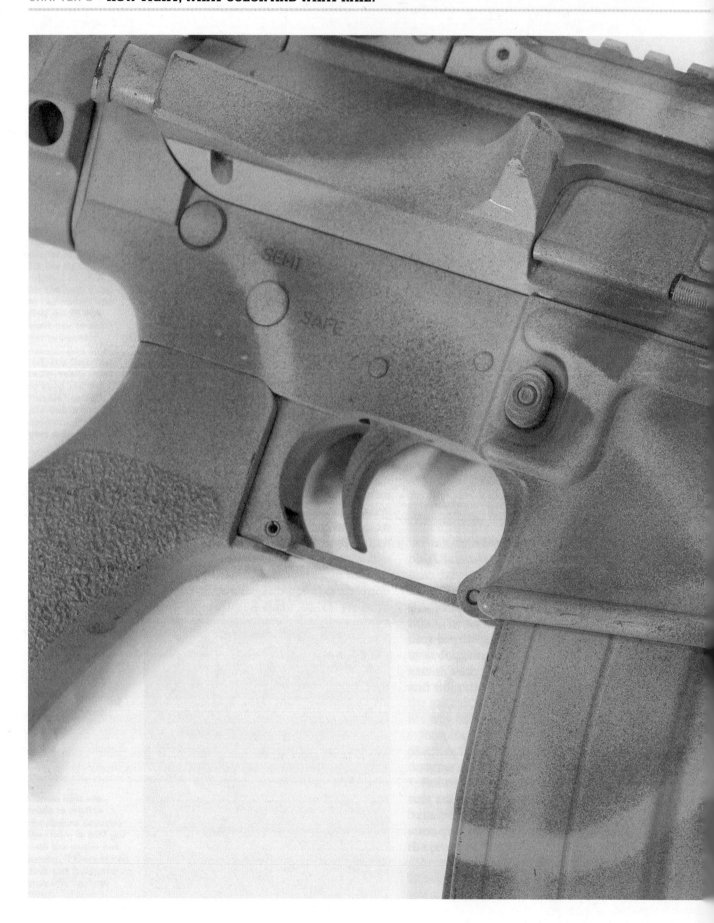

ent front sight assembly. Well, the new sight assembly, in its parkerized finish, does not match the rest of the rifle. I'd have to get the whole thing re-finished in order to match. Instead, I picked the closest color in a spray can, masked things off, degreased and then sprayed it.

The lesson here is simple: make sure your rifle is complete and exactly the way you want it before you send it off for an expensive, commercial camo job. Otherwise, changes show. On the other hand, if you do your own spray-paint job, you can blend and match the new parts to the old.

One last note, the idea of camo is to break up the appearance. In the military, things that catch the eye are colors that are off, patterns that stand out, shine, etc. Well, if you have a green rifle with a tan buttstock, FDE handguards, a black barrel, and so-on, you have made a non-matching color combo. That in itself goes a long way to being camouflaged, even if it isn't "camouflage."

This idea came to me as an interesting approach when I read of camouflage clothing observation experiments. Yes, patterns matter, and some are better than others. But the observers noted that simply wearing pants and shirts of different, solid colors went a long way to making the wearer harder to spot. That may not be enough to hide from a coyote, but it is a start.

So, if you want to paint it, paint it. After all, it is anodized aluminum and parkerized steel, paint remover will get the paint off if you change your mind. The polymer and plastic parts may not like it as much, but they are relatively inexpensive and can be replaced if the paint solvent dissolves them. Oops.

MODERN PATTERNS

We're seeing a surge of patterns in rifles and carbines that are commercially available. These come to us via one of two routes: patterned anodizing and dipped coatings.

The patterned anodizing is simply an applied pattern as dye is applied to the anodizing in the final steps. Short of super-aggressive chemicals (stuff you won't want to be using, trust me), you will not be able to remove the pattern. You can paint over

it if you wish, but it is there just as if it were the black of regular anodizing.

Dipping is something else. This is a multi-step process that cannot be done at home any more than anodizing can. It is applied over the anodizing, either bare or dyed black, if that is what the desired pattern calls for. Dipping is simple to describe, but the process was not easy to develop.

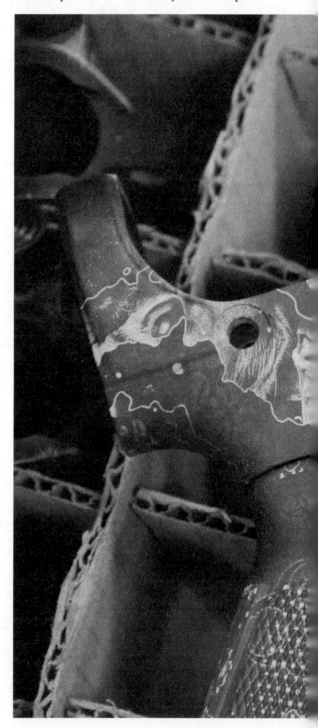

Use a computer-controlled printer to lay out an image on a plate. Then, submerge that plate so the image, in its entirety, floats on the surface. Now, take the object you seek to coat, submerge it next to the pattern, move it until it is under the pattern, then lift it up through the pattern, allowing the pattern to cling to the surface of the object. Then, dry and cure the pattern so it adheres to the object coated.

There, that was easy, wasn't it? Not at all. What ink or paint-like chemical solutions will be print-able? And then, how to make sure they stay as a solid sheet while floating? How to make them adhere to the surface of the object, instead of floating off to the side with the water as the water flows

Complex patterns are easy to put onto receivers, once the pattern has been made. This is a process known as dipping, and what you can do is quite amazing.

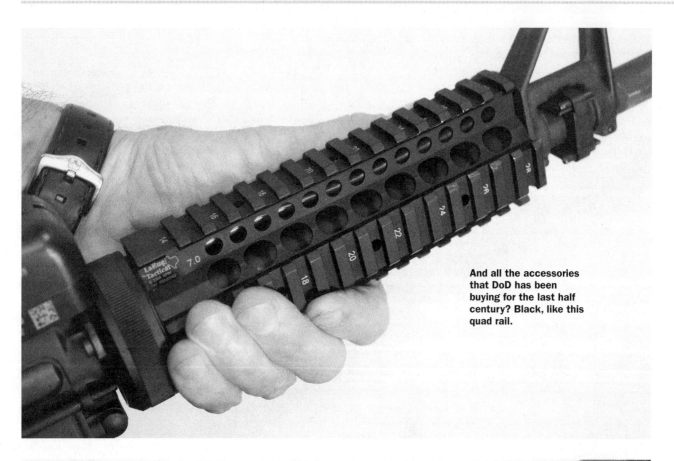

And all the accessories that DoD has been buying for the last half century? Black, like this quad rail.

Midwest Industries makes this slick, slim free-float handguard. Not only is it set up to add rails or accessories, it comes in a variety of colors, even black.

away? And then, what chemical solutions, having gone through all that, will adhere, cure, and retain their colors after exposure to light? You don't want your camo pattern to fade away, in the sun, right?

If it is all that difficult, why do it? Simple: you can apply an incredibly complex pattern to an AR-15, rapidly, repeatably, and once the capital investment and training is taken care of, at low cost. Compared to having an airbrush artist do it, you can run rifles through at 10 or 50 times the rate. But it is cost-effective only with complex patterns. You don't need this to duplicate a Rhodesian camo pattern, or a woodland camo pattern.

THE RAIL WARS

When we started wrestling scopes onto ARs back in the dark ages, we'd cut off the carry handle and then pin, screw, epoxy or otherwise secure a Weaver rail to the top of the receiver. When Colt came up with a flat-top receiver, they went with an improved design of the Weaver, which we have all come to call the "Picatinny" rail. Picatinny is an arsenal in the U.S. Defense department and they did not invent it. They just got the chance to name it after themselves.

As a scope-mounting platform on the top of a receiver, it is great. As a place to mount other accessories, it is overkill.

When it became necessary to mount other objects on rifles, like laser targeting designators and night vision gear, the only way to bolt it on was by using the "pic rail." When the rail on top was too short and making it longer still wasn't enough, we ended up with the quad-rail handguard. This was a problem.

If you use the four pic rails as your geometric mounting system, you need them far enough from the barrel that you can

Tan is the new black. You can have tan with paint, baked coatings or colored anodizing.

cool the barrel via airflow, and so objects on the rails don't interfere with the other objects on other rails. You can only make the quad rail so small before it becomes much less useful.

That size is a handful, too big for many hands. It is also a mass of sharp edges and corners. The "solution" to this was to install rail covers or ladders. This made it even bulkier.

An interim solution was to cut off the rails except where they'd really be needed, or to drill and tap the base tube and only mount rail sections where desired.

The real solution was called Keymod.

Here, the base tube was made as small in diameter as possible while still fitting over the barrel nut and providing airflow for cooling. Then, the tube was slotted for accessory mounting, and the mount hardware was to be built

into the accessory itself, or as an adapter mount. The end result was a tube small enough to handle easily, that you would mount accessories to only where you wanted or needed them.

Then came M-Lok. A different pattern, but the same approach, and the two were not compatible.

Competition is good, it improves the breed and it allows consumers to make choice.

The choosing seems to have been done, and M-Lok has won the rail wars. But that doesn't mean you

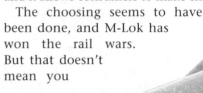

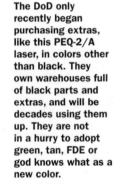

The DoD only recently began purchasing extras, like this PEQ-2/A laser, in colors other than black. They own warehouses full of black parts and extras, and will be decades using them up. They are not in a hurry to adopt green, tan, FDE or god knows what as a new color.

have to junk all your Keymod gear. All that gear still works, and until you use it up entirely and cannot find any more, if you like your Keymod, keep your Keymod.

M-Lok adopters, don't crow. In the course of our lifetimes I'm sure there will be an improved M-Lok, an M-Lok 2.0, or something to replace it as well.

Use what you want, what you like, what works for you, and don't worry about the fashion wars.

Make it the color you want and be happy. Just make it work. ■

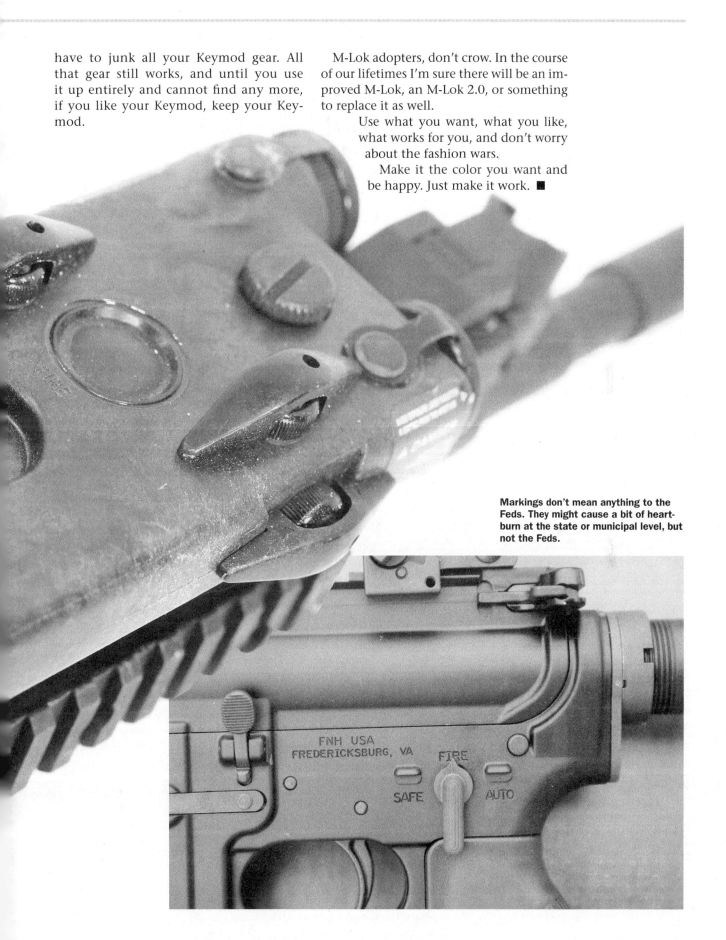

Markings don't mean anything to the Feds. They might cause a bit of heartburn at the state or municipal level, but not the Feds.

CHAPTER 9

The Truck Gun, Carbine & Handgun

Here is the truck gun carbine with the scope on top.

L et's go over a bit of background and exposition before we dive headlong into the truck gun and the other builds. What is a truck gun? And why are we building specialized ARs, anyway? Isn't the basic, M4gery the do-all and be-all rifle? The rifle that can do anything and everything? Well, yes and no.

Work with me for a moment. Walk into your kitchen, open the silverware drawer and look at the selection. Now look at the knives. Butter knives, steak knives, even that "what is this thing for?" fish knife.

Now turn around and look at the block holding your cooking knives. Big, little, wide, slim, knives of all sorts. (I did a quick count here at Gun Abuse Central, and without even trying, I found two dozen different sizes and shapes.)

If all knives cut, why so many? And we haven't even included the folder clipped to your pocket, the knives in the garage for working in the yard, and the knife or knives you have in your bug-out bag, your tac vest, the car/truck, and the ones buried in the gear on your shelves.

Why so many? Because there is no "one knife fits all" size and design. Cutting your steak with a bowie knife may work, but it gets old, fast.

So, we build specialized ARs for the various uses we find for them, to increase our performance in those endeavors. Which leads me to the first, the truck gun, and we build a carbine.

WHAT IS A TRUCK GUN?

A truck gun is the long gun you have in your truck, car or other vehicle for emergency use. For the longest time, the epitome of a truck gun was a .30-30 lever action, hung in the window rack of a pickup truck in a rural area. If kept out of sight, this also worked in a lot of other places.

We immediately have to make a decision: cost. Is the truck gun something essentially disposable, an item that can be subjected to the weather (trunks and pickup truck caps leak, it will get wet)? Will it not be a major economic loss when seized and logged as evidence in a court proceeding? Or, should it be the best tool for the job, regardless of cost, and the maintenance of keeping it up to snuff in the harsh environment considered just part of the cost?

I've been in the "cheap" group, and I've moved to not-so-much-the-cheap group.

The cheap group includes firearms such as a used Marlin .30-30 or .35 Remington lever-action or a worn-gray Mossberg 500. Or a military surplus Mauser bolt-action or a ratty-looking M1 Carbine. Things change, and those are not always the best or even a viable choice. The Mauser and the car-

bine are now pricey collector items. The lever gun is still a choice, god knows there are millions of them out there, but getting one loaded quickly won't be all that easy. (Most jurisdictions that are okay with a firearm in the trunk or the car require that it be transported unloaded.) That leaves the Mossberg, and it is still a good choice.

One of the guys in my gun club who kept a Mossberg in his trunk had the trunk built for it. The shotgun rested in its own rack, covered by a flap of vinyl to keep as much of the leaking as possible off of it. He had a special pouch up front that held his supply of 12-gauge buckshot or slugs. He practiced hitting the trunk latch button, grabbing the shells, getting back to the shotgun and loading it. He got so he could do it pretty quickly.

Well, times change. Now, a shotgun with five shells of buckshot or slugs in it is comforting but viewed as limited. A magazine of thirty rounds would be oh-so-more comforting. So we'll explore the low-cost end of the AR-15 as a truck gun, and see what we can do without breaking the bank or adding paperwork complexities.

SELECTING THE BASE GUN

The idea here is to start with a base gun, already assembled and ready to go off the rack, at a low

The truck gun AR pistol, with the SB Tactical arm brace installed. Yes, that's a suppressor mount on the muzzle, because this is America.

cost. Then we'll add a few extras that would be useful or even essential. I perused the rack here and came up with a likely candidate: the S&W M&P-15. The basic M&P-15 is a solid carbine, with a melonited barrel and built on mil-spec parts.

You can go with the standard basic M&P-15, or you can save a few more bucks by going with one of the price-point versions. You also have a choice between 5.56 and .300 Whisper/Blackout, but since the one in my rack for this chapter is a 5.56 version, that's what we'll work with.

First up, check the gas key and extractor, per the standard AR-15 checklist. At the slightest sign the key staking is less than excessive, I'd apply the MOACKS to it. (This rifle didn't need it.) I'd also attend to the extractor tension, to make sure it had all the boosting it could get. That would mean the installation of an O-ring or a D-Fender.

The SB Tactical PDW arm brace is adjustable, it locks open or closed.

Those checks out of the way (and a preliminary test-firing to make sure it worked and hit to the sights if it came with them and didn't need warranty work), and we're ready to get going.

THE BUILD

First, sights. If you picked up an M&P (or other carbine) cheap and it lacked sights, then you are spoiled for choice. To keep the costs low, the best option here is simple: Magpul. If your rifle has a fixed front sight, you need only the rear. If yours is a flat-top and flat gas block, you need both. The current cost on a set of those is less than $70 plus shipping. If you just need the rear, than you can manage that for less than $45 and shipping.

If you want something different, then that decision is one you, your wallet and your eyesight need to agree on. The "best" isn't much good if it is too expensive, and it isn't the "best" if you can't aim properly with it. The nice thing about the Magpuls is that they are a known quantity. You buy them, install them, try them. If they work, you're done. If they don't, you can always find someone at the gun club who will take them off your hands for a discount.

Next, we need a sling. This is also easy. You can simply install a military nylon webbing sling between the two sling swivels. Will it be "high-speed, low-drag"? No, but it will cost you less than ten bucks and keep your rifle off the ground when you aren't using it. Once you have it, you can then embark on a long test and evaluation process, to find the perfect sling for you.

Fair warning: this test will never end.

Magazines? That's even easier than the rest: use what you have, what is lawful where you live, and what works in your rifle. You should choose between 20-round and 30-round magazines. Don't go for the big-capacity ones, not because of any reason other than they tend to be bulky. Keeping a 50-, 60- or 100-round magazine stored in your car out of sight is a lot more difficult than keeping a flat and compact 20- or 30-round magazine stashed. Also, like my friend, you'll likely have to dash out of the car with the

magazine to grab the rifle and load it. That is a lot easier and less likely to be an fumblefest with a regular magazine.

Ammunition? You can spend even more time here than with the sling quest. My advice would be to find a source of bonded ammunition, something that works. Shoot enough in your rifle to make sure it works and hits to the sights. Load your ready magazine or magazines with it. Once you have something that works, then you can spend the time and effort to find something better. Or something "better."

One aspect of the truck/car gun is that, if you have it in a vehicle, you are then likely to be using it in or around vehicles. You want to use bonded ammunition because it gives you more performance through intermediate barriers. However, that applies for the other guy, as well. One trick you must pay attention to is that not all vehicles are the same.

If you find yourself in an altercation that involves vehicles, keep in mind two things: bullets skip off of sheet metal, and engines stop bullets. So, using the second point in your favor, use the engine as much as pos-

This sedan was plastered from stem to stern for a good fifteen minutes with rifles, pistols and machine guns. Notice the driver's door and compare that to the fender of the engine compartment. Where do you want to be?

sible, as both concealment and cover. (Cover stops bullets, concealment does not.) I've shot a few vehicles and seen a bunch of others shot up. The fender on the far side of the engine compartment from the incoming fire invariably has few if any bullet holes coming through it. The trunk? It might as well not be there.

But, hang back. If you are a few feet behind the fender and a bullet hits the engine hood and skips, those feet might let it pass over you instead of skipping into you. A bit grim and perhaps depressing to think about, but that's geometry.

Stocks and pistol grips? Here we have a wide-open field. Wide open because you should select what is comfortable for you, if you decide to change from the entirely adequate factory offerings.

Which leave us with the last, and most vexing choices: a light, and should we opt for optics? Let's do the easier one first: optics. If you need optical sighting on your car/truck gun, it should be a red-dot sight, unless you live someplace that is wide open and the engagement distances might actually be long. (I type this right after the Las Vegas incident, but the rarity of such a long–range shooting makes anything more than a red-dot sight really not much of a choice.) That said, if you know the trajectory of your round and the sight-in distance of your rifle, you can easily get hits to 300 meters with a 1X red-dot sight. I've done it plenty of times on the computer pop-ups at the National Guard base.

My choice here is the HiLux MM2 red-dot sight. It is a 2 MOA red dot that runs on a common-as-dirt battery, it is available with a co-witness or lower-third witness riser, and it costs all of $250 suggested retail. That means you can find it in lots of places for a bit less than that.

Keep the iron sights on, and fold them out of the way. Bolt on your HiLux, zero your rifle, and then turn the battery off. And here's a tip for you, when you do stash it in your car, truck, wherever, put a piece of masking tape on the side of the unit. Write the date on it. That way you'll have a clue about the battery age. But even if you forget to change batteries or the ride has been too rough, you still have the iron sights to use as back ups.

Tighten just as you would a regular castle nut, but you are tightening the buffer tube here.

Now, a light. As I've said before, half of the time it is dark outside, and inside it is dark a lot more than half the time. First, you need a place to attach the light, and that means a railed handguard. The simplest and least-expensive way to go is a replacement set of handguards with rails in them. No, no free-float, but that's the trade-off for lower cost.

You can get an all-aluminum quad rail handguard assembly from Blackhawk! for just over $150. Midwest Industries has an embarrassingly large selection, in lengths and colors, for $125. If you want to go on-line and search for Chinese knock-offs, I'm sure you can bury your front porch in them for less than $99 each.

With a handguard on, then it is a matter of selecting a light. Here again, you can go upscale and spend $300 to $500 for a sure-fire Scout light (we'll get to that in an upcoming chapter, don't worry), but if you are looking to get into this as inexpensively as possible, you can get a Streamlight on your rifle for a little more than $100.

THE AR-15 HANDGUN AS TRUCK GUN

Here we have a definitional and legal puzzle to parse before we can continue into equipment. What is an AR-15 handgun? At the Federal level it is a firearm that has never been a rifle, that is made without a stock, and has a barrel shorter than the required Federal minimum of sixteen inches. Actually, it can have a barrel longer than that, but a long barrel negates the utility of an AR-15 handgun.

So, the manufacturer (or you) starts with a receiver that has never had a stock on it. They (you, and I'll stop repeating this) install a buffer tube that is incapable of holding a stock. That's right, the buffer tube cannot in any way be able to hold, or have attached, a stock. This means you cannot use a regular carbine buffer tube, leave the stock off and call it a "handgun." Any fool can see it is a moment's work to slip the tele-slider on and you're stockin'. So, handgun buffer tubes are simple cylinder, sometimes with a sleeve of foam on them, as comfort for your face.

You aim by placing the tube up against your face and use the sights as you would

The SB Tactical PDW arm brace works just like a buffer tube, capturing the buffer retainer in the lower.

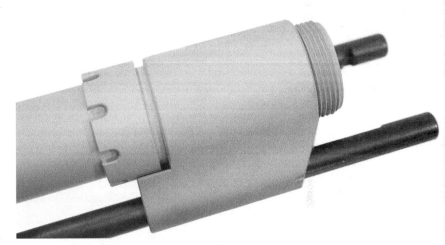

The SB Tactical PDW arm brace has the torque slots easily accessible. You can use a regular buffer tube castle nut wrench to tighten the assembly.

normally. If you are of shorter than average stature, you might even find that the back end of the tube, while not entirely comfortable, can rest against your chest as if it were a stock. (But it isn't.) When you are placing your handgun in the gun safe, you might even find that a rubber tip for a crutch on the end of the buffer tube keeps it from sliding around on the safe floor, preventing crashes of gear.

Here's the catch: unlike many other laws, where the Feds insist they have primacy, if a state has a stricter law on firearms, the Feds defer to the state. If your state does not recognize an AR-15 handgun as a handgun, you are out of luck. If they do, you are in.

The reason is another quirk in the law: most concealed carry laws and permits cover concealed handguns. A CPL does not

The SB Tactical PDW arm brace parts kit. You have to use the SB Tactical buffer tube, but you can use a regular buffer and spring inside it.

cover or permit a loaded rifle in the car with you. (Blame the DNR and their maniacal insistence that anything is a tool of poaching.) But, if what you have is a handgun, then the law allows it.

You must, absolutely must, check with your attorney on these things, as I take no responsibility for mis-steps on this.

If this works for you, you gain two advantages. The first is that you do not have to depend on the rifle, unloaded, in the trunk. It can be in the car or truck cab with you. (This of course, also gives you the burden of securing it while you are out of the vehicle. Always remember that.) The second is that you have a much handier firearm, since you can now go down from the 16" minimum length, with a stock on the end, to an 11.5" barrel, and no stock.

This creates a very handy firearm. I would not be keen on going much shorter than the 11.5" length, as barrel length testing has shown me that going shorter loses lots more velocity and increases muzzle blast to an alarming degree.

But, it gets better.

You can install an arm brace, such as one of the ones from SB Tactical. This provides a better aiming experience, and avoids going the SBR route or the bare-tube-on-your-face option.

Two braces come to mind, so I set about installing and testing them.

The first is the SBM4, which in profile has a triangular profile. It comes in black or FDE, and slides (with quite a bit of struggling, you want it to be snug) over the bare pistol tube on the back of your AR-15 handgun. Then, you use it as a brace while aiming.

The SB Tactical M4 brace used slides onto the KAK pistol buffer tube right up to the stop shoulder on the tube. Once there, it is snug and stays. If you find it shifts a bit, a small amount of a non-permanent adhesive will keep it in place.

The second is the SBPDW, which has the brace on a pair of runners, so it is adjustable to your arm length. The design calls for a new tube castle nut, and the rails for the adjustments have to run through a bracket, so the SBPDW is more expensive than the SBM4 ($299 vs. $149). It also requires that you pull the pistol buffer tube off of your handgun and install the new SB Tactical tube, but that's no big deal. It is a buffer tube installation the same as any other. (SB tactical did not see any need to re-invent the wheel while they were making our lives a lot more comfortable. Cheers to them.)

The buffer tube on the SB Tactical slides through the brace housing, and you use a standard castle nut wrench to tighten it. It, unlike the LWRC SBR stock (which, in its defense is much more compact, and an actual SBR), the SB Tactical uses the standard spring and buffer of a carbine with a tele-stock. SB Tactical has a video on their web

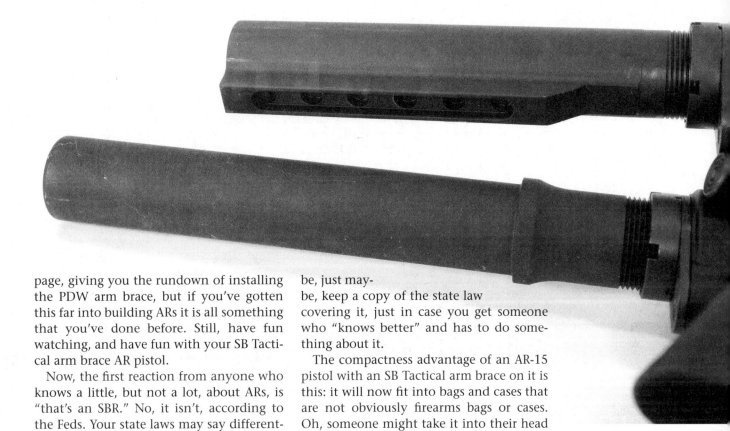

page, giving you the rundown of installing the PDW arm brace, but if you've gotten this far into building ARs it is all something that you've done before. Still, have fun watching, and have fun with your SB Tactical arm brace AR pistol.

Now, the first reaction from anyone who knows a little, but not a lot, about ARs, is "that's an SBR." No, it isn't, according to the Feds. Your state laws may say differently, and we've been over this. SB Tactical has the info on their web page, and includes it with each stock, so keep a copy. And may-

be, just may-
be, keep a copy of the state law covering it, just in case you get someone who "knows better" and has to do something about it.

The compactness advantage of an AR-15 pistol with an SB Tactical arm brace on it is this: it will now fit into bags and cases that are not obviously firearms bags or cases. Oh, someone might take it into their head to steal your obviously expensive tennis racquet if you leave the case in plain sight. But a nondescript gym bag? ∎

To make a truck gun pistol, you must start with a lower that has never had a stock on it. Then, you have to install a pistol buffer tube, one that has no provision whatsoever for attaching a stock. Above, a regular carbine buffer tube. Below, the KAK pistol buffer tube.

If you want rails but don't need free-float, then Blackhawk handguards replace your existing ones and off you go.

CHAPTER 10

The Truck Gun, SBR

Once installed, the collapsed LWRC PDW stock is very compact. It'll store in a very small space, even with optics on the upper receiver of your SBR.

Here we take a different tack. We bite the bullet, accept that we'll have to pay for the transfer tax, and build an honest-to-god SBR truck gun. Since we're all-in on this, there's no point in going half-measures on the parts and the build. So, we start by….. wait a minute, we don't start. We plan.

You cannot proceed in any way to making or buying an SBR until you have the approved form, with its tax stamp, in your grubby paws. Oh, you can have a rifle and the handguards, muzzle brake/flash hider, light, optics, etc., but you cannot have

The buffer tube notches for torque are hidden by the stock housing, and you will need the included LWRC wrench to reach them and tighten the tube.

The big advantage of an SBR is that even with a suppressor it isn't any longer than a regular carbine.

the barrel on-premises until you have the stamp. And I'd even be leery of something cute, like having the SBR barrel, which you will install after you get the stamp, stored up at your cabin by the lake.

You still own it, have access to it, and unless the cabin is by a lake that requires an

Here is a ready-
to-go SBR, a Sig
M400 with a factory
11.5" barrel. Put a
compact can on it
and you have a very
handy package. Or,
build a clone of it.

The LWRC stock uses a proprietary spring and buffer weight/cushion that fits on the back of the carrier. Right now, it is for the LWRC piston system, but there is a DI gas system model on the way.

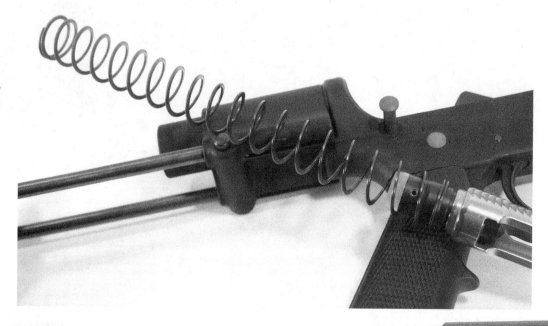

The LWRC PDW stock is very compact, but has some quirks to it.

airline flight, it is easy to get to. No, do this by the book, buy the barrel only after you have the stamp.

Or, just buy the SBR, complete, but built/assembled to your specs.

Me, I grabbed one out of the rack. (To steal a line from the late Alan Rickman: "Benefits of a classical education." In this case, years as a gun writer.) I used an SBR lower from Primary Weapons Systems. It was built with one of their piston-system 7" barrels on it, and it has worked very well. It's been reliable and accurate, but the muzzle blast is ….oppressive. Seven inches is just too short,

1DIV.=½@100Y

DOWN

RIGHT

Once extended, the assembly is long enough to be used as a stock, albeit a short one.

the blast is bad, and the velocity loss is too great. But boy, is it handy.

So, I replaced the upper with a BCM 11.5 slimline upper. This is a direct-impingement system, the traditional AR system. The handguard is a free-float design, it comes directly from Bravo Company, and is called their KMR. It has KeyMod slots (you can also have M-Lok if you wish) and comes out 10" from the receiver, close up behind the flash hider on an 11.5" barrel. It is slim, and I can really wrap my hand around it. It uses a proprietary barrel nut, and the clamping screws pass through the clearance slot in the nut, so the handguard is rigidly attached to the upper.

Above: As fun as they are to train and compete with, a pistol-caliber SBR as a truck gun is not the best choice. Vehicles are hard to get into or through, and using a pistol caliber makes it harder. That said, the 9mm carbine or SBR is fun, inexpensive to practice with, and easy on target steel.

Upper Right: When you're building your SBR, you have to get it approved as an SBR build before you build it or even acquire the important part – the short barrel.

Right: Yep, SBRs have lots of flash. Ammo selection can cut that down, but the best choice is a suppressor.

This was built with a BCM barrel, 11.5" long, and put into an M4 upper.

For the lower, I used an SBR'd lower, and installed the LWRC PDW stock on it. This is a telescoping stock that is the absolute shortest a stock can be. It requires a re-placement carrier, since the buffer weight is pinned to the carrier. And, you have to choose between DI and piston.

The buffer tube of the LWRC PDW stock is shorter than any other, and this requires that they include a socket for your torque wrench, to reach into the housing and mesh with the castle nut teeth, to tighten the stock assembly. Once it is in place, the SBR can't be assembled or taken apart as a hinge-open firearm. You have to press both takedown pins out, and then lift and pull the upper assembly off of the lower. To re-assemble, you have to put the carrier and bolt into the upper, and the spring in the lower, and then use the carrier tail to compress the spring back into the lower as you join the upper and lower. It is a bit involved at first, but once you learn the trick, you're fine. ∎

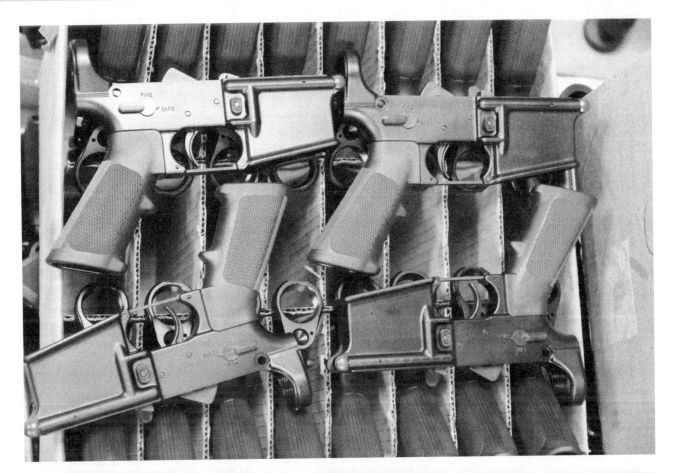

CHAPTER 11

Mk 12, Mod 0 and Mod 1

After the original Mk 12, the government used Knight's handguards for the Mod 1 version of the Mk 12. If that's the one you want, then go forth and find Knight's hardware to build with.

The genesis of the Mk 12 was the desire in some quarters for an accurate but not heavy (these things are relative) sniper rifle. The Navy had just adopted the Mk 11, which was the Knight's M110, a rifle chambered in .308, a.k.a. 7.62 Nato. But, not every job calls for a .308, and not every mission can take the weight. A loaded M110 has a "book" weight of 15.3 pounds. As if. In addition to the optics and the loaded magazine, the already-bipodded rifle gets more gear. Add a sling. Add a laser targeting designator. Add a suppressor. The rifle is soon up to

or even over 20 pounds, and that is before the end-user starts stuffing loaded magazines into his tac vest.

All that gear will add to the full-up weight of a 5.56 rifle, but it will at least start at a lighter weight, and offer more shots per added pound of payload to the tac vest.

It would seem obvious that rifles are tools used to shoot one's enemies. And in order to do that, they must be accurate. Well, it took a while for that to become common knowledge, apparently. I embarked on this quest with the idea that I'd have to muddle through and search for info, and instead fell into a bonanza. It seems that I had, unbeknownst to me, been emailing with a gentleman who was deeply familiar with the project. You see, he was for the Mk 12 project (the DoD one), one of a number of DOD Cage code contractors. "Cage code?" Yes, you see, the world of mil-spec has advanced a great deal since the early days. (And some might say not for the better, but that's a different story.)

A Cage code contractor (might I try using the CCC contraction?) is a commercial and government entity, a contractor who has jumped through the hoops. They have been checked out (this can be easy, such as providing chocolate chip cookies to the services), or difficult (working on top secret items), and once approved, they are issued a unique identifier.

This code then is marked on everything they produce for the government, and identifies them on each contract, invoice, purchase order, etc. No Cage code? Then you don't really make things for the government. At least, not the Defense side of the government.

The muzzle brake is also the suppressor thread part, and you need to get the brake aligned so the openings are to the sides.

As discussed in the chapter on barrel fitting, you want a tight fit of the barrel extension in the upper receiver if you wish to wring all the accuracy out of your barrel.

The Leupold 3.5-10 scope goes on top, in ARMS 22 medium-height rings. The rings are quick-detach, not that you'll be taking the scope off and putting it back on much. You do it because that's the way the military built it.

So, this fellow worked directly on the Mk 12 project for the government, and he provided me with a wealth of information. Starting with why was the barrel 18" in length? Well, you see, the idea was to make a super-accurate rifle that was able to deal with military uses. They built some experimental rifles, using match-grade 20" barrels, and doggone, they shot brilliantly with the right ammo. They then applied to have them type-approved, so they could start the process of issuing contracts for parts. (There is a lot of "mother may I" in government procurement, even in the black ops section, as everyone is deathly afraid of being accused of mismanagement of taxpayers' money.) Type-approved is where the powers-that-be look over a particular item. They then write up what it is, what it isn't, and that description is cast in stone. Once the details are nailed down, the manufacturer makes it for the government to fit the details so-listed.

This leads to some interesting philosophical questions. As an example, for instance, we use the M41A rifle, made by Arbat Battlefield Systems. If Arbat finds a way to greatly improve the M41A, but in so-doing they deviate from the detailed description, is it an M41A? No, it isn't. Will the government buy it? No, they will not. If someone else makes a detail-perfect M41A, but that company isn't Arbat, will the government buy it? No. And, it isn't an M41A, because the contract says only Arbat can make one.

So, the people assigned to desks in-between other assignments drew up the Mk 12 definition, and did their jobs as the jobs were described. And the powers-that-be said to them (yea, verily, comes to mind), "We have warehouses full of 20" barrels, so those will be easy to source." The end-users knew what that meant. All their efforts would be for naught, as they would be stuck with vanilla-plain A2 or

HBar barrels, whatever barrels the government already had in inventory.

Uhh, wait a minute. We have an update. The end-users report that the 20" barrel version is too long for some operations. They have reported to us that what they need is a rifle that is 2" shorter. "We need 18" barrels."

"And who makes barrels of that length?"

"We have a source."

So, in short, the only way for the end-users to get the accuracy they needed/desired, was to request a non-standard barrel length, one produced only by custom, match barrel makers. (Insert author shaking his head at this point, in awe of creative thinking.)

Do not blame the guys sitting at desks. They did their jobs. The job just didn't have a box to check marked "match-grade accuracy" is all.

So, the process went something like this. (I'm deliberately blurring some aspects, in the interest of keeping people out of trouble, and not raising the hackles of others.)

The M12 rifles started as barrel blanks. These were shipped by the barrel maker Douglas, and given a close-enough external diameter shape, before being shipped to the precision rifle smith. The barrels were air-gauged premium blanks, made of 416R stainless, button-rifled and with a twist of 1/7. Once with the rifle smith, they were lathe-turned down to final dimensions. He then installed the barrel extension, reamed the chamber, drilled the gas port to rifle-gas-system location, and then shipped them back. They then had a single round of M197 Proof Load fired in the barrel (using the provided bolt, and while sitting in a special fixture to do this) and inspected before being sent onwards.

The inspection was magnetic particle inspection, to ensure that there were no defective bolts or barrels sent onwards. (None were, my source tells me.)

Of course you check alignment during assembly. You don't want to Loctite or Rocksett parts in place that don't line up. And you use a Geissele tool to check alignment.

They then went to the government arsenal where the barrels were installed into flat-top uppers and married to M16A1 lowers. Why M16A1s? At first, the idea was to build with what there was, as much as possible. The problem with the M16A2 is the three-round burst. The cams in the mechanism result in three different single-shot pulls, and this is something that the Marines had noticed early on. They went so far as to dry-fire an A2 twice, to get back the same, least-ugly, pull in the trigger, for slow fire match shooting.

With the M16A1, that problem wasn't there. (And with the M4A1, as well.)

The flat-top uppers also used M4 ramps, so the barrels had those as well.

From this point forward, the Mk12 was a PRI and ARMS parade.

The barrel was enclosed in a PRI carbon-fiber free-float handguard. The handguard has short rail sections at the 3, 6 and 9 o'clock positions. On the top, the rail of the flat-top receiver and the 12 o'clock rail on the handguard are connected by means of an ARMS SWAN sleeve. This is an extra rail that bridges the two sections and runs the full length of the receiver and handguard. Why? Back then, there were no one-piece upper receivers, nor sectioned ones that had continuous rails.

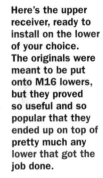

Here's the upper receiver, ready to install on the lower of your choice. The originals were meant to be put onto M16 lowers, but they proved so useful and so popular that they ended up on top of pretty much any lower that got the job done.

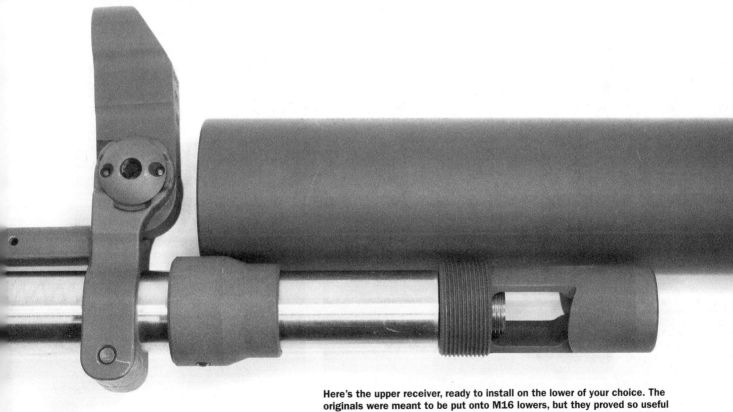

Here's the upper receiver, ready to install on the lower of your choice. The originals were meant to be put onto M16 lowers, but they proved so useful and so popular that they ended up on top of pretty much any lower that got the job done.

The SWAN sleeve (a.k.a. SPR MOD or #38 SPR) provides both a means of increasing the rigidity of the assembly, and also of keeping things aligned. The rear sight was the ARMS #40 folding rear, and the PRI folding front. The ARMS rear fits behind the SWAN rail, and the PRI rides on the barrel, in front of the SWAN rail.

You see, the military was going to be mounting a lot more gear there than we might. We'd put a good (or fabulous) scope on top and pretty much call it a day. If we needed more, we'd put a light or laser on one of the short rails on the handguard.

Well, in addition to the scope, which on the originals was going to be a Leupold 3.5-10x40 LR M3, the end-users were for sure going to mount a laser targeting designator. This is a powerful infra-red laser, which puts a useful beam on things out to incredible distances. How does it work? Simple: you "paint" the object you want blown up, and a large piece of ordnance, falling out of the sky, steers itself towards the IR dot it can "see." That building that was laser-tagged 2,000 yards away? It just got the gift of a 1,000 lb laser-guided bomb.

I realize this might be old hat to a lot of readers, but there are new readers, and it never hurts to review the good stuff.

The laser, either the old, blocky, AN/PEQ-2/A, or the newer, much more compact AN/PEQ-15 (ATPIAL), has one problem: it isn't visible in the spectrum we see. Well, that is a big advantage in that the bad guys can't see it. But that means you can't "eyeball" the dot on a target. It has to be carefully aligned with the reticle of the rifle scope, and then you simply use the scope to point the dot. (It does mean you have to be aware of what range setting you have "clicked" up or down, but that's relatively easy.) So, to drop a guided bomb onto a building or a location of interest and annoyance, you aim the rifle with the aligned laser at the object. You hold it steady, then switch on the laser. Once you get an "OK" from the voice in the sky, you stay there until the boom.

That is about as simple a description that requires much, much, much training on both ends, steady nerves, expensive equipment, and a supply chain like no other in the world.

Having the laser on a loose or vibrating handguard defeats the purpose. The million-dollar bomb (about ten grand for the case and explosives, the rest is electronics and guidance), dropped off of the fifty-million dollar aircraft, misses the mark.

Then there are other optics. One would be a forward-mount NVG. Here, you take an optoelectric multiplier, a night-vision scope, and you park it in front of your regular optic. The big advantage is that you don't have to worry about changing zero

The suppressor alignment collar rests on the shoulder turned into the barrel and is held in place with a simple screw. Ideally, once everything is checked, you'll go back, dimple the barrel at the locking screw location and Loctite the collar on.

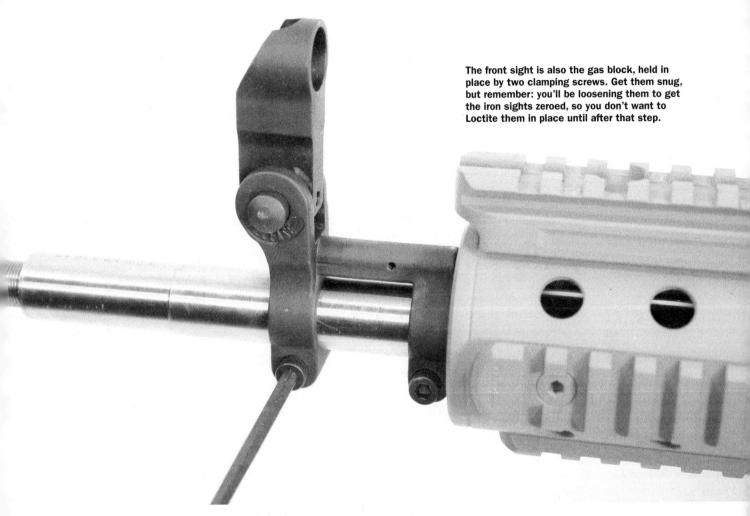

The front sight is also the gas block, held in place by two clamping screws. Get them snug, but remember: you'll be loosening them to get the iron sights zeroed, so you don't want to Loctite them in place until after that step.

by taking the optics off and replacing them with a dedicated NVG sighting system. And then off again the next morning and repeat.

The NVG simply provides an electronically enhanced image in front of the regular scope. NVGs detect incoming light and magnify it many times to produce a useable image. This image is projected on a screen and you see the image on the screen. Think of it as a tiny TV screen, and not a hi-res one.

There lies the drawback of this system. When you zoom up your optics, mounted behind the NVG, you are simply zooming up a larger image of the existing pixels. Instead

The last bolt is down through the top of the top rail, and secures it to the handguard along a different axis than the other locking bolts. If you do your part, this is not going to move.

of a 3.5X view of a 640 x 480 pixel array, you are seeing a 10X view of the same array.

The resolution of the NVG is the limiting factor. However, if you are willing to spend money, you can get more resolution.

But we risk straying far from the subject. Let's wrap that up by noting that there also can be a light, or lights, visible and IR, mounted on the rifle. For most of us, the world is dark half of the time. But for those using this rifle, a lot of their work time might be in the dark, and light is good. Better yet if it is IR illumination, and only they have IR viewers (which describes a lot of NVG).

The barrel on the Mk12 would be given a baked-on epoxy coating of medium gray. The receivers would be left black, and the handguard and other hardware would be in black as well.

The originals were made with fixed stocks, but it wasn't long before they were re-built with carbine stocks.

On the front end, the Mk12 rifles received a non-standard set of accoutrements.

The rifle was meant from the beginning to be suppressor-equipped. The suppressor selected for the Mod 0 was the OPS Inc 12th Model SPR muzzle brake, a.k.a. the OPS Inc suppressor. The design is a reflex design, where the expansion chamber is in the tube surrounding the barrel behind the muzzle. This provides any given length-and-diameter tube more expansion volume, since it extends back over the barrel. This also means that for any given internal volume, the suppressor will be shorter and/or smaller in diameter than one that extends solely forward from the muzzle.

It does pose a problem, in that the back end of the suppressor has to be a tight fit around the barrel, or there is the chance of wobble or mis-alignment. The was handled simply by fitting the barrel with a coned bearing sleeve ahead of the PRI folding front sight. The coned face of the sleeve provided a uniform and self-centering bearing surface for the rear of the suppressor.

The muzzle brake on the end of the barrel is where the suppressor threads on. You might overlook this, as the threaded portion of the muzzle brake also came with a thread cover, which was usually in place if the suppressor wasn't installed. So, if you pore over photos of the Mk12 you might not see threads.

For those looking for the gory details of minutia, the Mod 0 went through a couple of variants, with minor changes in bits and bobs. For instance, an Mk12 with a PRI front sight but with an ARMS #8 PEQ-2-3 is a Variant 1 of the Mod 0. (Head spinning yet?) And once issued, things got really different, but more on that in a bit.

MK 12 MOD 1

The PRI parts on the Mk 12 were durable, rigid and certainly got the job done. But

The ARMS 40 is designed to ride on the rear of the upper receiver and clear the back end of the added top rail that you will be bolting in place.

some things simply cannot be left alone, and so the Mk 12 was changed to the Mod 1. This involved changing the handguard and sights. The handguard was changed to the Knight's M4 Match Free-Floating Rail Adapter system. The part number for this is KAC 99167. Due to the larger barrel nut used on the KAC handguard, the Swan rail on the Mod 0 doesn't fit. The KAC requires the Swan #38 SPR PEQ-2-3.

One change to the SPR from the Mod 0 to the Mod 1, the rail, means that there is no longer a continuous top rail. The barrel nut prevents that, and the gap there complicates optics mounting. This is a detail that some complained about, but in the military, you use what they issue.

The sights were changed from the folding PRI, which was mounted on the barrel and also acted as the gas block, to a folding KAC sight mounted on the handguard. This sight is the KAC number 99051. For the rear sight, the Mod 1 gets the KAC folding 600 meter sight, #98474. Since the front sight was no longer the gas block, this required a new, low-profile gas block, and this can be seen forward of the KAC handguard.

Why the change? The end result of using the Mod 1 parts was to take a total of more than a pound. Still, at a bare weight of 10 pounds before you add on the suppressor, light, PEQ, sling, and god knows what else, I'm not sure the missing pound is noticed much.

If you want to see the Mk 12 Mod 1 on the screen, check out a copy of Lone Survivor from the local library (the only place to go, since video clubs folded a decade or more ago) and have a gander.

BUILDING A MK12 MOD 0

This is involved, partly because so much of it is not like your normal AR-15 assembly, and partly because the desired end result is an accurate, reliable rifle, and if you cut corners you won't get that.

Start with a ready-to-go lower, because that is not unusual. Ideally, you'd use a retro-style A1 lower, but since the Mk 12 was meant to go on whatever was available, you can get away with using an A2 and few will complain. (Oh, someone will, but ignore him.)

The first thing you have to do is source a barrel. After all, the Mk12 is meant to be a really accurate rifle, so building one that won't shoot well is kind of pointless. I opted to go with a BCM Mk12 barrel, because I have had good luck with BCM gear and in fitting and using their parts.

The barrel is a bull barrel, stainless steel, and with a 1/8 twist. To gain the most accuracy from it, it should be properly bedded into the upper receiver. You can do fine just bolting it in, but to wring the last few bits of accuracy out of it, go with the full-on barrel installation as described in the barrel chapter.

Next up, the PRI handguard.

The PRI handguard uses a proprietary barrel nut, so you'll have to plan ahead and do a bit of juggling. The nut also includes a rear locking cap. Put the cap on, then the barrel nut, and tighten the barrel nut. You'll have to align the barrel nut for a

The top rail bolts to the upper receive by means of through bolts that pass along the notches in the upper receiver rail.

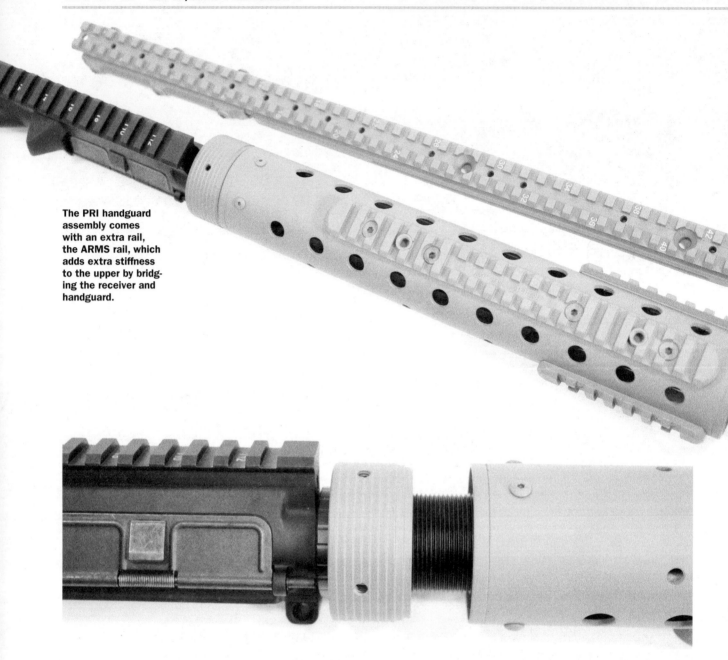

The PRI handguard assembly comes with an extra rail, the ARMS rail, which adds extra stiffness to the upper by bridging the receiver and handguard.

perfect gas tube clearance, and then use the alignment studs on the rear of the handguard tube, inserting them into the front of the barrel nut.

Now, Gen I of the PRI handguard uses a larger-diameter nut than the handguard tube. The Gen II has a locking nut that is the same size as the tube, but the process is the same. You have to get the nuts precisely aligned, for gas tube clearance and to align the top rail and receiver with the handguard rail.

This is where you want to be careful and precise. The handguard aligns on the barrel nut. The handguard also has to allow for the top rail to be bolted across he handguard rail and the upper receiver rail. If the handguard tube is the least bit mis-aligned, you will find the two rails and the top connector won't play well with each other. If you try to get it "close enough," you'll have a situation where the tightened-down top rail is stressing the handguard, receiver or both.

Keep adjusting and checking until there is no disagreement and the two rails (handguard and receiver) are in agreement that they are straight and will smoothly be clamped by the top rail. Use a strap wrench to tighten the barrel nut cap. Then install

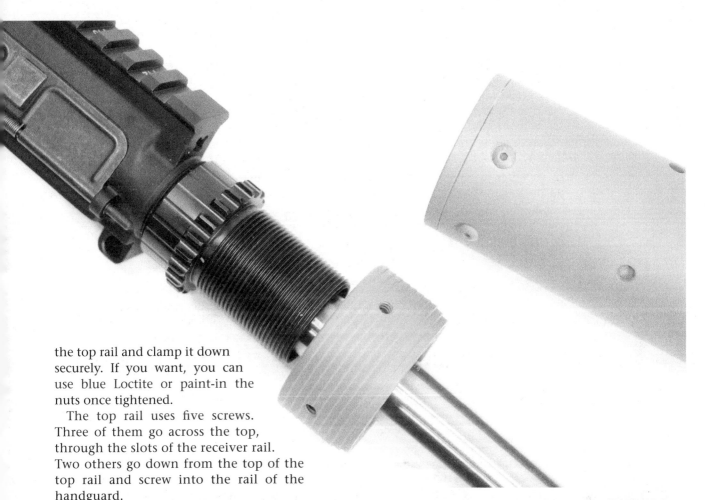

the top rail and clamp it down securely. If you want, you can use blue Loctite or paint-in the nuts once tightened.

The top rail uses five screws. Three of them go across the top, through the slots of the receiver rail. Two others go down from the top of the top rail and screw into the rail of the handguard.

Install the rear sight and paint it in as well. Now we're ready to get to the test-fire stage, once we get the gas block/front sight on.

Once you have the barrel nut in the right place, slide on the gas block/front sight assembly, align the gas tube and tighten the clamping screws. Don't Loctite them yet. Next up, range trip. Use common, inexpensive ammo, and if you are in favor of this process, use the opportunity to break in the barrel. Me, I don't care.

Ideally, you do this at the gun club, with the range to yourself, and on a nice, sunny, dry day. Make sure your rear sight is at the exact center of its adjustment range. Load one round, use the iron sights, an aim at an obvious mark on the hill. Fire. Where did it hit? It most likely was not on-center. If it hit left, your front sight is too-far right. And vice-versa. Loosen the screws, tip the sight a small amount in the correct direction and tighten the screws. Now take a moment to make sure your gas tube is still properly aligned. Fire again. Repeat this boring, de-

tail-oriented process until your iron sights are hitting dead-center. Your front sight is now aligned and centered, and life is good.

Back to the shop, to finish the rest of the build. Once there, loosen one of the two front sight screws, but do not remove it. Hose it and its recess in the sight assembly with wicking Loctite. Tighten and leave it alone. The next day, do the same to the other screw.

Next up, fitting the muzzle brake and suppressor mount. The suppressor alignment collar slides over the barrel, down to the step in front of the gas block/front sight assembly. There is a small setscrew to hold it in place. In talking about this with my contact, I asked if they did anything more than tighten it. "We used a bit of Loctite to hold the setscrew in place. It held, even without the barrel being dimpled, as you suggested."

I don't want to argue with real-world success, but I'd feel a lot better if the collar was more secure than that. But that's for the end of this process.

The PRI Mk 12 Gen II handguard uses a proprietary nut and handguard locking assembly.

With the collar in place, use the setscrew to keep it there and not rattle around or spin. Screw the muzzle brake on, and get it more than hand-tight. Don't worry if it isn't timed properly, not yet.

Now, spin off the knurled collar you see on the muzzle brake. That covers the threads for the suppressor. Spin the suppressor on, bring it down to seat on the collar, and then use your Geissele alignment rod to check alignment. It should be just fine, everyone involved in this has worked hard to keep things correct. If not, you will have to adjust the fit until your suppressor is aligned and central on the bore axis.

The suppressor, if a proper Mk 12 one, is now being made by Allen Engineering, and Ron Allen, the owner, was the guy who made them for the company who was making them for the government. The model is now called the AEM5, and it is a reflex suppressor. Instead of all of it being forward of the muzzle except for the mounting hardware, a reflex suppressor fits over the barrel. This provides a greater volume for the same overall length, and the first chamber, the expansion chamber, is also much greater in volume. The design also offers greater support for alignment. The two bearing areas, the threads up front and the collar in the rear, keep the suppressor aligned even when banged around.

Reflex suppressors have the disadvantage of being limited to barrels no larger in diameter than the inside of the suppressor overlap tube. But, you get more volume and more quiet without an extra foot of tube on the end of the barrel.

Once you know the suppressor is aligned, you're ready to wrap this part up. Tighten the setscrew enough to mark the barrel. Take it off, dimple the barrel, re-install, and check suppressor fit again. Still good? Pull it off, degrease everything, hose in the Loctite, slide the collar back on and tighten the setscrew.

Now loosen the muzzle brake and hand-turn it until it is as close to the stop shoulder as possible and correctly aligned. This is with the venting directly to each side. Use a feeler gauge to measure the gap. Assemble a stack of flat washers of that thickness to fill the gap. Hand-screw the muzzle brake on and check. If it stops at about 10 o'clock short, good. If it hand-tightens all the way up to twelve, re-do your washer stack a bit thicker. This is one of those cut-and-try processes; it can't be reduced to a chart of "if this much, use that washer."

Once you have the washer stack the proper thickness, remove all of the brake and washers, degrease the threads, brake, and washer, and re-assemble (once dry) with Rocksett. Torque up to top dead center. Leave the upper alone for a day. You have Loctite and Rocksett curing, leave them be. Check the assembly in an hour or less, and if you see any of the goo leaking out, wipe up the excess.

The ARMS 40 rear sight is the correct one for your Mk 12 build.

OPTICS

Once the locking stuff has cured, you are ready to install the optics.

The scope for the Mk 12 is/was the Leupold Mk4, either the 3.5-10x40 M3 or the Mark 4 2.5-8x36. The Mk4 is no longer being commercially made, but you can, if you must have the absolute correct optics, have one made by the custom shop for you. Rather than do that, I opted for a more modern Leupold, the 3.5x10.

When the Mk 12 was being developed there were choices for scope mounts. However, since the top rail, rear sight and other gear came from A.R.M.S., then the scope rings did as well. These are 30mm, throw-lever, individual rings and bases, mounted where the operator finds most comfortable and useful, and allows for the use of other gear. Put your scope where it works for you, and do not get too wrapped up in poring over photos trying to find the exact set of slots in the top rail "used by SEALs."

The big advantage of the Mod 0 over the Mod 1 is the continuous top rail. You can mount the scope or other optics anywhere along the rail, and not have to deal with the gap between receiver and handguard that the Mod 1 presents.

ZERO

Where you zero it to depends on where you will be using it. If you are going to run through a 3-gun or multi-gun match with your Mk 12, well, good for you. Zero for the distances that will work best in the match, and remember, most match organizers will put you in Open or Tactical Division if you run it with the suppressor on it. You'll be running and gunning against the guys and gals with super-tuned competition rifles. Have fun.

If you will use your Mk 12 as a varmint rifle and hose prairie dogs, then again, zero at the distance most effective for your uses.

If you want to zero it "at the distance operators used," well, I've got some news for you: there's the "book solution" and then there is the real-world solution. Once an operator got to where he was going to be using his rifle, he figured out what worked best, adjusted, kept notes, and worked with it.

It's your rifle, not the government's, do what works for you.

USE

The Mk 12 got used a lot in Iraq and Afghanistan. As a precise bullet-delivery tool out to moderate ranges it was just the ticket. One example would be a team going into a village, not a large one, and putting a fire team with Mk 12 gunner on overwatch, on a hill on the outside. (Better yet, two of them, at a ninety degree angle to each other, so you get as much coverage as possible.)

Having used magnified optics on the computer pop-up course out to 300 meters, a 10X scope makes a shot like that pretty much like plinking. Stretching it to 400 or 500 meters is a matter of knowing the drop and calling the wind, something in which a Mk 12 operator would have been well-schooled.

Beyond 500 meters, you really need a bigger caliber than the 5.56, as loss in velocity starts to become a real problem. The best ammo for use in this would be the M262 Mod 0 or Mod 1. That 77-grain bullet, by 500 yards, is going less than 1,700 fps and takes three-quarters of a second to get there.

But you can easily hit a 5" circle at that distance, once you know the drop, which can be pretty steep by then and still, a hit is a hit. With a 300-yard zero, your drop at 500 is 26.5 inches, and that's a bunch to keep track of.

If you are a movie buff and a gun buff, then the movie Lone Survivor has Mk 12s used in it. It could also give you ideas about how to paint your Mk 12 once it is done, and what other added accessories might be correct.

A LAST NOTE

If you really want a Mk 12 but find that building one is going beyond your abilities (heresy, in a book like this, but what are you gonna do?) you can always buy one. Yes, PRI and Bravo Company offer complete uppers. Well, complete except for the optics and mounts. And you can hit up Brownells for uppers or complete rifles. The price will be steep, but it saves time, and you have a ready-to-go, guaranteed rifle. ∎

CHAPTER 12

Mk 18

Not only are ships cramped, but getting there isn't easy. Is this the place to be packing a full-sized M16A2? I think not.

The "Mark Eighteen" is the ultra-short carbine you will see in naval operations known as VBSS. That stands for "Visit, Board, Search & Seizure." This could be as simple as the naval equivalent of "I'll need to see your license, registration and proof of insurance," right up to "Pull over, we're boarding because it was that or sink you."

The origins of the Mk 18 are not as clean as you'd like them to be. When I started asking about this I was put in touch with

some insiders, and my first question was, how did this come about?

The reply was "Navy Tier 1 types wanted something better than the MP5s they'd been using. They wanted an XM177, but they were told no." Basically, they were told, "We don't have any of those old Vietnam-era carbines on hand, and if we did, they didn't work anyway."

This, despite the Air Force having used the GAU-5/5A during and since Vietnam, and not having any problems with it. Colt had perfected the M4, and those lessons directly applied to their Commando models, which have 11.5" barrels.

So, the Tier 1 types did what any self-respecting cool group does, they started experimenting in their free time.

The process was simple. How short could they make it, and could they make it run reliably when it was as short as they could make it? The answers were: very, and with a bunch of work. The starting point was the basic M4 carbine, the M4A1, and to make those more handy in their work, they started lopping off barrel length. Once they had worked out the details of an ultra-short barrel and the gas port size they needed, then it was back to the workshop to thread those short barrels and fit

the Knight's suppressor on them. More testing and adjusting.

This led me to the next question. Why did they settle on such an odd length, 10.3 inches? The answer, as it has been for an embarrassingly large number of situations with the Stoner-system rifle, was the bayonet lug. The Mk 18 was that length because that was as short as they could make it and still be able to fasten the suppressor in use at that time, the Knight's KAC M4QD. The M4QD was by then a standard Sopmod equipment item, and the units that could request suppressors could count on those being the ones they would get. Later, other suppressors were available, but at the time, the M4QD was it. And so, the Mk 18 is set up for that suppressor.

The Mk 18 barrel has a larger gas port than an M4 because of the much shorter dwell time. Look at the Mk 18 barrel in stainless. The barrel stops just about where the M4 barrel steps down for the M203 clamp.

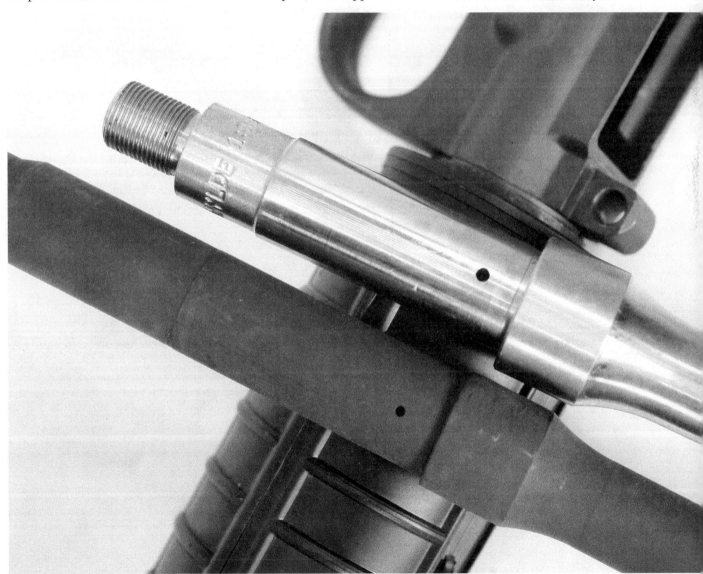

Once they had working carbines and were ready, the real work began: getting approval. First, the government still had/has racks full of MP5s in armories across the country (and in naval bases around the world), so why did they need this? And who gave them permission to chop off perfectly good M4 barrels, anyway? But, there was a need and sanity prevailed and the Mk 18 was type-approved.

Building your Mk 18 clone involves a few steps. The first of those is the simple fact that it is an SBR and you'll need to get your lower approved, and the tax stamp in hand, before you can begin.

Then there is the matter of which one. You see, there have been three generations of Mk 18 since the beginning, and the nomenclature isn't consistent. The first was the Mk 18, Mod 0. (Of course, when it was the first and only, it was simply "Mk 18" since there'd be no reason for a Mod 0, but that's getting really pedantic.) Second came the M4A1 CQBR Block 1, followed by M4A1 CQBR Block II.

If you really wanted to be OCD correct, you would not mix and match the hardware from Mod 0 to Block I and Block II. But, here's a dirty little secret: the government isn't so picky. A sailor assigned to VBSS, or a Tier 1 (hey, we all know them as SEALs, right?) operator will be handed a rifle and that's what

Here we see the Daniel Defense handguard rear clamping plate, ready to start our Mk 18 build.

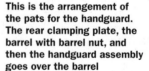

This is the arrangement of the pats for the handguard. The rear clamping plate, the barrel with barrel nut, and then the handguard assembly goes over the barrel

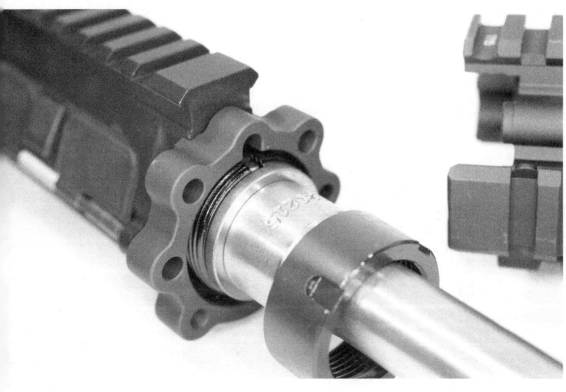

Make sure the clamping plate is all the way to the rear when you thread on the barrel nut.

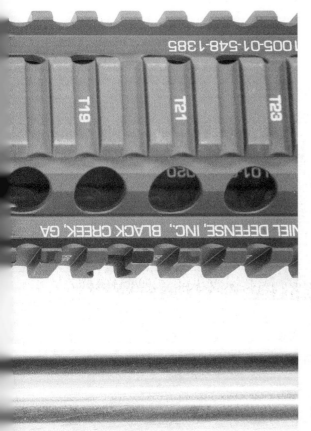

he uses. Now, depending on the assignment and the people in charge, the SEAL is going to have a lot more leeway in making changes. Most won't, and they'll use whatever comes out of the arms room. But long before a carbine gets to any particular arms room, someone had to build it or overhaul it using approved parts. So we end up with rifles and carbines known as "mix-masters." That is, a mixture of Mod 0, Block I and Block II parts.

For instance, it would not be beyond reason for a Mk 18 to be handed over the counter from the armorer, with a (just to mix things up) Mod 0 pistol grip and stock, a Block I rail, and a Block II light. If they all work, and that's what the armorer has, that's what they get. And if the SEAL doesn't like some parts on it, he can swap them with parts the armorer has in the back, or just hand it back and say, "Got anything else?" (By the time someone makes it to a team, they've been in the Navy long enough to know how things work. And, they have a certain amount of leeway in some things. Not cart blanche, but leeway.)

I've seen photos of some pretty egregiously altered Mk 18s, just starting with paint jobs instead of the issued flat black anodizing. So, if you want to make changes to

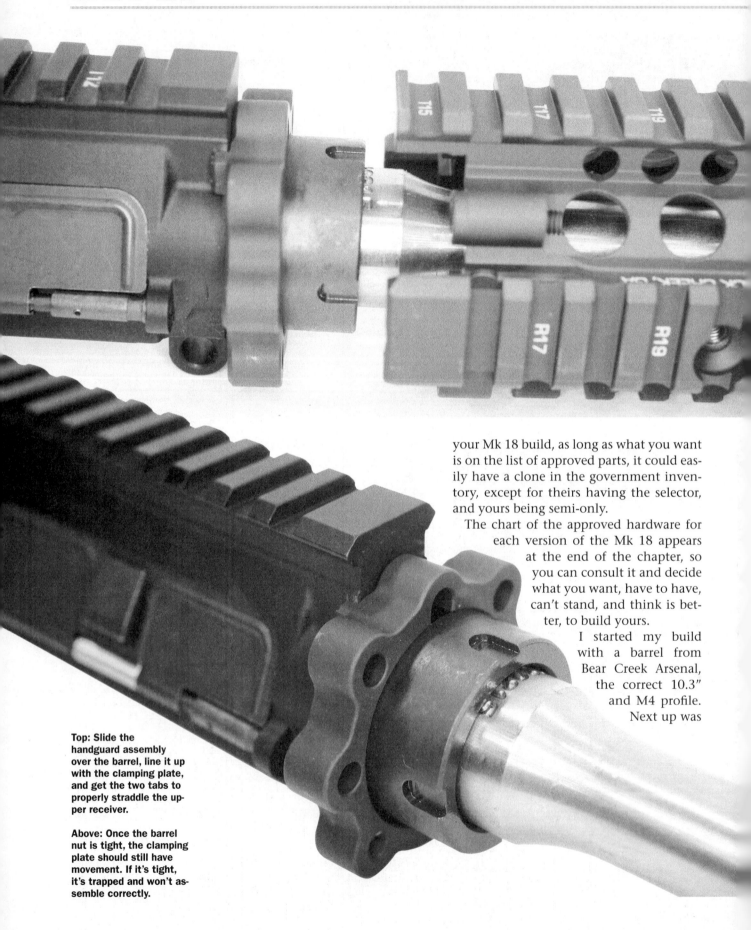

your Mk 18 build, as long as what you want is on the list of approved parts, it could easily have a clone in the government inventory, except for theirs having the selector, and yours being semi-only.

The chart of the approved hardware for each version of the Mk 18 appears at the end of the chapter, so you can consult it and decide what you want, have to have, can't stand, and think is better, to build yours.

I started my build with a barrel from Bear Creek Arsenal, the correct 10.3" and M4 profile. Next up was

Top: Slide the handguard assembly over the barrel, line it up with the clamping plate, and get the two tabs to properly straddle the upper receiver.

Above: Once the barrel nut is tight, the clamping plate should still have movement. If it's tight, it's trapped and won't assemble correctly.

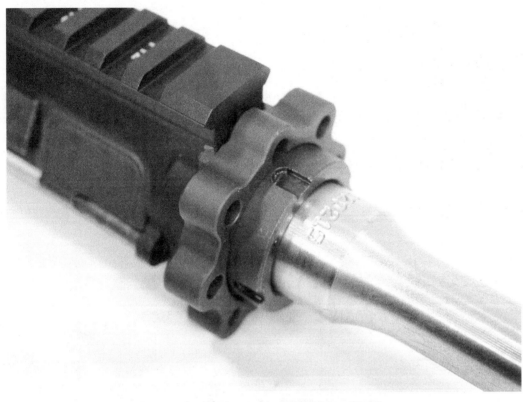

If at any time you find things binding or not fitting, remove the screws and start over. Trial fitting by hand is not only acceptable, it's clever.

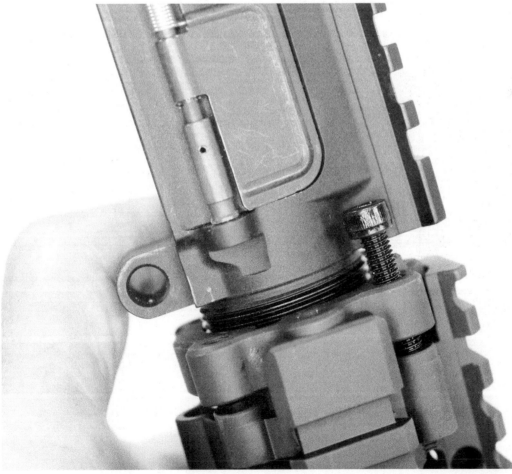

Start the bolts by hand and finger-tighten them to bring the parts together. Some are inserted from the rear, some from the front.

The end users are able to mix-n-match the stock they want. Or at least, one that is available in inventory. This Rock River Operator stock is really comfortable, and would work well on your Mk 18 build.

the selection of handguards. While I'm not a fan of quad rails (the world has moved on, and KeyMod and MLok handguards are slimmer) that is what the Mk 18 has always had, so the choices were Knight's or Daniel Defense. I opted for DD, in part because it was the newest. That, and the rail is easy to install, I know it, and I have one. Having is a good reason for using, don't you think?

I don't use a single-point sling, if at all possible I want to use a two-point, so that made the "correct" sling swivel selection a moot point. For those who must be correct, the one to use is the CQD rear plate, where you clip on a single point sling. I got over using that kind of a system a long time ago, so I'll take the points deduction for not hewing to OCD hardware.

On the stock there's more leeway. The original the Mk 18 Mod 0 used the first-generation Sopmod stock. While it was a great leap forward, it is heavier than a stock needs to be, and the Block I and Block II carbines can be made/had/issued with an M4 stock, the Sopmod, the CTR, and "others". Whatever that means. I figure the "others" means that someone with sense decided that, with the government buying all kinds of stocks for all kinds of rifles and carbines, there wasn't any point in restricting the Mk 18 to just one. And no need to go through the hassle of adding a new one to the approved list, in the future, and the attendant time spent.

The matter of optics is a really personal one. And in use, it's a headache for those using them on the job. If you are boarding a 40-foot fishing vessel, you really don't need a 4X optic on your rifle. A 1X red dot would be just the ticket. However,

Once you have the upper assembled, then it's a matter of picking sights. As with the real-world end users, you should select the right tools for the job. If you feel this is the perfect CQB tool, then red dots it is. If you think it makes a really handy medium distance sniper rifle, then a variable, magnifying optic will be the choice. Ditto with flash hiders or suppressor mounts.

if you are boarding a 300-foot cargo vessel, you may find that a 4X optic is really useful if some knothead is banging away at you from the superstructure 75 yards away and 50 feet up. And if you found yourself boarding a really big cargo vessel, one of the Panamax boats just short of a thousand feet long, you'll need someone with a bigger scope than that on overwatch. I'd say here you should work from the list and pick the one you find most useful, enjoyable, or allows you to do your best shooting.

For handguards, the DD RIS II works just like their lightweight free float handguard, except with quad rails. Because the government wants quad rails. And, I found out

talking with my contact at DD, a quad rail is just a little bit more stable. When you are zeroing and then using an IR targeting laser out to 1,000 yards or more, holding zero becomes important.

Here's how the mounting works. Take the bare receiver and slide the back bracket of the RAS II onto it. (You can do this after the barrel is in, but check anyway.) It goes on with the two prongs back, towards the receiver. Press the barrel in.

Now slide the barrel nut down and tighten it down to hold the barrel. The rear bracket will still be loose. No problem, it is supposed to be.

Once the barrel nut is tight, slide the handguard down over the barrel and line

This USCG boarding party has three different stocks and three different sights on their Mk 18s. So, there is not one definitive setup you have to adhere to. Build yours the way you want.

Part	Mk 18 Mod 0	Block I	Block II
Lower	A1	A2	A2
Stock	Gen 1 Sopmod	M4, CAR, Sopmod, CTR, other	Same as B I
Pistol Grip	A1	A2, Ergo & others	Same as B I
Rear Sling Plate	CQD	CQD	CQD
Upper	M4	M4	M4
Barrel	10.3" w/1-7 twist	10.3" w/1-7 twist	10.3" w/1-7 twist
Rail	KAC RIS	KAC RAS	DD Mk 18 RIS II
Rear Buis	LMT Fixed	LMT Fixed, Matech, others	Matech, KAC 300M
F Sight	A2 FSB	A2 FSB	
Front Sling	FBS Sling Swivel	FBS Sling Swivel	CQD
Muzzle	KAC M4QD	KAC M4QD	Surefire FH556RC
Suppressor	None	KAC QDSS NT4	Surefire Socom 556
Laser	None	PEQ-2	LA-5
Light	Surefire M962	Surefire M952, M962	Insight M3X/ WMX200
Optic	Comp M2, Wilcox MT	Comp M2, QRP MT	EOTech 553

it up with the bracket. There are five screws on the interface, and they do not all go on the same direction. Some from the front, some from the rear. Line them up and tighten them. DD recommends 29 to 32 in-lbs.

That's it for the handguard.

For the rest of the rifle, since you are using the DD RAS II, you'll have to go with a low-profile gas block and a handguard-mounted front sight. The correct spec is the Knights 99051, which runs $70 or so, and in the world of KAS parts, is reasonable. If you want to use something else, go ahead, since we've discussed how much "churn" there is in government property.

With the Daniel Defense handguard on your papered SBR, you can kit it out to your heart's content. If you really want to score points in the verisimilitude department with your gun club buddies and "authentic" builds, cruise the Department of Defense web page image sections and find the Mk 18 that looks like you want yours to look. Then build it. ■

CHAPTER 13

The Varminter

Leupold Mark AR, 6-18 x 40, Mil Dot Adjustable Objective, Matte, 1"

The point of a varminting AR is to whack nuisance little critters at distances from which they cannot see you, or at least have little chance of seeing you. This means absolute accuracy, mild recoil, immediate terminal effectiveness, and all at a reasonable, or at least not obnoxious cost. Classic varminting is prairie dog shooting, not the same as a modern variant of shooting nuisance predators. Prairie-dogging is a picnic-like affair, shooting "colonies" or "towns" of many targets in a small area. Predator shooting is more like classic sniping in the military, with rifle and shooter fully camouflaged, motionless, and in the case of predators, luring them in with cries of anguish of their favorite prey.

We're looking at prairie dogs.

The choice here is between an old one in its purest and a new one.

The old one is the .223 using lightweight bullets. The "heavyweight" here would be a 52-grain match or varmint bullet. Bullets for this use in the .223 go all the way down to 35 grains, and it should be obvious that for maximum terminal effectiveness you want a thin, fragile jacket on bullets.

This leads to the inescapable conclusion that the fast-twist barrels are off the table. Even a 1/9 would be too fast, so for pure varminting, you need only consider a 1/12-twist barrel.

Now, if you have a rifle that is suitable for, or you just must have a go at prairie dog sniping and have a rifle with a fast-twist barrel, go for it. Just realize that you will be limited in your ammunition selections, and the lightest, fastest, most-effective bullets and loadings will not be possible.

I had an example of this more than 30 years ago. Our club treasurer had tired of shooting our then-new 3-gun matches with his FAL. The recoil and slow reloads were just killing his scores. So he took his FAL to a gun show and traded it for a new Colt HBar, a scope, a basket full of magazines and a stack of cartons of ammo. Why so much? The FAL was one of the ones imported by Browning and was marked "Browning." That made it rare. It was also one of the grandfathered Brownings that had a select-fire receiver, even though it had been built and imported as a semi-

auto rifle. That made it rare and valuable.

He went and shot the rifle stage, and there were no holes on the targets at 100 yards. You guessed it, he had gotten varmint ammo, loaded with 40-grain "Blitz" bullets. They were literally disintegrating on the way to the 100-yard targets. They had stayed together long enough for him to get a basic zero at 25 yard, but past that, no go.

He went back to the next gun show and traded that varmint ammo for twice as much 55-grain fmj "ball" ammo. Yes, he was really good at wheeling and dealing.

So, you want a 1/12-twist barrel and a pile of ammo with lightweight bullets if you are going to shoot .223. The other choice? .204 Ruger.

Developed by Ruger and Hornady, it is the .222 Remington Magnum necked down to .20. It uses bullets of .204" diameter, and the weights there are from 32 to 45 grains. It fits into the magazine of a .223/5.56 rifle, so the only difference between this and the .223 is the barrel. With the lighter weights, it offers the lowest re-

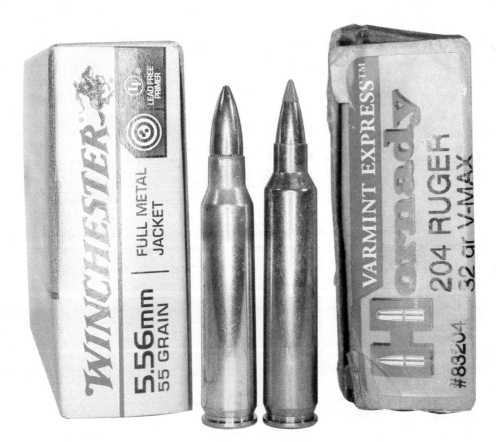

The .204 Ruger uses a lighter, smaller-diameter bullet, at a higher velocity, to extirpate varmints at absurd distances, with little recoil.

The ALG Defense Ergonomic Modular Rail (EMR) V3 with M-LOK is a cost effective, lightweight, ergonomic and modular handguard

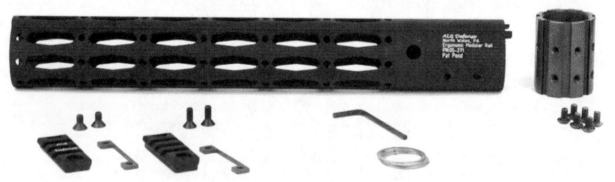

coil and a trajectory that is a bit flatter. A 32-grain bullet in .204" will, all other things being equal, have a better BC than the same weight in .224" diameter. A better BC means less trajectory drop and less drift. Interestingly, the differences are not large, but they can be critical.

A comparison: a .204 Ruger with a 32-grain V-Max bullet has a BC of .210. At 4,200 fps, zeroed for 300 yards, it will drop 1.8" at 400 and 4.2" at 500. The wind drift for a 10 mph wind will be 6.2" at 500 yards. A .223, with a 35-grain NTX bullet has a BC of .177. Its starting velocity is 4,000 fps, and if zeroed at 300 yards, the change is significant. At 400 yards the drop is 2.4", and at 500 it is 5.8. The wind drift at 400 is 6.1", and at 500 it is 8.6.

The differences are enough to cause a miss, as your target is a couple of inches wide at best, and not much more vertically.

They are commonly reloaded for lowest cost and to be tuned to the particular rifle and use. The ammo costs are pretty much the same, and the choice is almost one of fashion, as it is utility.

BARRELS

The twist is known, the choice now is weight. You will use a free-float handguard, there really is no other choice when you are talking about accuracy differences of fractions of an inch at multiple football fields distances. Heavy or not-heavy? A heavy barrel will have less felt recoil. It will be slower to heat up, but it will also be slower to cool off. Many varminters use multiple rifles, or multiple up-

pers on a lower with a fabulous trigger, so one can cool while using the other. Or, as I used to do at the Second Chance Bowling Pin Shoot, rotate through three identical uppers, letting them cool in turn, after "punching" the bore with a patch with bore solvent on it.

There are now battery-powered fans that will pump air down the bore of an AR to cool it faster.

HANDGUARDS

As mentioned, free-float is it. Which you use is up to you, because when you are shooting prone over sandbags they are all the same. If they are not, then that makes the decision for you.

OPTICS

Lots of magnification, a side knob for parallax or focus is good, and how you mount it hardly matters. You aren't going to swap it from rifle to rifle, you aren't going to use NVG, thermal or other gear, you just want something to see small critters at distance. 4-12 is a starting point, 5-25 is another choice, and it goes up from there, depending on your preferences.

MUZZLE DEVICES

Varminting is done in the open air and with hearing protection. So if you want to use a muzzle brake, you can. Or a suppressor, but you will still want to have some hearing protection. A suppressor is good, but the supersonic crack of hundreds of rounds in an afternoon, or a thousand over the course of a weekend, is not good for your hearing.

Go with what works, what maintains accuracy, what you like, or what is stylish, it's all the same.

VARMINTING MINI-MAX

So, to the end of making a varminter, I took a Rock River Arms stainless fluted bull barrel, plugged it into an M4 upper, put an ALG Defense handguard on it, and then found my highest-end Leupold scope to put on it (a 5-25 meant for just this task). ∎

CHAPTER 14

Competition AR Open

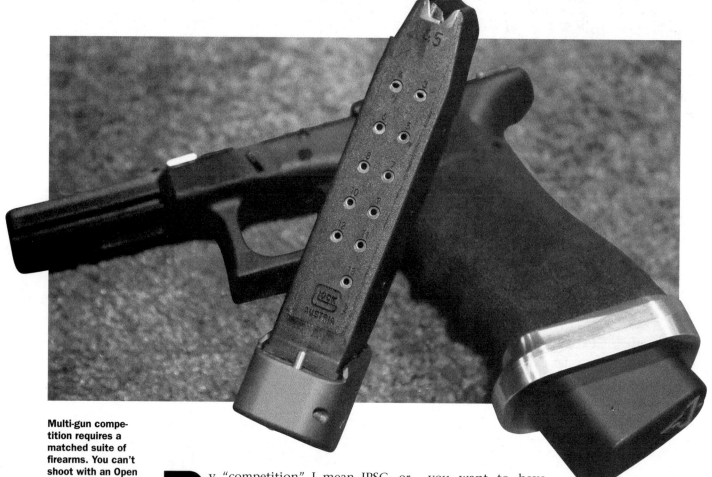

Multi-gun competition requires a matched suite of firearms. You can't shoot with an Open rifle, a Limited handgun, and a Heavy Metal shogun. At least, not outside of your home club. Keep that in mind when planning your rifle build.

By "competition" I mean IPSC, or practical shooting match rifles. Actually, more than one. There are three divisions of equipment in which you can compete in USPSA (the U.S. organization of IPSC): Open, Tactical, and Limited.

The road to these divisions was long and rocky. It took a few years, back in "the day," to hammer out what mattered, what didn't and what would be allowed.

In Open, you are allowed to use magnifying optics, a magazine as large as you can manage, a bipod, back-up sights of any kind, a muzzle brake of any kind, and even a suppressor (where locally permitted). If you want to have a flashlight on your rifle, you can.

In Tactical the limits start coming down on you. You are allowed only one optical sight. That means a red-dot or magnifying scope. If you have a back-up, the sights must be "iron" sights, regular sights. You can have a muzzle brake, but it cannot be more than 3" long, nor more than 1" in diameter. No bipod, but you can have an extra-capacity magazine if you wish. And a suppressor.

It is in Limited that the rules come down hard on gear. Here, you can again only have a small brake (1"x3"), you cannot have magnification in your optic if you have one, and you are permitted one only. No bipod, no flashlight, but a suppressor is a yes.

All three rifles will have a few things in common at the top end of competition. They will have the best trigger the shooter using them can handle. They will be fitted and tuned to the owner. (Using a borrowed rifle may be awkward, if something has been so modified that it doesn't fit you.) And they will probably have an adjustable gas system or gas block. More on that later.

In all three of these, to be scored Major you have to deliver a power factor of 320, and for Minor, a PF of 150. It is not possible to deliver a Major PF with a rifle chambered in .223/5.56, so everyone who uses one shoots Minor. A 320 PF is attainable with a caliber less than .308 Winchester, and those who wish to try it can do so with a host of calibers, but the limiting factor is always the rifle. We will limit ourselves to the .223/5.56 for this chapter, and consider Heavy Metal in a separate chapter. (That division requires a .308 chambering, so it is a separate chapter.)

The form of the base rifle in Open/Tactical/Limited in 5.56 has settled down to pretty much a standard configuration.

They are all built on a flat-top upper with a continuous rail the length of the top. The lower is whatever the owner wants, likes or gets from a sponsor. That is, it might be forged, billet, it can be any color, and unless it is brand-new, it will be dinged, scarred, worn bright on the edges and the magazine well opening will be chewed, gnawed and dinged from thousands of reloads at speed.

Those rifles will generally be barreled with a stainless barrel, 18" long, with a mid-length or rifle-length gas system. Piston systems are rare. They are compensated, i.e., have a muzzle brake on them. The use of an extra large muzzle brake is not as common as it used to be, as the smaller brakes have proven tune-able to keep recoil down.

Around the barrel, there's a slim and compact free-float handguard, typically out to the back of the muzzle brake. The current en vogue shooting style is with the left, or support, arm out almost straight, and the thumb wrapped up over the top of the handguard.

They all have a match trigger, clean and crisp. The pistol grip is whatever the individual shooter finds comfortable. Stocks will usually be one or another carbine-type stock, adjustable for length, but with a proper shape for a good cheek weld. That is, it won't be a plain M4 style stock.

Where they differ is in the bipod (Open has one, the others don't) and the sights. An Open rifle will have two optics, a magnifying one on the top rail, and a red-dot mounted on the side. A Tactical rifle will have a magnifying scope on top and iron sights mounted at an angle. The Limited rifle will typically have a red-dot sight, and if there are iron sights, they may be on top and folding, or mounted at an angle. This isn't common, simply because of the use the tilted sights get put to.

Competition rifles get more-aggressive gear. Geissele makes these oversized charging handles so you won't miss them when you have to chamber a round. Some stage designers might have you start with the chamber empty, and it hurts your time (and score) to miss the charging handle at the start.

The magnifying scope is usually a zoom scope, and it has a lever on the ring for fast zooming in and out. Magnifying optics allow for precise aiming. However, the limits of zoom make it easier to use a second set of sights for really close targets. Let's say you are at a match where the stage designer has placed an array of steel targets at 100 to 200 yards. You use whatever magnification works for you on those, and then run to the next shooting position. There, the designer has placed an array of paper targets that are 3 to 10 yards away. The next shooting position is again targets past 100 yards.

What to do with the really close paper ones? Well, you can crank the scope down to 1X and then back up again for the next position, but there's a faster way. If you have a compact red dot sight mounted at an angle on the right side of the rifle, when it comes time to shoot the close targets, you simply rotate the rifle.

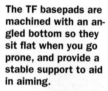

The TF basepads are machined with an angled bottom so they sit flat when you go prone, and provide a stable support to aid in aiming.

Think of it as if you were screwing the rifle into your shoulder. The rotation brings the red-dot sight in line with your eye, you simply shoot with the dot, and then rotate back to the normal position for the next set of further targets.

For Tactical, substitute a set of iron sights for the red-dot sight. For Limited? The red-dot is plenty fast as-is on the close targets, you simply have to work to get your hits at 200 with the red-dot alone.

The question then becomes, which Division? That depends on your other gear as well. You see, most rifle competition in USPSA is part of the match design known as multi-gun. It used to be "3-gun," but the difference is this: in the old 3-gun format, each stage was a single type of shooting. You shot the handgun stage(s), the rifle stage(s) and the shotgun stage(s). In multi-gun, you use two or all three in each stage. You use what are known as "dump barrels" with the rifle and/or shotgun, and then draw your handgun to finish. (It is not permitted for a stage designer to require you to re-holster, to go from handgun to rifle or shotgun.)

You start with one long gun, engage the designated targets for it, then unload it (rifle or shotgun) and shove it, unloaded, muzzle first into a padded barrel where it remains until you are done with that stage.

As a result, multi-gun gear has to be quite robust, as your rifle will get shoved into a barrel on every stage you use it in. If your

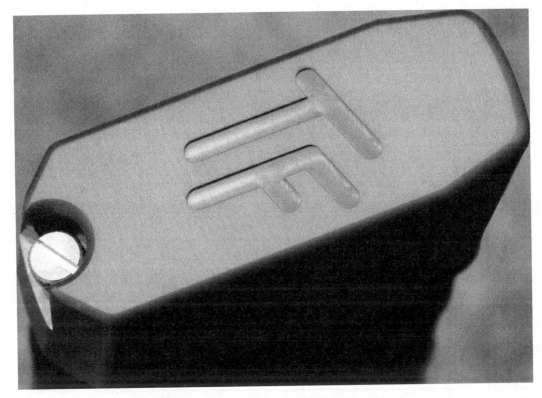

Taylor Preelance makes mag base-pads that not only add weight, and a few rounds, too, but you can bolt the mags together through the TF base-pads, and have 60+ rounds that you can actually go prone with.

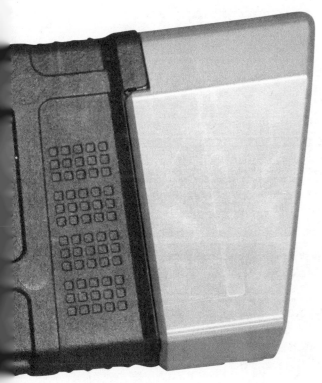

scope mount is at all weak, it will lose its zero or even break or fall off.

When you decide to engage in multi-gun competition, you have to use a rifle, shotgun and handgun that each fit the rules of that division. You can't shoot, for example, with an Open rifle, a Tactical shotgun, and a Limited handgun. So you have to pick a division.

What most shooters do is the prudent course, even though they do it for economic reasons. Most new gun owners, and even some who have owned guns for a while but are new to the AR, will be the proud owners of a vanilla-plain M4 clone. It will have iron sights, a set of mil-spec plastic handguards, a 16" barrel with a flash hider, an M4 stock and a standard trigger. Good.

If you want to give multi-gun competition a try, buy a not-expensive red-dot scope. Ignore the mil-spec maven who tells you that you must have the "combat rugged and proven" very expensive red-dot scope. Buy what looks good to you. You will use it to learn if you like this and what works for you, and you will discard it when you finally break it. Then you buy the expensive one, once you know what works for you and what you like.

Take the rear sight off of your M4 or, if it folds, fold it down and forget it. Mount the red-dot scope, zero it, and ignore the front sight post and pillar sticking up in your field of view.

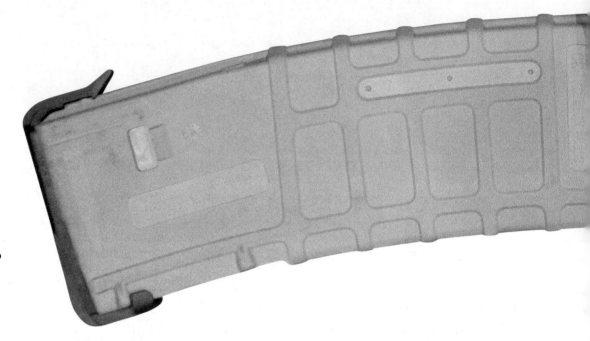

And sometimes you want as much ammo as you can possibly get, which this California Competition Pmag coupler gets you. Yes, that is a 60-round magazine.

Why this? Because you probably also have a vanilla-plain handgun and shotgun to complete your multi-gun ensemble. With a red-dot scope, some spare magazines, and the belt holders and holster to wear what you need, you can take the firearms you already have and compete. You won't need more than a couple of hundred bucks more to get into competition.

If you find you like competition, then keep using what you have, learn what you need, and re-build your gear in the off-season. If you find you don't like competition, then you haven't

spent much to find that out. You could easily spend 4-5 thousand dollars getting the "best" equipment to compete in multi-gun. If you do that and find out you don't like it, you are going to be selling your lightly-used

Open guns can have any-sized muzzle brake on them that you want. This JP Tank Brake stops recoil and might set fire to nearby objects. The smaller A2-like brake will pass muster for the other divisions.

competition gear for half what you paid, or less. If you can afford to lose a couple of grand finding that out, great. The rest of us have better uses for our money.

So, you've shot in the club matches for a season and you like it. You want better gear for next year, once you settle on a division. The upper is easy, as you can simply swap out the M4 upper for a complete upper that meets the rules. You take your M4 stock and replace it with a more comfortable one. (This is the good part of using the M4 the first season, you can try other rifles and see what stocks you like. Then put one on your rifle.)

Then drop in a better trigger set or pack and you are ready to go. Well, almost.

You see, you'll have to tune your new rifle. We'll get into that in a little bit, but first, let's assume you have built a rifle as a base. I have one that fits the bill already, a Rock River Arms competition rifle, so I'll use that as the model for building up a rifle that can be in any division.

I already have the rifle, but you will be building yours to the point of this rifle without much of a problem. You get to select the length and weight of the barrel you want; the handguard style, size and length you want; and the muzzle brake you want, all based on your experience in the season of competition. We'll simply assume that the rifle I'm using is the one you built, and if there are differences, they will be mostly cosmetic.

The process starts where you might think it would end up, and works in a way that seems backwards. You develop a load. To make a Minor power factor of 150, you simply need a 50-grain bullet traveling 3,000 fps. By going up to a 52- or 55-grain match bullet, you get a margin of error, and not much extra recoil, staying with the even 3,000 fps figure. The factory standard here would be the XM-193 from Federal, which is a 55-grain bullet that, out of an 18" barrel, can easily be going 3,200 fps. So, a 55 at 3,000 is not pushing any limits in pressure, or powder in case volume used.

The next step is an either/or process.

You can develop a load that is the most accurate (while still being 100% reliable) for your rifle, and then tune the brake. Or, select a powder that works the brake to your satisfaction, and settle for whatever accuracy you get. If you use good bullets and have a good barrel, you will most likely find that it is easy to get 1-MOA results. If you really need better than 1 MOA, then you'll have to develop the ammo, and then tune the brake.

TESTING, ONE

Testing for brake-ammo compatibility is easy. Use whatever powder you have, with the bullets you have selected, and chrono

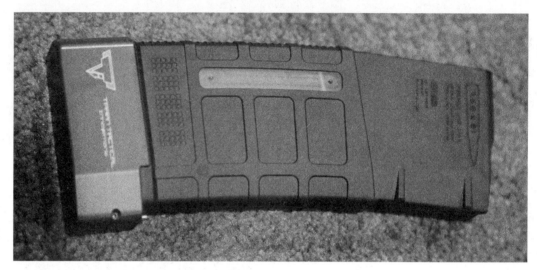

Sometimes you want just a few more rounds and a safe-solid baseplate on your magazine. Taran Tactical makes such a beast.

until it meets the Minor threshold plus whatever margin you want. Then, use a 100-yard target. Aim on the target in your offhand shooting position, and start shooting. Watch the movement of the dot or reticle on the target. If it moves up, or up and to one side or another, you are not feeding the brake enough gas. If it moves down, you are feeding it too much.

To adjust, change the powder charge or the powder type. A slower-burning powder (it won't take much of a change) will feed more gas, a faster-burning less.

The brake makers here have been on your side. They know the likely barrel lengths and powders being used, and will have produced a muzzle brake that is pretty close to what you need, with the most common combinations.

And what if the reticle or dot simply moves up a little bit, but to one side or the other? You're there, you just need to "clock" the brake. That is, tilt it so it is pushing at a slight angle. That angle will depend on your exact shooting style, and how the rifle recoils on you.

A muzzle brake diverts gases in a direction and in a volume to counteract the felt recoil of the rifle. A good brake, with ammo suited to it, keeps the muzzle on-target to the point that you can see the bullet impact on steel, and thus know it hit before you hear the "twang."

TESTING, TWO

With an adjustable gas block, you now dial back the gas traveling to the carrier.

The idea is simple: to reduce the amount of gas traveling back to the carrier, reduce the force with which it is hurled to the rear, until the gas delivers just enough force to cycle the rifle and is not causing the buffer to bottom out in the tube. Most rifles are over-gassed. That is, they are set up to deliver more gas than needed, so they will still run reliably when fed under-powered ammo.

When used with full-power ammo, the carrier is hurled back with such force that the system bounces against the back of the tube, or the spring completely cycles until it becomes a rigid cylinder of steel. This force then gets transmitted to your shoulder, increasing felt recoil.

By reducing the amount of gas, the carrier doesn't bottom out. The method is simple. Load a single round in a magazine, then chamber that round. Fire it and see if the bolt locks open. If it does, reduce the gas volume by one step in the adjustment and repeat. Keep doing this until the bolt does not travel back far enough to lock open. Then open the gas flow up an adjustment step or two, for an operating margin. Competition experience will tell you if this is enough of a margin. If you find, in a club match, that this isn't quite enough, then when you next clean your rifle, adjust the gas flow up one more step.

This process really comes into use when you build the next-step-up competition rifle and use a lightweight carrier or a lightweight buffer. By reducing the cycling mass, you reduce the effects of felt recoil, but the decreased mass calls for a radically different amount of gas. Much less than normal.

So, do not use a lightweight carrier or buffer unless you have an adjustable gas block. To use them with a normal gas lock is asking for parts breakage, and quickly, as the lighter parts will be rocket-propelled in cycling.

DRAWBACKS

The distance the AR bolt travels behind the bolt hold-open is not large. The margin between bottoming out and not traveling far enough to lock open is easy to see. Lock the bolt open. Now, with it held in a cleaning cradle and with it unloaded (always), push the charging handle back while looking into the ejection port. See how little it goes back, before it stops? That's your margin.

You want to reduce the bottom-out bounce but not cut into the over-travel margin. That's not easy, and that is why carrier manufacturers who make lightweight carriers tell you not to use them in duty or defensive rifles. And it's why competition shooters are very careful to keep their rifles as clean as they need to be.

OPTICS

The Open gun is allowed pretty much any aiming equipment you care to bolt on. For the dedicated Open shooter, this means a variable scope, with a big throw-lever, so they can quickly change power. But also, there is a small red-dot scope bolted on. This is bolted at an angel, either using a ring clamped on the scope itself or an angled mount on the rail. The red dot is perched on the right side, at a thirty-degree angle or so.

You may have seen something like this on the Acog, with the red-dot optic mounted on the Acog, up on top. This came from the SpecOps community, and while I have to applaud them for trying, they did it wrong. By putting the red-dot up there, they made it slower and made worse the bore offset.

Your scope is not on the bore axis. It is above it. As a result, when you fire the rifle has to be pitched up to get the bullet up to the line of sight. At close range, the difference can matter. Your eye is 2.6" above the bore on your AR-15. At distances inside of 25 yards you will hit lower than your aiming point. Inside of 25 yards, you want to be at maximum speed, in a match, or tactically.

Mounted on top, the red-dot is now more than 3" over your bore, making the "hitting low in close" problem worse. And, up there, you have no cheek support and will be slower and sloppier when aiming.

So, on an Open gun, the red-dot is at or below the scope, it is on the side, and to aim you simply rotate the rifle. Essentially screw it into your shoulder, turning the scope away and bringing the red-dot up. It is closer to the bore, and thus the offset is so small it doesn't matter. And your face has full support, so you are wicked fast.

One big variance from mil-spec

Well, one of many. While the mil-spec crowd is arguing about charging handles ("Is an ambi, or a big-hook extra, really tactical?") the competition crowd has already found an answer: there's no such thing as too big. As long as it doesn't get hooked on something, the bigger the better. If you have to chamber a round against the clock, or deal with a malfunction, you want a handle big enough to wrap your fist around.

So don't be surprised at the size, shape, color and inventiveness of the charging handles you'll see in a 3-gun or multi-gun match.

APPEARANCE

If you decide to go into 3-gun or multi-gun matches, be aware that you will be entering a technicolor world. The rifles will be bright colors, painted or anodized, they will be billet and sculpted, in configurations not seen in the mil-spec world. Your all-black rifle may seem rather plain. If your scores are as good as the rest of them, don't worry about looks. If you are to the point of having worn out your starter rifle, then you can certainly look into receiver sets that better reflect your personality.

MAGAZINES

The old adage, "One cannot be too rich, nor too thin," may have applied to society women a century ago. Today, who knows. When it comes to mags, you can't have too much. Stage designers love to pose problems, and a problem can be as simple as a 36-round stage and everyone has 30-round

In a multi-gun match, you rifle and shotgun will get safely ditched into the barrel, and you motor on with your handgun. This is not the place for a fragile build, you want a solidly constructed rifle.

magazines. Well, Taylor Freelance and Taran Tactical both have solution. They offer a magazine extension for your AR that adds rounds. How many? You can have +3, +4 or +5 magazine extensions.

If those aren't enough, you can use a mag doubler from California Competition that fits two PMags together, to get you 60 rounds. Or go with a Surefire 60- or 100-round magazine. Fair warning: these can get bulky, heavy and awkward.

3-GUN VS. MULTI-GUN?

In the beginning, the earth had barely begun to cool and we were not entirely happy "just" shooting IPSC with handguns. We expanded to shooting it with all the handguns we could figure out how to shoot. This soon encompassed more than we could handle. We had Pin (now Open, more or less), Stock (now Limited, more or less) and revolver (still the same).

We dabbled with "pocket guns," which were compact .380 and .32 pistols. Acquiring enough magazines for any of them was a problem. And, finding holsters. We also in the very early days had a more-expansive scoring system. Well, at least, our club did.

Current power factor is score Major-Minor. We had a scoring system of Magnum-Major-Minor-Micro. Yes, we scored a .44 Magnum, full-power load, better than a .45 ACP. Or at least we did until we acquired our first set of falling steel plates, known as pepper poppers. Those plates were relatively mild steel, and magnums dented them. So we dropped them, and disallowed them in the matches. (Not many people shot Magnum, truth be told.)

When we began to shoot rifles and shotguns, we did so in a format called "3-gun." We'd shoot a stage of handgun, a stage of rifle, and a stage of shotgun. That would be a club match. A bigger match would bet two or three of each, but not mixing.

A multi-gun match mixes the types. In a stage, you shoot a designated set of targets with a rifle, then safely rack or store the rifle, draw your handgun, and finish on the handguns stages, all in one run, all timed start to finish. This is obviously more complicated, but it's also more of a burden on the club running it.

In a 3-gun match, you could shoot the handgun stage on a 25-yard range, the rifle stage on the 100-yard range, and the shotgun (no slugs or buckshot) in an open area, as long as there was enough room behind the targets for the shot to fall to the ground. No need for a back berm.

Well, if you are going to mix them up, you need ranges with berms on three sides, for all stages, and with enough elbow room, side-to-side and to the back, to handle the target arrays. However, multi-gun has become so popular, and so much the default arrangement, that it is rare to see a pure 3-gun match these days. A multi-gun match will likely have stages of rifle-pistol, shotgun-pistol, rifle-shotgun-pistol and/or shotgun-rifle-pistol. You will notice that the pistol always comes last. That is simple: the rules prohibit requiring shooters to re-holster a loaded handgun. If the pistol came first, you'd have to unload it (magazine out, round out of the chamber, ditch it in a safe box) to go to the next firearm.

With long guns, the process is much simpler. When you get to it, you pick it up off of the rack or table, chamber a round and fire. When done, make sure it is on Safe (you will be DQ'd otherwise) and then shove it, muzzle down, into the barrel or sloped rack provided.

Welcome to multi-gun. ∎

CHAPTER 15

USPSA
Tactical Limited

The Tactical and the Limited rifles for USPSA are basically Open rifles that have been stripped down. That wasn't always the case. In the old days, the Open gun was the one that had to be special-built. To take a rifle built as a competition rifle and build it for Tactical or Limited, you need a copy of the rule book in hand.

You'll need to make sure your muzzle brake is inside the dimensions the rules require. Most come that way, it is one of the things you have to jump up to to make an Open rifle. The specs are 1" in diameter, and 3" long, max. Why? Circular logic, in a way.

Back when the Assault Weapons Ban was in effect, the makers put on muzzle brakes instead of flash hiders. Since they didn't want to go to any more expense than necessary, they used 1" bar stock. Three inches was plenty long enough to get some ports on there and actually dampen felt recoil.

Since all rifles were coming with muzzle

Left: Do not mount your fast, close-range sights up on top of the scope. Mount them on the side and rotate the rifle, like this.

Above And when you need the optics again, just rotate the rifle back upright and you're good to do.

Competition shooters will use whatever it takes to win. Not all the rifles you see on the range will be ARs, but don't let that bother you.

brakes, when the USPSA decided to have rifle equipment divisions, they went with the flow. The flow was that 1" by 3" covered all the brakes, so that became the default.

Next up, aiming. A Tactical rifle is allowed a magnifying optic. So, for the close targets, Tactical shooters use angled iron sights, like those from Barry Deuck. You use them the

Here is what the rifle looks like on your shoulder when using the angled sights, with irons like these, or a small red dot.

same way the Open shooter does, screwing the rifle into your shoulder to rotate it and bring the sights in line.

For Limited, you have the same irons as your close sights, but you aren't allowed a magnifying optic, so you have a red-dot on top. You have the same brake limit, and a lot of shooters start their 3-gun or multi-gun shooting with a rifle like this. Basically, you take your M4gery, put a red-dot on top, and frankly, most don't bother with a set of irons as the close-in sights. They simply keep in mind that they will be hitting an inch or two low at close range and account for it. At 25 yards and on out, they will most likely have hits inside the diameter of their aiming dot, and that's all they need to know.

If you are thinking of trying your hand at 3-gun shooting, then this is the way to start in the rifle category. Of course, your handgun and shotgun also have to fit the rules for Limited, but if your rifle is this basic, then your handgun and shotgun probably are, also. ∎

The Dueck Defense sights are made to be offset and angled. You rotate the rifle in your shoulder to aim with them.

DUECKDEFENSE.COM

RTS-1

PATENT PENDING

T48

CHAPTER 16

Heavy Metal

The Heavy Metal division is a step back in time, especially when it comes to caliber and sights. A rifle used in Heavy Metal division can only be chambered in .308 Winchester/7.62 NATO. You can only shoot Major ammunition, there is no Minor in Heavy Metal. So, that means a 320 power factor, and for a 150-grain bullet, that means a velocity of at least 2,100 fps. Since the factory loadings

When Heavy Metal began, iron sights ruled and life was good. Then a lot of shooters got older and found optics were better. Thus, Heavy Metal Tactical was born.

of .308 will usually fire a 150-grain bullet at 2,400 to 2,500 fps, making Major is easy. It is dealing with the recoil that is hard.

A Heavy Metal rifle is allowed a muzzle brake, but it cannot be lager in diameter than 1", nor longer than 3". On a .223/5.56 rifle, a brake or comp that size is all you really need. On a .308 rifle, that is asking a lot of a brake. While a muzzle brake that small can take the sting or thump out of shooting a .308, it won't make it as soft to shoot as that same size would on a .223.

You are limited to magazines that hold 20 rounds. In the beginning of Heavy Metal, only iron sights were allowed, but once more shooters wanted to try it (and the shooters who were doing it got a bit older), Heavy Metal Tactical was created, and one optical sight was permitted. That is one sight, red-dot or magnifying, period. Heavy Metal Limited still does not allow an optical sight. No bipod, no flashlight, but a suppressor is permitted.

Heavy Metal was a way for traditional rifle shooters, or rather, shooters of traditional rifles, to compete, and not be put at a disadvantage compared to a tuned AR-15. Back in "the day" this meant M1As, FALs, the occasional Garand, and various HK rifles. Now, with the advent of the modern AR-10 variant, you see AR-10s. When we started this, the only .308 ARs to be had

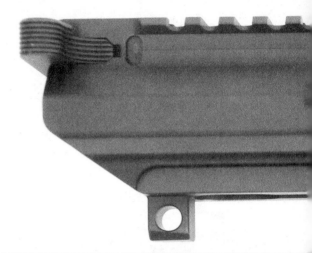

were rarities, original AR-10s, usually select-fire. But now the .30 AR is pretty common, and that's what you see.

I built mine on a Mega Machine receiver set. The receivers, barrel, bolt and handguard came as a set, and that's all you really need to get started, because the rest of it is all standard AR-15. Yep, triggers, pistol grips, stock, those are all regular items out of Brownells or from AR makers that you can use to finish the build of your Heavy Metal thumper.

One drawback to the AR-10 is that there is no mil-spec, so, each maker has had to

Armalite makes a 7.62 rifle. The older version uses modified M14 magazines.

Here is the Mega Machine .308, at the start.

re-invent and de-bug the design themselves. Once you go with a maker, you are stuck with them for parts. At least, the proprietary parts. As a result, you'll find that you can do the externals and the common parts, and thank goodness, the magazines, in common. Most will work with Magpul 7.62 magazines. One exemplar is Armalite. They started this before Magpul was around, and as a result, Armalite modified M14 magazines to work in their AR-10. So there are older Armalites that use those proprietary magazines. Otherwise, everyone uses Magpuls.

So, you have to use the proprietary parts of the manufacturer. You get us use all the other standard AR-15 items, you get to use the most-excellent Magpuls, and you get to shoot a "real" rifle in .30.

What's not to like? ∎

CHAPTER 17

USMC M16A4

H aving done the heavy lifting to create the M16A2 back in the 1980s, the USMC was a bit late to the party when it came time to make improvements to that rifle. The Army had started fielding the M4 in numbers in the late 1990s, but the Corps stuck with the full-sized rifle for much of a decade after that.

There were objections to the reliability and durability of the M4, but I'm convinced that the main reason was simple:

Top, the A4 with ACOG. Bottom, the A2 with iron sights, now an essentially obsolete arrangement.

marksmanship. Shooting a passing score on the USMC annual qualification course with a full-sized rifle and iron sights is not particularly difficult. Well, once you have successfully passed Primary Marksmanship School, it isn't. But, to do the same with an M4 is much more difficult. Since your rifle score is part of your permanent record in the marines, who wants to take that hit? The Army adopted the M4 as a supplementary rifle, and then once we were in the Global War on Terror, wholesale. The Marines instead went with the M16A4, which is/was/is the M16A2, but with a flat-top upper receiver.

When the Army went with the M4, they also started adopting the railed handguard known as the "quad rail." This is a free-float handguard (it does not touch the barrel) with four "Picatinny" rails on it – at the top, bottom and each side. This was done to provide mounting locations for the extra equipment now used in modern warfare. This includes a white light, a laser targeting designator, night vision equipment and more.

Opposit Left: The USMC is moving ahead, even if the rest of DoD isn't. Here is a DMR (designated Marksman Rifle) and it is new new new. It has the 4X ACOG, uses a piston system and has a suppressor. What next, phased plasma rifles in the 40-watt range?

The Marines were not as quick to adopt a railed handguard, but when they did they used one from Knight's Armament that would fit their M16A4, the M5 RAS.

The Knight's handguard can be had in two versions, the free-float RAS and the RAS (Rail Adapter System). The free-float does exactly that, it uses a proprietary barrel nut, and the handguard does not otherwise touch the barrel. This improves accuracy, but with most military ammo the improvement is marginal. After all, if you are using issue M855 "green tip" with a best-expectation accuracy of 3 MOA, free-floating the barrel doesn't do much. Switch to something more accurate and you can see a difference.

The handguard was there to provide locations for lasers, in particular the PEQ-2 or 2/A.

The A4 was there to provide a location for the optics, which in the Corps was the Trijicon TA31RCO ACOG, a 4X magnification,

known as the AN/PVQ-31 Rifle Combat Optic in the Marine Corps.

The Trijicon ACOG was and is a huge advance in rifle optics. It's a solid, dependable magnifying optic, one that requires almost no maintenance.

I had an occasion to visit Trijicon a while back, and in the factory floor was a bin, the size of a compact car, full of piled-in ACOGs. "What's all that? Broken scopes?"

The answer was both informative and disheartening. "No, those are returns from DoD."

"You know, if you check those out, and make sure they meet spec, even though they are beat to hell, you can make a pretty penny re-selling them. People would pay good money for a scope that might well have been used in Iraq or Afghanistan."

"Nope, the contract requires that we destroy them. We can't even tear them apart and use them for spare parts."

And you can blame Bill Clinton for that.

I don't know where to begin. This is an M4 with an ambidextrous selector, a suppressor, a CAR stock from the 1970s and a Magpul angled vertical foregrip. What has happened to the world?

The lower has its own compression spring.

There's a tensioning spring and plunger at the front of the Knight's handguard assembly, and you'll have to compress this spring as you install the upper handguard.

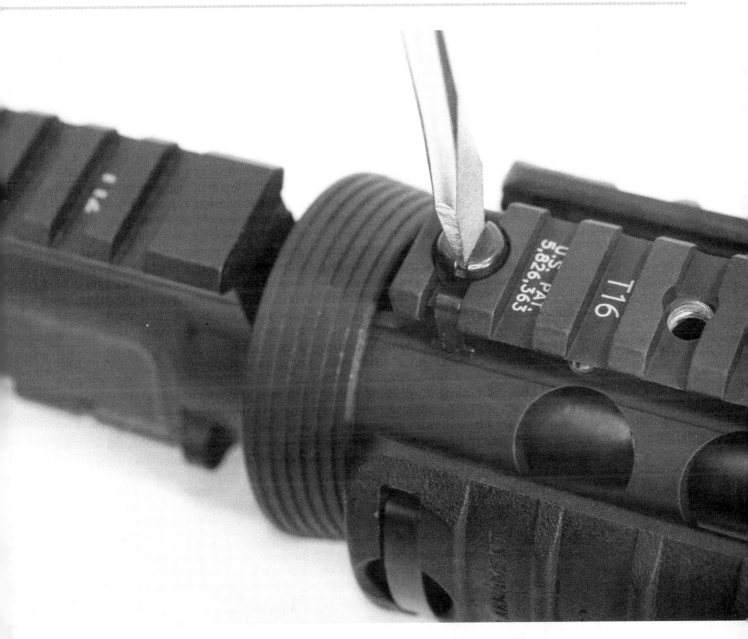

5.56x45mm NATO MFR 12238 MP CHROME BORE 1–7

Anyway, building an M16A4 clone is pretty easy. First, you'll need an A2 configuration lower with an A2 stock. You need an M4 upper, and an A2 rifle barrel.

Install your Knight's RAS, standard or free-float (your choice, there's about $100 difference between them) and you are set.

I opted for the non-free-float, just to see how it worked. (I've got a rack full of rifles and carbines with free-float handguards on them.)

The A2 barrel profile is small under the handguards for an absurd reason: to make the millions of rifles fit the ten thousand M203 grenade launchers. I kid you not.

The Marines are big on marksmanship. They adopted the ACOG as an across-the-board infantry aiming device, and if you are building an M16A4 clone you'll need one as well.

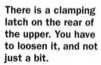

There is a clamping latch on the rear of the upper. You have to loosen it, and not just a bit.

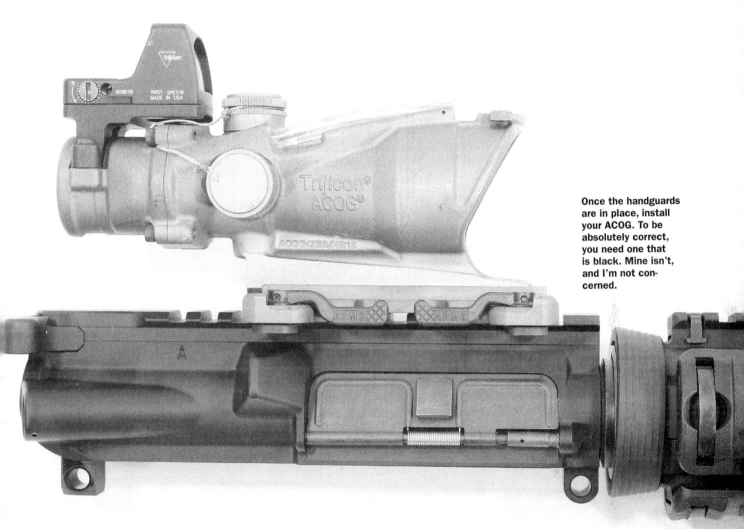

Once the handguards are in place, install your ACOG. To be absolutely correct, you need one that is black. Mine isn't, and I'm not concerned.

The RAS has a couple of interesting extra details to it. First, the top handguard goes on first. The front end has a spring-loaded plunger. You need to press this against the front handguard retained, to get the handguard in. On the rear there is a clamping screw. Loosen this until the clamp drops free. Now install the handguard as you would any other. Once it is in place, tighten the top screw (that's the rear clamp). Knights recommends only 20 in-lbs.

Now install the lower like any other A2 lower. The big deal with the Knights', in addition to having rails (and rail covers that can be removed easily), is that I can accept an M203 if you happen to have one. Or a 37mm flare launcher clone.

On top, put an ACOG. Now, if you want to be absolutely correct, you'll go with a black TA31RCO in 4X. You could even use

this in a Service Rifle match, and while you will be achingly correct, your scores will suffer in comparison to those who build rifles for the match.

However, if you want to use some other version of the ACOG, 3.5X, or a different reticle, different color housing, or other mount, I'm not sure anyone will complain.

As to the trigger, to be correct I'd stick with something that looks right in the trigger bow and delivers a 4.5 pound trigger at the lightest. That way it looks right, it is Service Rifle match correct, and you can still do some good shooting with it.

And to be absolutely correct, keep the A2 stock on it, regardless of how much you want to make it a telestock. Oh, the USMC will get around to that (they already have some built that way), but if you're going classic, old-school, and borderline retro, then stick with the A2. ∎

CHAPTER 18

Service Rifle

When the rule-makers allowed 4X optics to be used as Service Rifle aiming systems, I'm sure they were thinking of this: an ACOG against an A2. Competition shooters don't think like that.

Things have changed since we last covered this as a rifle build. Back then, to make a service rifle that fit the rules for NRA High Power competition, you basically built a precision M16A2. The sights would have been re-built for more-consistent changes, and even increase the number of clicks per change. The sights would have looked like any other A2 sights, but they were still iron sights. The real trickery was in the handguard. There, we'd re-build it to hide a free-float tube, and then fasten the shells of the handguard to the tube. Externally, it looked just like an M16A2, but internally it was more like a Nascar rifle. (Now there's a thought.)

Well, life has moved on. The armed forces now use lots and lots of rifles and carbines with free-float quad rails, and a lot of them in combat use do not even have iron sights, regular or backup sights. Plus, the military has gone to the red-dot and the low-power magnified sight in a big way. If you peruse photos from Iraq and Afghanistan, then and now, you'll see lots of Aimpoint, EO-Tech and ACOG sights on rifles and carbines.

The purpose of the Service Rifle matches has always been to enter into competition using the service rifle of the United States. When that rifle was the '03 Springfield, that's what competitors used. When we switched to the Garand, the rules reflected that change. Ditto the M14 and its semi-auto clone, the M1A.

Well, the Marine Corps now issues fleets of M16A4 rifles, with free-float Knight's handguards and an ACOG on top of the flat-top rail. If the people running the Service Rifle matches are serious (and they are) they would have to acknowledge that, and they have.

The rule changes are subtle, but they are there. In the rule 3.1 Service Rifle (c) the bullet point number seven reads: "The rifle may have an optical sight (reflective sights are considered optical sights) with a maximum power of 4.5X installed on the receiver. Variable scopes with a maximum of 4.5X are permitted."

What this means is simple: the military now issues an optical sight, and therefore the Service Rifle matches now also permit them. Of course, this means that those who insist in still using iron sights on a Service Rifle will be competing in a different class than those using optics, but scopes are permitted.

That's not all. 3.1 service Rifle (c) bullet point nine reads: "Butt-stocks may vary in length and be either fixed or collapsible. Collapsible or adjustable length stocks may

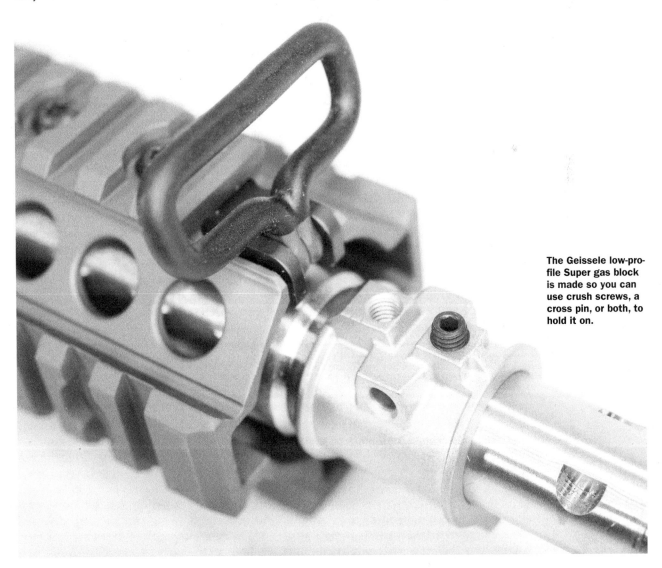

The Geissele low-profile Super gas block is made so you can use crush screws, a cross pin, or both, to hold it on.

The Geissele hand-guard comes with its own wrench, since it uses its own barrel nut.

The services are now using lots of rifles with adjustable telestocks, so the Service Rifle rules have been adjusted to allow for them.

be adjusted during an event, but butt-stocks that allow for other adjustments such as the cheek-piece height or butt-plate location may not be used."

Again, since the military now issues rifles and carbines with carbine-type stocks assemblies on them, such are permitted on a Service Rifle. This does not mean, however, that you can go and install a stock with

If you are going to invest in a fabulous barrel, then sort through a bin of uppers until you find one that is a tight fit. A very tight fit.

For Service Rifle use, your trigger has to hold a certain amount of weight, And it will be tested, with literal weights of steel. So, use a trigger/hammer set designed, made and tested for that use, like this one.

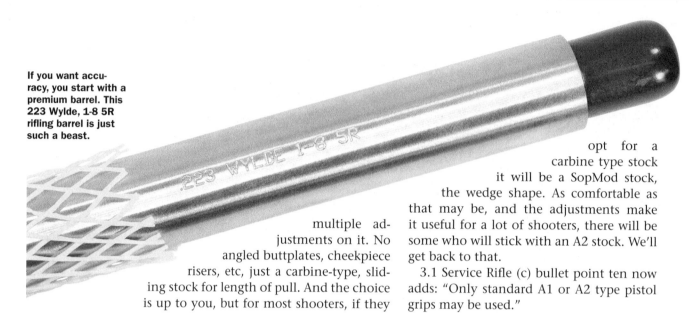

If you want accuracy, you start with a premium barrel. This 223 Wylde, 1-8 5R rifling barrel is just such a beast.

multiple adjustments on it. No angled buttplates, cheekpiece risers, etc, just a carbine-type, sliding stock for length of pull. And the choice is up to you, but for most shooters, if they opt for a carbine type stock it will be a SopMod stock, the wedge shape. As comfortable as that may be, and the adjustments make it useful for a lot of shooters, there will be some who will stick with an A2 stock. We'll get back to that.

3.1 Service Rifle (c) bullet point ten now adds: "Only standard A1 or A2 type pistol grips may be used."

Here you can see how the clamping bolts pass through the grooves in the barrel nut, and secure the handguard to the nut and receiver.

Once the barrel nut is tight, and before you do the final tightening of the cross bolts, use the small alignment screws to get the upper rail of the handguard precisely aligned with the receiver. Be fussy, it will pay big dividends in the future.

This means you have to use a mil-spec pistol grip, no matter how much you love something else. The DoD doesn't issue a [fill in the blank] and despite it being something "used by SEALs/SocomOperators" etc, you have to use an A1 or an A2. Even a real-deal SEAL or SpecOps service member would have to use an A1 or A2 pistol grip in a Service match. So it isn't like they are gaining an advantage.

The last bullet point is by far the most interesting. There, a simple statement tells us: "Quad rails or similar hand guards may be used."

And why not? The Army has been handing out carbines with quad rails on them like party favors for over a decade now. The USMC uses the Knight's handguard, either the captured or the free-float, for as long. If you wanted to shoot in Service Rifle matches, you could simply take the A4 being built in another chapter and show up on the line with it.

Of course, the other rules still have to be observed and some things don't change. Your trigger still has to have a pull not lighter than 4.5 pounds. This is tested at a match in the simplest way possible. The person or persons checking will have a weight of 4.5 pounds, they will hook it on the trigger of the unloaded rifle, and with muzzle pointed straight up and the safety off, they will pick up the weight using the rifle.

If a bull-barreled, full-weight handguard rifle is still too light for you, you can use the lead weights Geissele makes, to up the net weight of your Service Rifle. They slide in on the sides, and you attach them with the provided screws.

If the trigger holds the weight without dry-firing, you're in. If it fails, you are not. Depending on the match, you can probably step off the line (if there's time) to find an armorer and have your trigger re-worked so it holds the required weight. If not, well, you can still shoot the match, but your Service Rifle will now be in competition with the rifles that fall into Match Rifle rules. Those are built to out-perform a Service Rifle, and your score will suffer in comparison. But it beats going home without competing.

What doesn't change is the weight. A Service Rifle benefits from added weight, at least in the opinion of those competing with them. Since they don't have to "run 'n gun" in a 3-gun or multi-gun match with it, extra weight

is good in a Service Rifle. It helps the rifle stay on target in rapid fire, and it allows for a steadier hold in slow fire. At least for as long as you have the strength to hold it. A heavy rifle can get too heavy, pretty quickly.

As a result, it is not uncommon for a serious competitor, or one who seriously intends to get good, to add weight to a rifle. This means a lead weight in the stock and lead strips inside the handguard. That's why some competitors still use an A2 stock instead of a tele-stock. The trapdoor in the buttplate for a cleaning kit can hold a lead triangle, which by itself can add more than 3.5 pounds to the full-up weight of the rifle. Also, the barrel will be a full-diameter tube underneath the handguard. (It has to remain standard diameter forward of the gas block, to look like a real Service Rifle.) That's not all. Some handguards are built to accept extra lead

weights. With the bull barrel, lead in the handguard and stock, and a scope in rings on top, this ends up being the definition of an anvil.

It is not unusual for a fully-massed Service Rifle to tip the scales at close to twenty pounds. There's no recoil, but you definitely have to eat your Wheaties to shoot one for any length of time.

With that in mind, let's get to the build.

SERVICE RIFLE, 21ST-CENTURY STYLE

I started with a basic carbine that had the bore shot out. Really hosed. I stripped off the barrel and handguards, and took the old-style telestock off. On the back end, I installed a spare A2 stock buffer tube and buffer weight and spring assembly. I waited until it was all together before installing the 3 pounds, 11 ounces of lead weight from Brownells.

Inside, I yanked out the mil-spec trigger parts and installed a Geissele Hi-speed national match trigger set. This is a two-stage trigger designed to provide a clean, crisp trigger pull, but one that will, right out of

If you are shooting optics, you want them to be as solidly attached to the rifle as possible, short of welding. Geissele makes a bomb-proof mount, and it comes in any diameter in which scopes are made.

the box, hold the required 4.5-pound trigger test weight.

The top end received a Brownells match heavy barrel 5.56 20" tube. Actually, the chambering is .223 Wylde, which is a 5.56 throat tightened a bit to increase accuracy. Made of 416 stainless steel, it has 5R rifling and a twist of 1/8. It is a medium contour, so it isn't the absolute heaviest barrel that could be fit underneath the handguards, but it comes close, and offers performance and weight without being a truck axle.

The gas block is a Geissele low-profile block, and it fits a rifle-length gas tube.

Out on the end, I hand-fitted an A2 flash hider by filing the back of the A2 until it timed up properly when only hand-tight. I then used high-strength Loctite to hold it in place.

And what to enclose all this? A Geissele Mk 7 Super Modular National Match rail set. Complete with included lead weights, direct from Geissele.

The Mk 7 installs just like the other Geissele handguards. They use a proprietary barrel nut, which is okay for Service Rifle use. You see, if the changes to the rifle

are hidden from view, as far as the Service Rifle rules are concerned, they don't exist.

Then, a pair of cross bolts, going through the bottom flanges of the handguard, pass through grooves in the barrel nut, and securely clamp the handguard down on the nut. Two small alignment screws on the bottom of the handguard allow you to get the top rail of the Geissele in perfect agreement with the receiver rail.

Once the handguard is locked in place, there is simply the matter of a scope. One approach is to use a low-power variable, such as the HiLux XTC14x34 HI Power, which is legal for Service rifle match use. But the rules are clear, any scope that fits the power range is okay for use. Knock yourself out. And the rules are also utterly unconcerned with the mounting system. So if you want to use the biggest, strongest, and perhaps the most

If you're mounting a scope that will be solidly attached, you will have to work very hard to beat Geissele.

portly mount to be had, to add a few more ounces, you could.

For that, I'd opt for Geissele again. Their Super Precision mounts are precision-reamed for absolute alignment. They clamp on with big bolts, and the rings have four screws each. The come in colors, and they can be had in 30mm and 34mm ring diameters. You can have them with zero or 20 MOA down-pitch, and you can have them in black or a color they call Desert Dirt.

Why the 20 MOA down-pitch? If you are doing extreme long-range shooting (past the 600 yards of National Match competition), you need the extra down-pitch to get the rifle up-pitched and keep your scope adjustments in the range you need.

As a last selection, you can choose from three lengths. That is, where the rings are in relation to the clamping base, and thus the upper receiver. This is to allow you the choice of scopes that might be longer in tube length, or with scopes that have the adjustment turrets in a spot farther forward than a more-compact scope.

The Geissele mount is a smidgen over 7 ounces, almost 8. The Hi-Lux scope, in 30mm, is a pound and almost an ounce. That puts the set at a pound and a half, by themselves.

All-up, with sling, an empty magazine, the rifle is just over 17 pounds. I'm going to have to eat my Wheaties. ∎

CHAPTER 19

Hog Guns & Blackout

This is a FLIR thermal optic on a .300 Blackout carbine. It offers an affordable thermal sight, with a cost under three grand, and ruggedness enough to last through a lot of nighttime hog-whacking.

The world is being over-run. On the seas, the water is filling with jellyfish. On land, hogs. Or so it seems, at times. Hogs are productive (at least when it comes to making more hogs), adaptable and smart. They are also quite destructive, at least from the perspective of farmers and ranchers. A squadron of hogs can pretty much reduce a plot of crops to a muddy mess in the course of a weekend. Shooting them is not considered hunting in most locales, especially the ones that suffer from their presence. No, it is pest eradication.

The process is not sniping or whacking a single hog, the big, trophy hog. No, the idea is to get as many of them as possible at each opportunity.

Complicating this is the cleverness of the hogs. They are smart enough to know what is going on, and ornery enough to not like it. If you hunt hogs, they will adapt. Quickly. Ambush a new fleet of them on a nice sunny day, and they will move to dawn and dusk. Go after them then, and they will hole up in the light hours and come out only at night. This doesn't take long if the ones you are hunting having been briefed by others, and they are already starting at night.

So, you'll be using specialty optics. Before we get to that, there is the matter of caliber.

I've been told that the .223/5.56 is marginal, that the .300 Blackout is enough or marginal, and that everything up to a tactical nuke is "marginal." Yes, they are tough,

but they are not all the size of Buicks. You can use whatever you want, like, have or are recommended. My suggestion on caliber is this: consider the biggest one with the stoutest load that you can shoot quickly and accurately. A .300 blackout that you can hit with at the rate of 3-4 shots per second is probably better than a .458 Socom that you can hit with at the rate of 3-4 shots in ten seconds.

Use the biggest caliber that you can hit fast with.

Then scope it up.

Since the hogs will be out at night, you will want to use night vision gear. Also known by the acronym NVG, or NODs,

This EOTech LWTS is a thermal sight that will let you rapidly depopulate the hog cohorts. The only problem is the price, currently $14,000. That's a lot of hog-shooting expense, but at night, it rules.

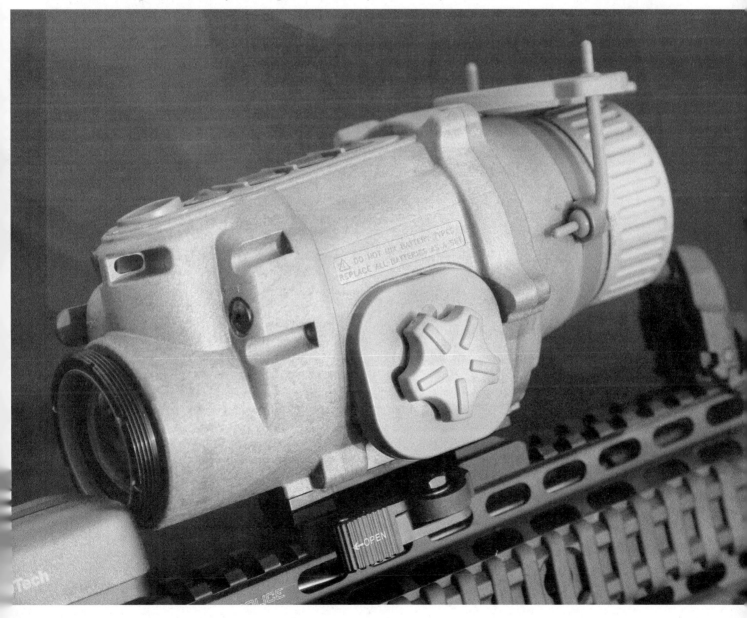

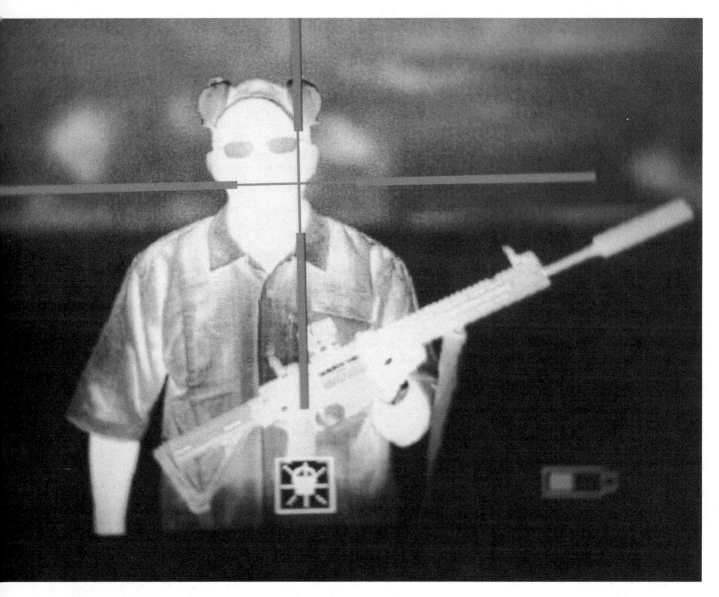

This is what a thermal image looks like. What's hot is white (unless the setting is "hot is black") and the hotter, the whiter. No, this was not on a rifle at the time the image was taken.

these are photomultipliers that let you see in dim light. Starlight, in fact. Even a hint of moon helps, but it helps the hogs, too. Overcast makes NVG useless, as it hasn't anything to magnify.

NVG

Night vision comes in two types, add-ons and weaponsights. The add-ons are just night vision multipliers. They take in the ambient light, crank it up thousands of times, and pump it out as a video picture in a small TV screen on the back of the unit. This is the ubiquitous "green screen" image we see in movies and TV shows. The image is not nearly as hi-res as your smartphone, in part because the expense of making it

such would be hideous, and in part because the volume of production can't support that cost. Each pixel you see in the image on your NVG is a "pipe" of the multiplier. If you wanted to double the resolution, you would have to double the number of microscopic pipes that are used by the photomultiplier to produce that image.

You mount the NVG on your rifle with your regular aiming optic already mounted behind it. You look through your scope, at the image of the NVG, and as long as your scope was properly zeroed, you get hits. The big advantage here is that you can install the scope, zero it, and know it is on. Then put the NVG on when you need it, and take it off when you don't, and not change your zero.

A removable night vision scope is great for night-time pest control. You can move it from one rifle to another and not change zero, since the zero is in the optic that this sits in front of.

The ATN Night Arrow is an integrated night vision and optic with a built-in reticle. You only need it, not an optic and an NVG.

Here you see the setup: the ATN in front of the magnifying optic.

The disadvantage is that you have two scopes, with their combined weight, on the rifle at night. When night shooting was sniping and single shots, this wasn't a problem. When trying to whack a whole herd of hogs before they can flee, extra weight is a problem.

The setup is exemplified by my ATN NVG. This is a day/night system, where you mount it for night and take it off for the day. This is not to be confused with a Day-Night scope, which can be used at both times of day. Behind it, use the scope of your choice. I generally don't use any-

thing with more magnification than 10X. The reason is simple: you are not magnifying 10X on the NVG as you would be in the day. The daytime "resolution" of the world is beyond the parameters of the 2K, 4K, 8K digital methodology. When you zoom up in your scope, you see 10X closer of an object that can be viewed microscopically if you had the gear.

When you zoom up to 10X on an NVG display, you are zooming up on a screen that is 640x480 in resolution. If you go X enough, you simply see pixels you can't turn into an image.

Hogs are not easy to stop. The more horsepower you can bring to the party, the better. The Wilson Combat in .338 Federal has plenty of horsepower.

So, use as much as you want, but realize that you run into the law of diminishing returns really quickly.

WEAPONMOUNT

Here, the NVG device has an aiming reticle built in. The advantage is simple: you only have the one device to deal with, and no extra weight. (Assuming your weapon mount NVG is no heavier than the plain NVG.) The disadvantages are many, even if each is minor.

You are stuck with the reticle it came with, or the reticle choices you could order it in. If you don't like what they offer, too bad. It only works at night. Oh, makers offer a front cap with a pinhole in it, for "use in the daylight," but this is a pretty marginal compromise. And if the cap comes off in the daytime when you have the NVG turned on, you risk burning it

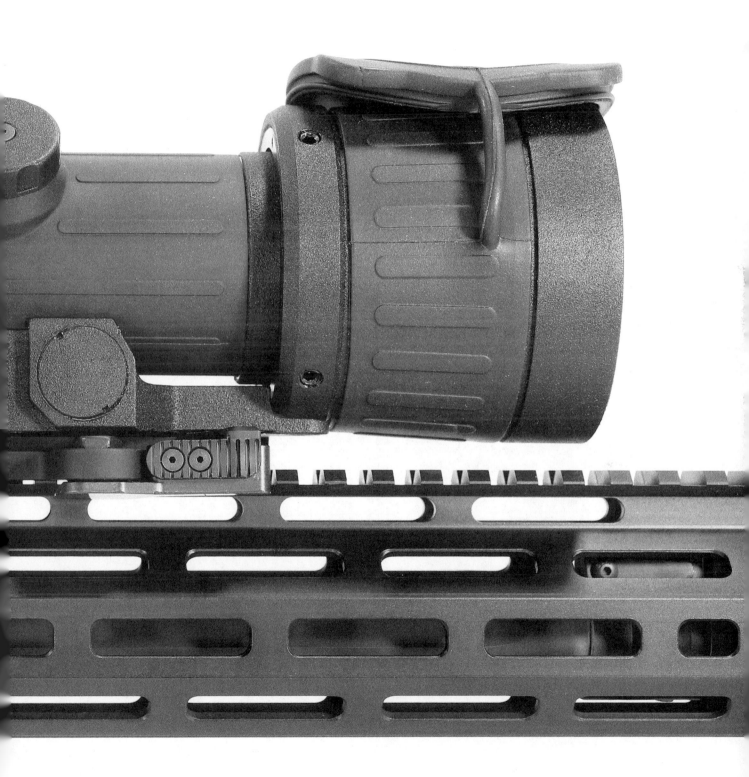

Yes, it is not uncommon for there to be a bit of misalignment between the magnifying optic and the NVG. This can be corrected with a set of rings to adjust the optic to the axis of the NVG. A small problem in the scheme of things, and a slight mismatch isn't an impediment to good shooting.

out in short order. If you are only ever going to use it for night-time hog shooting, no problem. But if it is your one-and-only AR, problem.

There will be little, if any, magnification. You have what amounts to a night vision equivalent of a red-dot scope.

GENERATIONS

The technology used to produce an intensified image is rated by what "generation" it hails from. Basically, the lower the gen, the older the tech and the lower the results. The generations are 1, 2 and 3. There are other descriptors used by manufacturers, and there are some who are using a "Gen 4" description, but that isn't an official government generation.

Basically, the newer the technology the more a unit costs, even if the housing and all the details are the same. In one instance, going from a Gen 2+ (some enhancements over a Gen 2, but not an official designation) up to a Gen 4 (again, not official) brings the cost from $1,700 up to $6,000.

There is also the matter of quality. The multipliers are made by bundling the microfibers together, processing them to create the core of the system, and then measuring them for performance. A core with a "dead" or inoperative tube will have a black spot in the image. The manufacturing process is still art as much as science. The government has a standing order for the top-quality cores. If there are any left over after the government nabs all the ones they want/need, then the top-quality ones come down to use. Otherwise, we get the ones with the occasional black dot in the image.

When you use NVG, you are magnifying existing light. To get more light, you need an illumination device that projects a beam in the infrared. Surefire can do that for you, with the Vampire, a white light or IR selectable light.

NVG BOOSTERS

You can see more at night with NVG if there is light to see by. The way to do that is with infra-red. NVG is somewhat sensitive to IR, and if you use an IR floodlight or laser, you can boost what you see. Also, if you are in a hunting party for hogs using NVG, if anyone has an IR flood then everyone has one, at least where the flood is pointed.

HEAT

Then there are "thermal" sights. These are sensitive to the infra-red spectrum. Now, the NVG gear is, also, but it isn't sensitive enough to "see" anything but an IR laser. (That's the green beam, in the green screen, you see in action movies.)

Thermal is the new NVG, and the prices are coming down while the resolution is going up. By seeing the infra-red spectrum, thermal sees where image intensifiers don't. Even a little bit of a brush screen can hide something from a NVG. But if it is giving off heat, the thermal will see right through the thin screen of brush. It takes a lot to hide thermal.

Thermals, like NVG, come in viewers and aiming optics.

Being new, you can take the price of a regular NVG, multiply it by five or six, and you have the price of a similar thermal.

SOUND

Suppressors don't hide the sound of the shot well enough to keep hogs from knowing they've been shot at. And they certainly don't hide the "thump" of the bullet hitting a hog in the group, which alerts the rest, even if the reaction of the one being hit hadn't so-warned them. But it can hide the location of the shot well enough that they don't know which direction to run for safety. A group will scatter, and some may even run towards you, as well as some away and to the side.

If you are going to hunt hogs at night, you'll need some sort of image improvement and aiming system and a suppressor. Otherwise you're just wasting your time. ■

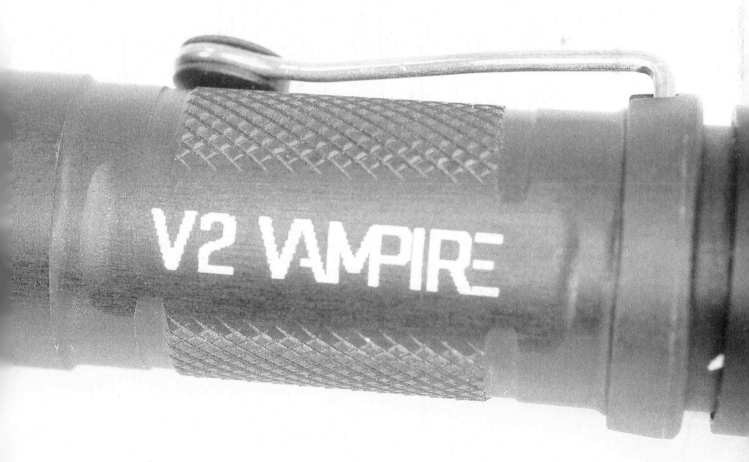

CHAPTER 20

Serious .30 with Wilson 7.62x40

You can load your own, or you can get loaded ammo direct from Wilson Combat. Buy the ammo, save the brass, load your own and see if you can make your own ammo as good as Bill's.

I still remember the late night work sessions, fixing customers' guns before opening day. I had just finished working on a rifle chambered in .30 Remington and was getting ready to head home. There was a box of .30 Remington ammunition on the bench, and a magazine for an AR-15 caught my eye. "I wonder," I thought to myself. Yep, the round would fit under the feed lips of the magazine. It was too long, but that could have been corrected.

That was in the middle 1980s, and I was one step from the 6.8 Remington SPC and other calibers. I abandoned the idea for two reasons. One, my lathe was not big, precise and powerful enough to have done the work opening up a bolt face, and threading the back of a barrel blank to put an AR-15 barrel extension on it. And two, back then, the only people who wanted something bigger than the .223/5.56 were not going to settle for anything smaller than the 7.62 NATO.

A lot has changed since then, and one of those changes is the idea that we absolutely must have the NATO round, and nothing between it and 5.56 will do. The 6.8 Remington SPC and the 6.5 Grendel are two of those. But here we're looking at .30 rifles.

One other approach is the .300 Blackout, which is a pretty darned good cartridge,

The 7.62x40 WT was developed by Wilson Combat to a reliable .30 caliber solution for the AR platform with enhanced power, range and accuracy over other .30 caliber AR chamberings.

Match Grade Barrel, 7.62x40 WT, Recon Tactical, 14.7", 1-12 Twist, Stainless

Complete Upper Assembly, 7.62x40 WT, Recon Tactical, 20", Non-Threaded, 1-12 Twist.

but it is set up for one main focus: subsonic projectiles. The idea there is to use a 200- to 240-grain bullet, at less than supersonic, to provide a compact, hard-hitting and very quiet rifle. Essentially, a .45 ACP equivalent, without the downsides of that cartridge in a carbine.

But, when you boost it up to supersonic speeds, you run out of case capacity. Yes, it comes up to a useful speed, but not all it could be.

That's where the Wilson 7.62x40 comes in. Here, the case is made as long as it can be and still fit a .30 bullet in it, and still have all that fit into the magazine. What is the difference? A .300 Blackout (the Whisper does the same), with a 110-grain bullet in it, tops out at 2,300 fps, more or less. The same weight bullet in the Wilson gives 2,500 fps or more. The actual numbers depend on barrel length and the individual barrels involved. It is useful to note that, of the two, the Wilson benefits more from a longer barrel, as the greater case volume keeps the expansion ratio in favor of the Wilson.

The gap is similar as the weights increase. By the time you get up to 135-140 grains, the Blackout will drop below 2,000 fps (especially out of a carbine) while the Wilson retains the 200 fps advantage.

Unlike my perusal of the .30 Remington, the 7.62x40 does not need any bolt work. It uses the same bolt as the AR-15 in .223/5.56, because the Wilson is based on that case.

What Bill Wilson did was simple. He cut off 5.56 cases, necked them to .30, and kept adjusting the dimensions through testing until he had the longest case that would hold a .30 bullet, in a magazine-length package.

And since the operating pressure of the .223/5.56 is 55,000 PSI, he could get .30-30 ballistics out of an AR-15 package. Well, the classic .30-30 loading, since the .30-30 has been getting something of a facelift these days. The classic .30-30 load came out of a Winchester M-94 or Marlin 336. The 16" barrel of a carbine one of those (the 20" barrel delivered more speed, but were uncommon in the hunting fields) delivered a 170-grain bullet at 1,900 to 2,000 fps, and a 150 at 2,100 to 2,200 fps.

If we take a 16" barrel AR, in .300 and 7.62x40, we can get close in weight, 135 grains, and into the velocity range of the 150-grain bullet in the .30-30.

Close enough that a white-tailed deer won't notice.

And that is a big part of the focus of the 7.62x40. A lot of state DNR regs do not allow a .22 for deer hunting. Some do, as long as it isn't a rimfire, but most don't. That leaves your AR-15 in the rack when it comes to deer season. You could buy another rifle, but why? A barrel from Wilson Combat will run you less than $300, they also sell ammo for it, and if you are a reloader, you can easily get dies and reload the empties for practice. Or to use the bullet you feel is the perfect whitetail-slaying projectile.

The conversion requires only a new barrel, which you can acquire form Wilson Combat or other custom barrel makers. So, you pull out the shot-out tube on an AR you already have, or you build up a new upper, with a barrel and receiver. (You can use the bolt/carrier assembly and charging handle from another rifle until you want to spring for the cost of its own, dedicated set.)

The trick here is making it a handy hunting rifle and getting the performance you want.

So, this build starts with a Wilson combat 20" barrel in 7.62x40. I plugged it into an M4 flat-top upper, since I wanted to put a scope on it and wasn't worried about back up iron sights. Over the barrel, I used an ALG Defense free-float tube. This is slim and circular, so it won't be too big even for a small shooter using gloves in hunting season.

The barrel gets a no-name low profile gas block and standard gas tube, as well as an A2 flash hider.

ADDENDA

There is one more detail to keep in mind: the 7.62x40 is not prone to the problem, albeit rare, that the .300 can fall prey to. A loaded .300 Blackout/Whisper, if the bullet is too short or the neck tension not enough to support the impact, can chamber, and the bolt close, in a rifle chambered in .223/5.56. Yes, wince, it is as bad as that.

Back in the 1960s, the *American Rifleman* had a column in the technical section about a Japanese Arisaka originally chambered in 6.5 Arisaka that had been re-chambered to .30-06. Why? The common re-chambering back then was to take a 7.7 Arisaka and ream the chamber out to accept a .30-06.

The 7.7 bullet diameter is .312" (more or less) while the .30-06 is the familiar .308". Post-war, hunting ammo in 7.7 Jap, as it was called, was ultra-rare. Reloading? Get real. But .30-06 was common as dirt. Literally available at many hardware stores and even gas stations.

It was common enough to re-chamber 7.7 Arisakas to .30-06 that finding one not so reworked is becoming difficult.

Well, the owner didn't know it was 6.5

and not 7.7. The "gunsmith" who did the work even had to make allowances, and didn't think it through that the pilot of the chamber reamer wouldn't fit, as-is.

The end result was a hard-kicking rifle that took several deer before it came to light and got tested. A test-fired .308" bullet came out the muzzle at .264" and was visibly longer. The headspace did not change, so regardless of the chamber pressure (and it had to be impressively high) the rifle held together.

Well, the AR isn't so strong as the Arisaka, which is a clone of the Mauser 1898.

A poorly reloaded .300 can have the bullet set back in the case when the bolt drives it into the chamber. A .308" bullet trying to go down a .224" barrel just isn't going to work. I'm not sure if even the Arisaka could hold together, there. (Not that I'm ever going to try, you understand.....)

The 7.62x40, with its longer case, simply can't be closed that way. ■

The 7.62 x 40 WT was designed for tactical/defense applications as well as hunting for medium sized game such as deer and feral hogs.

CHAPTER 21

Long Range 6.5 Grendel

The 6.5 does not have the raw horsepower of the .308, but for flat trajectory and retained energy at distance, the 6.5 punches above its weight class.

It was a warm summer day. We were a bunch of gun writers on a PR trip, and we had exclusive use of a 600-yard rifle range. At the back end, behind the target frames, was a steel half-silhouette. We lasered it at 640 yards. We got a rifle zeroed to the point that it was hitting that steel, and someone came up with the idea of a contest. But what kind? Well, most hits. Hmmm, we have a squad of competitive types and a mountain of ammo. Who wants to see a barrel burned up as we try to make it 20-30-40 hits in a row?

Best hits out of five shots. Yes, and when we've all shot five hits, then what? OK, here's the plan: five shots, scored the most hits. Shortest time is the tie-breaker, but to add pressure, any shot over ten seconds doesn't count.

Use anything on the range, table, chairs, bench, sandbags, to build a shooting position that isn't prone. Time starts on the beep.

For the longest time, four hits in just under ten seconds was the winning score. Then I found a shooting position that worked for me. It was awkward to look at, it had nothing in common with the classic shooting positions, but it afforded me one great advantage: I could see my hits (and misses) through the scope. On my last run I hit the steel five times in five shots, in just over seven seconds. Winnah!

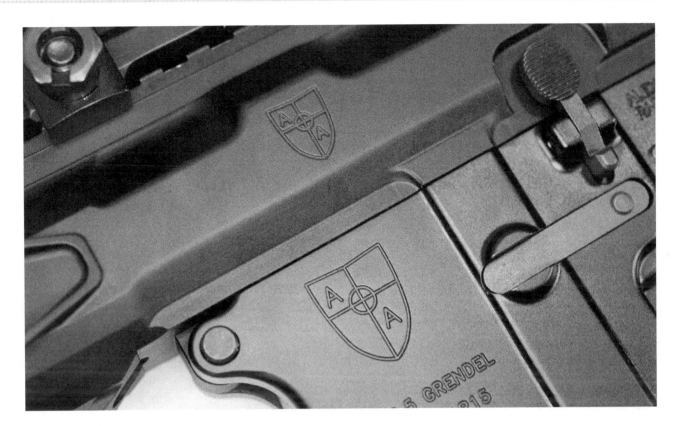

The rifle was an Alexander Arms 6.5 Grendel with a 20" barrel and a Leupold 3.5-10 on top. Having won the contest for the day, I had to have a rifle, so I asked Bill Alexander to send me one exactly like it.

Bill designed the 6.5 Grendel to be the best medium-bore hunting cartridge to be had in the AR. The bonus was the case length allows for long, high-BC (ballistic coefficient, a measure of how easily it slices through the air) bullets in 6.5, and that means it is a really good long-range cartridge as well. How much of a difference?

The competitor here is the 6.8 Remington SPC. A typical bullet for it weighs 120 grains and has a BC of .400. The 6.5 Grendel, with a similar bullet weight of 123 grains, has a BC of .510 (higher is better)

and you can buy or load 6.5 with bullets of 139 grains and a BC of .578.

A higher BC means, with all other things being equal, less drop and less wind drift. Drop wasn't the problem on that afternoon, but wind drift was. Once I knew the drift, I could hold off (Into the wind) and get my hits.

One conversion option of an AR to

The 6.5 Grendel is the brainchild of Bill Alexander, and he makes cracking good rifles chambered in it. That doesn't mean you can't make your own, and eventually you will. Trust me on this one.

At first glance, the 6.5 (right) and the 6.8 (left) are similar in performance. But the 6.5 can use bullets with much better BCs, and that makes the difference downrange.

This isn't the scope I used to whack steel at 640 yards, but were I to try that again, I'd be more than happy to do so with this optic. The performance of the 6.5 warrants the best glass you can park on top of it.

6.5 Grendel is to buy a complete upper from Alexander Arms. The advantage is that you have a ready-to-go upper that you can simply install on a ready-to-go lower.

If, however, you want to build one yourself, you need a barrel in 6.5 Grendel, obviously. Brownells lists and makes them. You also need a different bolt. The 6.5 Grendel used as its parent case the 7.62x39. The case was blown out, necked down, and the result was the 6.5. So, you need a 7.62x39 bolt to go with your barrel. (Again, Brownells.)

With bolt and barrel on hand, the rest is all straightforward AR building. The barrel and bolt are designed to fit into standard receivers and carriers, respectively.

I did just this, once I had the AA rifle on hand. My barrel came from a maker no longer in business, and fluted to boot.

I used a VLtor CASV handguard (which they have discontinued, unfortunately) for my build. This gave me a big-enough handguard to hold, without weight, and plenty of room for cooling. I then painted it tan and brown, in a pattern I call "ropeflage." Paint the base color, then drape rope across the surface and overspray the second color. The base color shows as stripes, in curves, in the overcoat.

Then it is simply a matter of what scope base and scope fit the job I have in mind for this, or the Alexander Arms 6.5.

Oh, and that afternoon? We heated that barrel up to the point of not being able to touch it, just shooting five-shot groups. And the AA 6.5 Grendel still held zero. Nice rifle, indeed. ■

CHAPTER 22

Retro, the M16A1 & XM177

The desire for light weight and modern may conflict with a period-correct build. But then, if they had had the choices we do, would they have not built something like this?

When I started on this life journey of working on guns, there was no such thing as retro ARs. There were the ARs that Colt made, and ARs that we could make from scratch from parts we could source.

The list was pretty short. For a while, there was your basic A1 with triangular handguards, or some sort of carbine-like rifle with a 16" barrel, circular handguards and maybe a tele-stock. And maybe not, as Colt was making a rifle called the Lightweight Sporter, which was a carbine with a fixed stock. And it wasn't a badly handling little rifle, by the way.

Then came the A2, with its heavier barrel, circular hand guards and longer stock. Oh, and a rear sight that could be adjusted without tools. With a few exceptions, there

This is an actual Vietnam-era M16A1. This is what you'll strive to duplicate in your retro build. Well, at least some retro builds.

The original Colt non-government rifles and carbines have a two-headed screw as the front takedown pin. This would not be right for a Vietnam-era retro build, unless you want a 1960's-era semi-auto rifle or carbine.

weren't many SBRs being made, in part because we just hadn't come to appreciate their handiness. And, it was still back in the dark ages, when a lot of states didn't allow them.

The sources of parts we had were few. Basically, you scoured the gun shows (which back then were not like today, and that's not just an old curmudgeon grumping) and bought whatever parts you could find, or

Pay attention to details. A period-correct build will have a "teardrop" forward assist, up to a certain date, and then not.

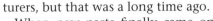

needed, or could trade to someone else who had what you needed. A lot of those parts were surplus, and a lot of them I'm sure were production over-runs that should not have been let out the door of the manufac-

turers, but that was a long time ago.

When new parts finally came onto the scene, they were not like the old parts. They were made for competition, or to improve on the plain old ARs that we'd been shooting. One example was tubular handguards. The first ones were just solid aluminum tubes with the barrel nut made as an integral part (or welded on the end of seamless aluminum tubing) so we could have a free-float barrel. They were a great leap forward, and they were horrible at the same time. They were heavy, they got hot (and didn't cool quickly), and if you wanted to attach anything to them, you had to drill and tap the tube and then bolt on your accessory or improvement.

But they were not the plain old ARs we'd been dealing with, and we were happy.

In time, we got actual free-float handguards, railed handguards and flat-top receivers (which meant that we didn't have to chop off carrying handles any more), and we realized we'd missed something. Oh, the new rifles were a lot more handy, useful and effective, but we had lost the plain, straight-forward rifles of the early days.

Ever wonder why rich people buy 1960s and 1970s muscle cars? Memories. There was a time before then, when their parents took old cars and built hotrods. The classic hotrod you see, in its bright paint scheme, started life as a plain, probably black, car. It ended up stripped, painted, chromed, re-engined and turned into a street-rod or hotrod. Then, when the supply of build-able old cars ran dry (the ones left were too valuable to be "chopped"), people started making the parts needed from scratch.

Honest. If today you wanted to build a classic hotrod, you no longer have to track down an original Ford Model T and start stripping and building. (Besides, if it is in build-able condition, it is too valuable to be rodded, it should and hopefully would be restored to original.) You can buy every part you need, from a custom hot-rod parts supplier, manufacturer or retailer, and then find a builder who can assemble it for you. You will have to learn practically a new language, as the vernacular of the rodding set can be quite detailed, and if you use it incorrectly you'll be a long time living it down.

Well, welcome to the brave new world of retro. You no longer have to find a buildable AR and then start swapping parts, making it more and more retro. You can buy all the parts you need (and a lot of the parts will be the same, retro or no) and then assemble it yourself. You can even buy new retro. No, not an oxymoron, Colt and others now make period-correct ARs, not the newest tacticoolest, but period correct. Hey, this is America, we do what we want, and we buy what we want.

Brownells jumped into this, and you can buy all the parts you need to build many of the period-correct models you may desire. When you want to build retro, you have to make some decisions. First, what time period and use? Second, what place or end-user? Those decisions will then determine what barrel, bolt and carrier, handguards, stock, sights and receivers you will use. A few guidelines follow here.

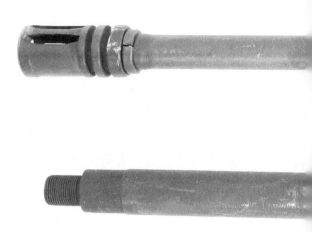

BARRELS

You have two choices here: twist and weight. For anything before the A2, select something slender, as heavy barrels were not common. The whole point of the AR when it came out was that it was lighter than the existing .30 rifles. So, you need a lightweight barrel, but there the shift in what is cool actually goes your way. After a years-long affectation for heavier barrels ("They're more accurate and don't get as hot"), a lightweight AR barrel and lightweight AR is now much more sought after.

The dividing time here is the Colt HBar. Before, with the A1 and A2 rifles, barrels were relatively trim. With the HBar, barrels got fat.

Barrel markings matter on a truly correct retro build. This is the correct marking line for a Colt rifle between the late 1960s and the early 1980s.

My XM177 clone weighs 5 pounds, 12 ounces. Your basic M4gery tips the scales at close to 2 pounds more than that, mostly barrel.

The big change is in twist. Back in "the day" there was just the one: 1 turn in 12 inches. It works fine with 55-grain FMJ bullets, and anything that has a lead core that weighs that or less. If you insist on an all-copper bullet, you will have to make sure the ammo you use is correct for a 1/12 twist. (The makers of all-copper-bullet ammunition are aware of this, and will mark the boxes of their products to let you know.) Or, you can use a faster twist. This may seem like heresy to some, but if your barrel profile is period-correct, I don't see a problem with using a 1/9 or 1/7 twist

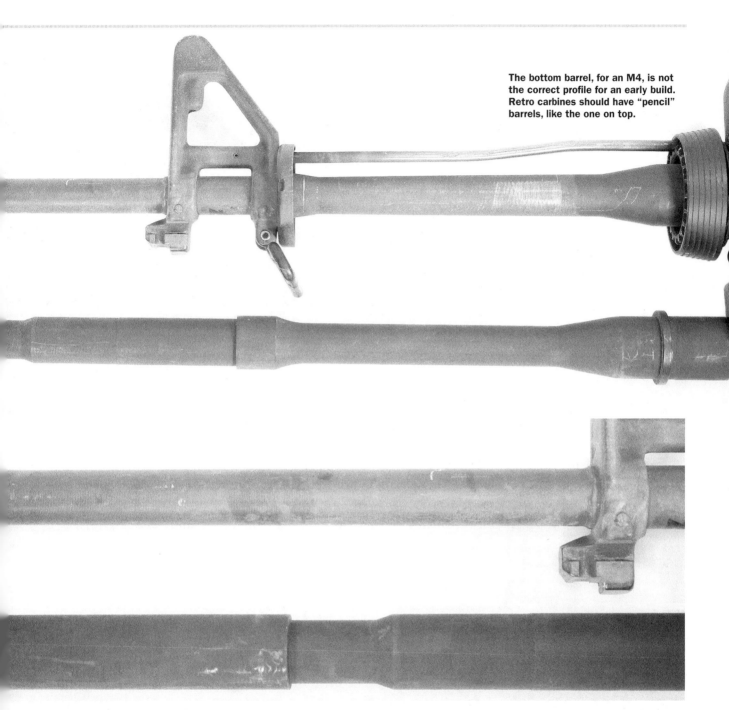

The bottom barrel, for an M4, is not the correct profile for an early build. Retro carbines should have "pencil" barrels, like the one on top.

The big giveaway that the bottom barrel is wrong is the groove turned in the barrel, where the grenade launcher for the M4 would clamp on.

bore inside. It will give you greater flexibility (especially the 1/9 twist) in ammo choices.

Brownells offers new barrels that have the correct profiles for XM177, carbine, A1 and A2 rifles. The first three will be 1/12 twist barrels, and the last will be 1/7 twist, which are correct for the time.

Now, if you want to take your kinda-sorta M4gery and make it as close to an actual M4 as you can, you need an "M4 profile barrel." And if you are making it truly as close to an M4 as possible, you

also need to apply for your tax stamp, because at 14.5" the M4 barrel will make your carbine into an SBR. The barrel profile difference? There is a circular recess turned in the profile that is there to be the clamping groove for the M203 grenade launcher.

Yep, that's right, they modified the barrels (well, the barrels-to-be of a million M4s to come) rather than modify the existing ten thousand (did they even have that many, in 1996?) M203 grenade launcher mounts. They had done the same thing

The slip ring on a build prior to an A2 should have a cylindrical shape, and not be the delta ring of the A2.

This upper receiver is perfect for a Canadian C7/C8 build. It has the forward assist, ejector lump and A1 rear sight.

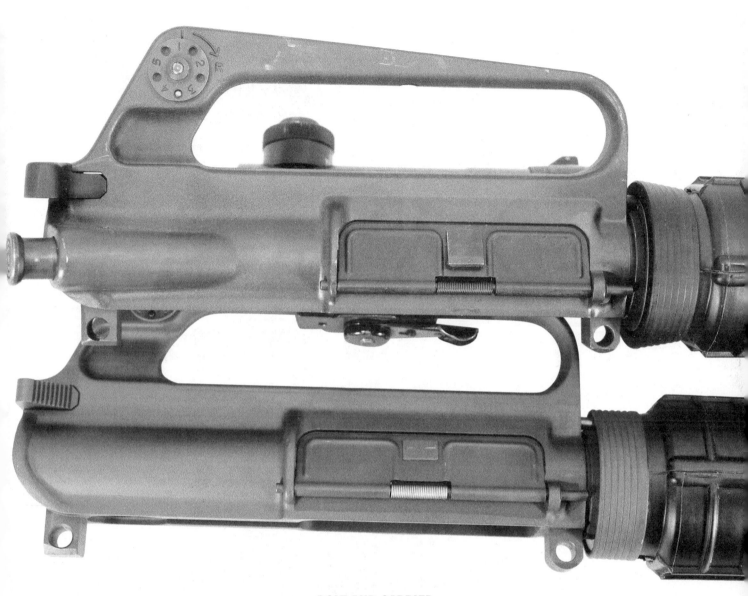

ten years before for the A2. The A2 was supposed to have a heavier-profile barrel, but the M203 as-is, wouldn't fit. So, they made the barrel smaller in diameter, under the handguards, to clear the launcher.

On the end of your barrel, you want an A1 or A2 flash hider, with two exceptions. If your retro is a very early clone, you need the three-prong open-end flash hider. Or, if you are making an XM177 clone, you'll need either a long flash hider that copies the 177 moderator, or a copy of the moderator itself. You can get either the three-prong flash hider or the XM177 moderator (that one is a suppressor, it will take the tax stamp and wait) from Innovative Industries.

BOLT AND CARRIER

The original bolt and carrier was chrome-plated for easier cleaning. This changed when the Army adopted the M16A1, as a chrome carrier was seen to be too flashy, too obvious, and it got changed to one that was parkerized.

After that, the only choice you had was parkerized. In the earliest years of building retro, it wasn't easy to course a chrome carrier, and almost impossible to source a chromed bolt. Now they are a lot more common, but you have to be careful. A modern, nickel-boron plated carrier, say one from LWRC, would work just fine. But it wouldn't look right, and we're here for the looks. (And the performance, there's no

Two uppers for retro builds. One (the lower) is a "slick-side" and lacks a forward assist. The upper one is an A1 with forward assist. Notice the anomaly? A button forward assist plunger. It should be a teardrop, and will get changed, pronto.

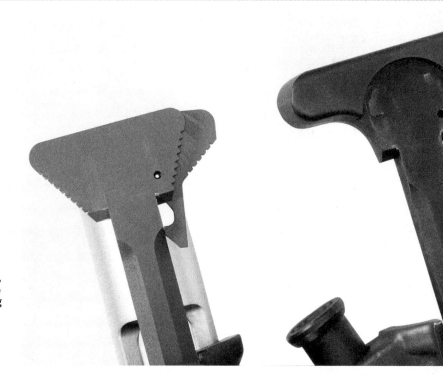

If you go far enough back in a retro build, you'll have to source a triangular charging handle like the one on the left. After that, everything will call for a plain one like on the right.

need to build an unreliable, nor inaccurate, retro clone.)

Well, Brownells again to the rescue. They offer chromed bolt carrier assemblies that will work with almost all of your retro builds. Well, the early ones, not the later ones. And not the earliest. An M16A1 clone will call for a parkerized carrier. An early XM177 can be chromed or parkerized. But here's one: the very earliest ARs, the ones lacking a forward assist? Their carrier did not have the sawtooth recesses for the forward assist. That will be tougher, as finding a smooth carrier, chromed and period-cor-

If your retro build doesn't call for a forward assist (a slickside upper), then you really ought to find a no-notch carrier to go in it. A chrome one would be correct.

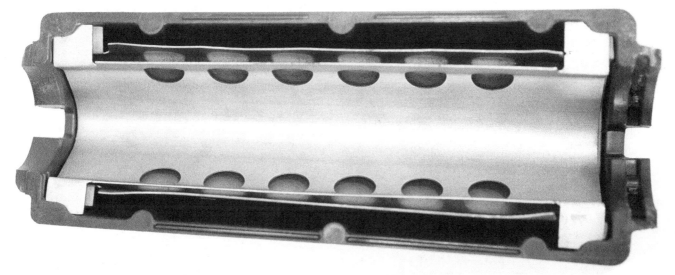

M4 handguards, in addition to being the wrong shape for a retro build, also have double heat shields inside.

rect, will be a lot more difficult.

But, wait! Since they are making retro builds easier, they are making or ordering (it makes no difference to use, Brownells as a company is accustomed to making sure the details are all correct) their chromed carriers "no serrations."

And if you cannot find a chromed bolt, don't worry. Bolts are considered consumable items in military use. It is entirely likely that a chromed-carrier early rifle or carbine would have a parkerized bolt in it after only a bit of use.

HANDGUARDS

The A1 rifle calls for triangular handguards, which are made in left and right sets.

The various carbines and XM177, the Air Force GAU-5, 5/A and 5/A/A models have the small-diameter round handguards. Those are made as interchangeable halves, installed as top and bottom, but interchangeable.

If you are building an A2, then you need the rifle-length round handguards, made the same way as the carbine handguards.

The big advantage to the A2, and the CAR before them, was in pairing. If a triangular handguard was damaged, you had to have the correct one to replace it. Broke a left? Having a bin of spare rights doesn't help. The A2 was not only stronger (material and design changes), but by being identical, if you broke one you didn't have to break up a set to replace it. You simply had a bin of spares.

A rarity would be the special handguard used when the military was installing M203 grenade launchers onto A2 rifles, and the handguard is just an upper, leaving the lower half clear for mounting the launcher.

Last of the regular handguards would be an M4 clone, with over-sized oval handguards (with a double heat shield) and made as interchangeable upper and lower pieces. After that, the world shifts to free-float and railed handguards, which is firmly out of the arena of "retro." Or at least, will be for a couple of decades. Who knows what will be collectible and desirable in 2040?

A small detail, but one worth noting: early rifles and carbines, the M16A1 and earlier, will have a handguard retainer that is cylindrical. The A2 will have the delta ring, the earlier ones are called a slip ring. That would be an obvious "oops" on an otherwise correct retro build.

As mentioned, the various railed or free-float handguards are not really part of the retro movement, and we have covered them in various builds already.

STOCK

The first stocks on AR rifles were the short length, the same length as the M16A1 stocks. But they did not have the trap door for a cleaning kit. The A1 rifles had the short stock with the trap door. The A2 used the longer stock, with a buttplate with a sharper edge on the contour of it, and a trapdoor. The early carbines, the XM177, used a telestock, but it only had two posi-

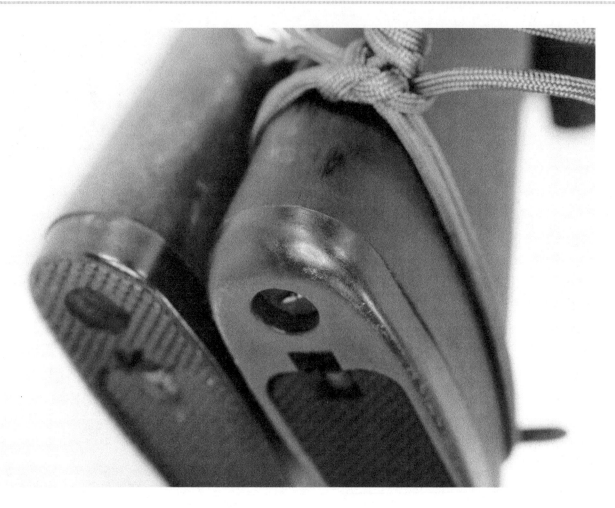

The A1 stock on the right has a shinier finish to the buttplate and the edges are more rounded than the A2 stock on the left. These things matter when your retro build is being judged.

tions: extended or collapsed. Only the later versions of the carbine, the Air Force GAU 5, 5A, etc., and the M4, have multi-stop telestocks. This is perhaps the most difficult part to source, as everyone who makes a telestock offers five, six or even seven stops, but few make a two-stop buffer tube. (The buffer tube, not the stock, is the part that "decides" how many stops the stock has.)

NoDak Spud offers this buffer tube with two positions in their retro lineup of build parts.

The carbines also have different sliders, the moving part on the stock assembly. The earliest ones are simple and plain, and have a rectangular loop on top of the stock. This was meant to be the sling attachment point. Original stocks were aluminum with a gloss black vinyl coating. After those came the same design done in a tough plastic. If you want to be period-correct, then adding the vinyl-coated aluminum stock will make it correct for the early guns, but will also add weight to your build. My XM177A1, for

example, would be over 6 pounds, empty, if I put in the aluminum stock. The later M4 stock has extra ribbing on the sides of the stock, to reinforce it, and lacks the top loop for a sling. Only the latest versions (again, not retro) have the wedge-shaped stocks patterned after the Sopmod stocks. Although it would not be beyond reason to build a GAU 5/A clone and then put a Sopmod stock on it. The part is in the government inventory, and if someone saw a way to grab one (in the military) it could happen.

SIGHTS

This comes along with the type of receiver. The A1 upper receiver has a rear sight that is adjustable only for windage and requires a tool. Oh, the various manuals you might read will tell you it can be adjusted using the tip of a loaded round, but that is just a cruel joke. The problem is that the tip of most FMJ bullets is too blunt

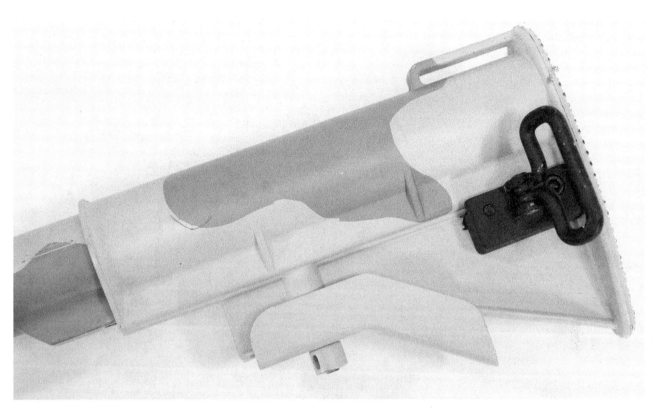

OK, the right shape and size. But with a Desert Camo coating, it would be "retro" only if you are building something for Desert Storm.

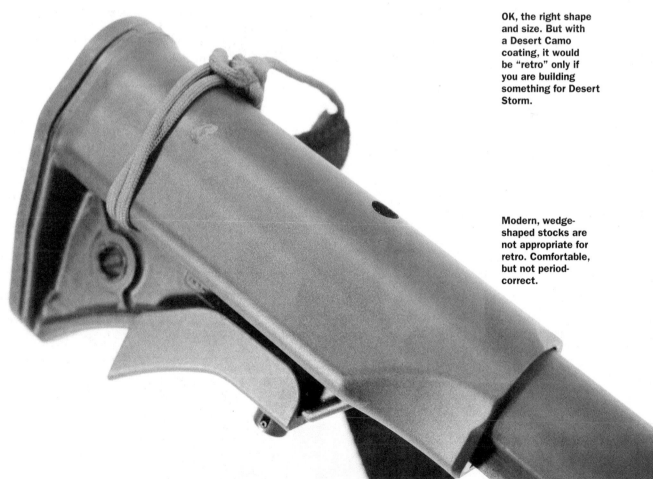

Modern, wedge-shaped stocks are not appropriate for retro. Comfortable, but not period-correct.

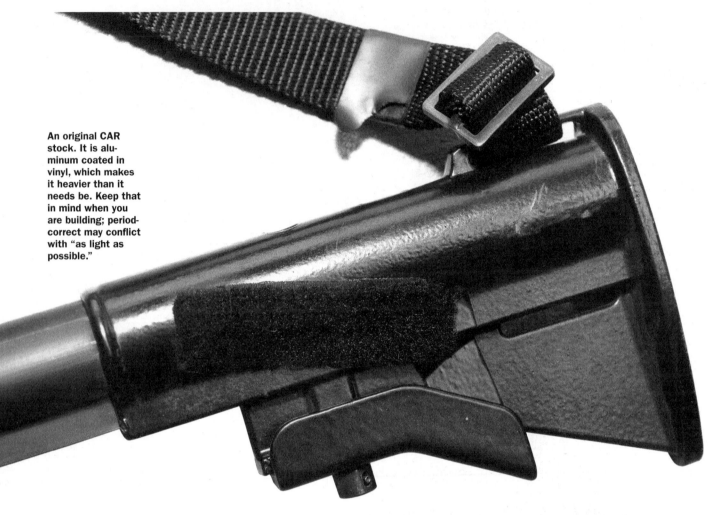

An original CAR stock. It is aluminum coated in vinyl, which makes it heavier than it needs be. Keep that in mind when you are building; period-correct may conflict with "as light as possible."

The very earliest ARs did not have a spring-loaded buffer retainer. Instead, there was a roll pin that went across the bottom lip of the tube and held the buffer in place. Luckily, the makers of retro lowers, NoDak Spud, put the hole there, but they also put the hole for the spring-loaded plunger. It looks correct but is modern convenient.

and won't depress the plunger enough to allow the plate to rotate. As a result, you end up with brass scratches on your carry handle from futile attempts to adjust the sights. Polymer tips break off, and hollow points, well, they just don't fare well when subjected to such abuse. Get the tool, use it when you need it, and try not to lose it until the next time.

A proper retro front sight would be the round-tip front, which has five notches for adjustment of elevation. The change to the A2, with four adjustment settings and a square cross-section, was done for marksmanship reasons. Essentially, a round post, when light hits it from the side, makes that side toward the sun disappear. You "see" a different center, of a thinner front post, and you end up "shooting into the sun." This was seen as a problem to the USMC. They qualify each year, and their scores are part of their permanent record. Hurting scores was not a good thing. (Plus, it makes a difference when trying to whack bad guys.) The flats prevent the sun effect, but the cost was only four "clicks" per rotation.

If you want the better front sight post and insist on installing an A2 post in your retro A1 or other rifle, you won't get any grief from me.

An A2 upper (rifle or carbine) will have the windage and elevation adjustable rear sight, in its housing in the carry handle. The rifle will have an elevation wheel regulated to 800 meters, and the carbine to 600 meters.

The zeroing of each is different. You use the front and rear of the A1 to get your rifle sighted-in. You use the rear to adjust windage and the front to adjust elevation. You move each to where it needs to be, to get the rifle hitting where you are aiming. For range adjustments, you have two options in the A1: hold over, or flip the rear sight to the "long range" setting. The L of the rear has apertures at two different heights. One is for regular range, and the other for long range.

On the A2, you only use the front sight to get the rear at the proper height for elevation for the mechanical and basic zero process. After that, if you need to adjust for range you use the rear sight with its click adjustments.

For those who favor such things, night sights have never been issued. You may want them, and you can certainly install them, but they are not retro. Also, it might bear repeating: flat-tops are not retro.

The A1 rear sight is adjustable only for windage, and then only with a lot of struggling. This is not a target sight.

RECEIVERS

This is the big choice, because there have been some obvious and cosmetic changes to the receivers over the decades. And when we first started seeing retro work being done, some years ago, some of it called for actually carving on receivers to return them to the retro configuration. Let's cover lowers first.

A1 VS. A2 LOWERS

The A2 receiver was upgraded from the final-configuration A1 with two changes. The first change is the hoops, or bolsters, on the front of the receiver, where the takedown pin went through. For the A2, they had the radius of their blend to the receiver front wall increased. This made them somewhat stronger, and made it an easy spot to tell them apart. A less-obvious change was at the other end of the receiver, where the receiver extension "hoop" was made stronger with some reinforcement sections added. The extra thickness of aluminum made the hoop stronger, at least where the reinforcements were. The top could not be made thicker, because that's where the upper receiver and the charging handle have to fit and work. Making the hoop thicker there would have blocked the charging handle, and that wouldn't have been an improvement.

The rest of the lower was left alone, because the final form of the A1 was pretty much not in need of improvements. In decades of working on ARs, I have not seen either the front takedown pin bolsters or the rear hoop broken. That doesn't mean that

the government didn't see those broken, just that neither I nor any of my customers abused our rifles in the way that service members might.

A1 LOWER VARIANTS

The A1 went through a bunch of changes before it reached its final configuration. The first stage was the "slickside lower." This had no reinforcement or protection rails on it at all, those being the rails commonly called the "fence." The magazine button was just out there for anything to bump into. And the front takedown pin was not secured. It used a small spring-loaded detent ball, built into the pin itself, to keep it in the assembled rifle. When you pulled it out to take the rifle apart, it came out of the rifle and could be lost. This had obvious problems, but rifles had been made with small parts that could be lost on disassembly for decades before then.

Top, a NoDak Spud partial-fence lower. This is correct for retro builds up to about 1965 or so. Below, a billet-cut modern receiver, not at all a candidate for a retro build. But this San Tan lower is first-rate for a modern build. As the British say, horses for courses.

Next came the short-rib, where the take-down pin now had a spring-loaded plunger (like the current one we are familiar with) to keep it on the lower when taking the rifle apart. This fence only extended partway back, along the top line of the lower receiver, and was there just to hold the spring and plunger retaining the front takedown pin.

Last up was the "full fence," which had the rib of the takedown pin spring housing extended the length of the receiver to the back of the magazine well, and the fence also extends halfway down the magazine well and surrounds the magazine button.

The full-fence version is the most common, as the earlier ones were transitional models.

If you are building an M16A1 Vietnam rifle clone, then you need a full-fence version. Anything earlier than that would call for one of the partial-fence or the slickside lowers.

Upper receivers are a similar progression. The earliest ones will not have the forward assist. These would be pre-A1 models. When the U.S. Army adopted the M16 and made it the M16A1, they insisted on the forward assist. This upper will have an A1 rear sight. Later, the A2 added the ejector wedge to the forward assist, to keep hot brass from hitting left-handed shooters. And, it'll have the A2 rear sight. Once you get to the flat-top upper receivers, you are out of the retro era, as those did not come along until the 1990s.

A slight diversion here, the forward assist will also be differently shaped, depending on the time. The early rifles, the A1 and XM177, will have the "teardrop" forward assist. This is a roughly oval-shaped head on the plunger. The A2 and the Air Force GAU versions would call for the later forward assist, called the "button." This has the head of the forward assist circular. This change was called for because the teardrop could get hung up on equipment, gear and underbrush. Also, the button shape could be easily formed in a simple lathe operation.

COMBINATIONS

The mix and match possibilities are limited. In chronological order, a slickside lower, to be correct, should only be with a slickside upper, lacking a forward assist. Then, you'd have the same slickside upper as a correct match with a partial-fence and then a full-fence lower. An upper with a forward assist would only be a correct match with a full-fence A1 lower.

And no A2 upper will be a correct match to an A1 lower, at least not as a retro build. As a later build, like the Mk 12, yes, with an M4 flat-top, but that's not retro.

Now, that's not to say that combos outside of the "correct" retro pairings don't exist. It is entirely possible that, in an arms room someplace, there is a partial-fence lower with an A2 upper, say an M4, on it. But sooner or later someone with the savvy to spot it will do an inventory and it will get yanked out of the rack, sent to the appropriate maintenance level for a rebuild (or more likely, to be scrapped), and replaced with a current build.

While I was in the process of wrapping up this chapter, I came across a photograph which I, unfortunately, can't show. It was of a secret-squirrel type, and not one who is "all show and no go." He went there, did that, and came back with the beard to prove it. (OK, a bit on the having-fun side, I'll admit.) The carbine he was holding in the photos was a mixture of A1 lower, an M4 upper, a CAR stock, an original-design Holosight (before EOTech made them shorter) and a free-float handguard right off of a 3-gun competition range. Before that photo, we all would have called such a rifle a "franken-rifle." Well, no more.

I suspect that, as more and more photos leak from the GWOT and the SpecOps community, we'll find that the boundaries of what is "allowed" as a "retro" build will pretty much go away.

And in some gun clubs, the only limit on what is allowed as a retro build is that you have to produce a photograph showing it was used someplace by our armed forces.

One interesting combination that differs is the Canadian C7 and C8. This is an A2 lower with a mostly A2 upper, but the upper has an A1 rear sight. This combination uses the forward assist, the ejector wedge, but an A1 rear sight. This was a combo designed before the widespread adoption of the M4 upper as the do-all upper, and the Canadians, while liking a lot of the A2 features, didn't see any point to an overly complex rear sight, and opted for one that could not easily be adjusted without tools.

A brief aside, all this is off the charts when discussing the Air Force. The various GAU 5/A and 5/A/A carbines are a headache to retro builders. Starting out with 11.5" barrels, sporting either the XM177 moderator or just an A1 flash hider, 1/12 twist carbines, they later received 14.5" M4 barrels, with 1/7 twist. (I suspect that they received them as the old ones wore out, until there was no more M-193 to feed the 1/12 barrels.) They can have slickside lowers, partial and full-fence lowers. They can have A1, A2 and even M4 flat-top uppers. They started out with XM177 tele-stocks, later got the plastic CAR ones, and have been seen with M4 and Sopmod stocks. They can have slender CAR handguards, or large M4 handguards, and either slip rings or delta rings. I have not seen a photo of them with a free-float or railed handguard.

The original Colt markings would have been left on, and each build by the USAF would have called for re-stamping the receivers. Some would have had the model designation milled out (a shallow slot) and

be re-stamped professionally. Others would have had the model designation X'd out, and hand-stamped. Some could be pretty ugly, in fact. And some would even have been given the designation "GUU-5P".

The Air Force, while willing to spend hundreds of millions of dollars on aircraft (even a billion each, for some models), really feels it proper to, as the saying goes, "Pinch a nickel until the buffalo moos." Good for them.

So, basically, you can build pretty much any SBR in that general form, and call it your "GAU-5/A clone" and be correct. Let's hear it for the USAF.

SOURCING

Finding these various receivers used to be difficult. Then, ten years ago or so, we started seeing them from a company called NoDak Spud. They made short runs of A1, slickside and other receivers. They added uppers a few years ago, and they were nicely made, dimensionally correct and period-correct. You can also find A1 uppers and lowers at Brownells. As for the Canadian C7 uppers, those can be found (depending on production runs) from Fulton Armory and Bushmaster. One minor note:

How much fence? On top, an A1 with a full fence. Below, a partial fence, appropriate for an early build.

After all the nagging about what is and isn't period-correct, the USMC goes and messes it up. This current photo shows an M4 with all the current parts on it, except for the stock. That could be right out of a photo from 1974.

the C7 is the full-sized A2 equivalent rifle, and the carbine is the C8. But they both use what is called the C7 upper.

FINISH

The current finish on mil-spec AR-15/M16 rifles and carbines is a Type 3 hard-coat anodizing, with an acetate seal, dyed black. Anodizing of this type is the most durable to be had. However, the A1 did not always come that way. The earliest color was a light gray. Then came a dark gray, before the military went to the black finish. The earlier your retro is placed, the lighter the finish. This, however, is subject to several caveats. It is entirely possible for a rifle with early features to be black, as it is possible to either re-anodize the receivers or to simply paint them or use a dry coat lubricant on them.

The Air Force is a particular example of this, as you can find photos of the GAU/GUU with mis-matched colors, light and dark, old and new.

The government has been providing M16A1 rifles to police departments (except for a short while when the loans were suspended during the Obama Administration)

and these rifles come right out of government storage. I have seen a bunch of them, and it is not unusual to see M16A1 rifles that are the current flat, jet black anodizing. Also, while many are sporting A1-era Colt-made barrels, I have seen brand-new A1 barrels, made by FN, on M16A1 rifles. And yes, they have 1/12 twist barrels. They may be getting new barrels, but they are M16A1 rifles, and the specs call for a 1/12 barrel twist on those. So they get them. Well, the Army ones do; the Air force, we've been over that.

And remember, the more they are used, the more shop-worn they appear. It is entirely possible for a rifle to be black except for the edges, which can easily be worn down to bare white aluminum. If you want to "age" your rifle, you are on your own, but you can get an idea of what it looks like by checking in with the folks at NoDak Spud.

If you are building a retro, you can send the aluminum parts to the correct place for a time-match, and that place is U.S. Anodizing. They regularly work on anodizing ARs, and can help you find the correct shade of gray for your build. Or, you can paint or use Norrels moly-resin. ■

CHAPTER 23

USPSA PCC

Built for the match, and not to a retro or mil-spec standard, this is the match-winning PCC and we can all learn from it. Photo courtesy Taylor Freelance.

PCC is Pistol Caliber Carbine. While I can't say for sure that my gun club invented it, we were the first I knew of, and for a long time pretty much the only club that held regular matches and scored them as a division in USPSA/IPSC matches.

PCC has come on strong in a short few years. Part of that is the competition format, and part of that is cost. There's also

the matter of being indoor-range friendly. At the moment, a thousand rounds of .223 ammo runs about $230 for steel-case, and $310 or so for brass-cased ammo. 9mm? $165 per thousand for steel-case, and $200 for brass-cased. Indoor ranges where you can shoot rifle calibers are not as common as ranges that allow handguns. And often the rifle-rated ranges require that you shoot only range-supplied ammo, to prevent steel bullets chewing up their backstops.

9mm shooters don't have that problem. Also, rifle calibers indoors are work. The .223 is so much louder that even using

foam plugs and muffs isn't enough to keep it from being tiring. 9mm is a lot more ear-friendly.

The match format is simple: you use a carbine or rifle, chambered in a handgun cartridge, in a handgun match. Not a rifle match, with targets at rifle distances, but in the same handgun stages that the handgun match is firing. This is also a boon to gun clubs that don't have rifle ranges, or have only the one 100-yard range that is usually used to sight in deer rifles. The PCC runs on the same ranges that the handguns do, in the same match.

When we did this, beginning in the 1980s, our club was packed with serious, high-volume competitors. At a time when a squad (a set of shooters going through the stages of a match as a group) in a local club match might be ten or twelve shooters, we'd have six-man squads. Why? Because each of us would be shooting the match 2-3 times, all at once. You'd shoot the match once in Open or Stock (that's what we called the non-comped guns before we split it into Limited, Limited 10 and Single Stack), then swap your gear and re-shoot the same stage with your other Stock or Open gun. (The first was your official match score, the second was your "bragging" score.)

Then, you'd swap your belt gear (or just wear everything you needed all the time) and re-shoot the stage once again, in PCC.

Six shooters, doing it three times each, was the match equivalent of eighteen shooters, so we had to work fast. But we did.

Some opted for a different mix, like Stock, Revolver and PCC. Since our club at one time or another recognized half a dozen different divisions (this being years before the USPSA started splitting equipment divisions), we had some pretty odd combos.

The gear in the early years was, well, mixed. We had some Colt 9mm ARs, as well as conversions built on Olympic Arms uppers. There was always someone trying to make a Marlin Camp Carbine work reliably enough to actually finish a match. They had ferocious ejection (sometimes over the side berm) and broke under heavy use.

When the Ruger PC9 and PC40 carbines arrived, they were reliable enough to finish a match and a season, but they were late to the party. By the time they arrived, in 1996, we had almost all gone to one variant or another of the AR in 9mm.

We also found that PCCs were markedly faster in the handgun matches than handguns were. A C-class shooter who practiced enough to be smooth with his/her PCC could shoot scores and times that rivaled the A and Master class handgun shooters' scores. And that was with iron sights. Given a red-dot sight (which was easier to mount and longer-lasting, back then, on a PCC than on a handgun), the C-class PCC shooter could post the match-winning score. Beat even the Master or GM in Open.

That should not have come as a surprise, but it was startling, nonetheless.

The Marlins and Rugers are gone now, or rarely seen, and then only by new-to-the-game shooters, who use them "because I already have it." Now, it is the realm of the AR in 9mm. But that is quickly shifting, as the Sig MPX seems poised to take over. The main reason for that is magazines, which we'll get into. But first, the AR-15 in 9mm for PCC competition. (Oh, and a really, really good home defense option, as well.)

OPERATION

The PCC in the AR-15 operates as a straight blowback system. The mass of the bolt and buffer, plus the force of the spring, keep the system closed at firing. The case thrust of the cartridge then blows the weights back against the spring, which compressing stores energy. Once the energy has been absorbed, it is used to feed the next round into the chamber.

The 9mm thus has no gas system, although there is the stub of a gas tube on the front sight, to keep the handguards from rotating. Lacking a gas system, the 9mm carrier (which is also the bolt) has just a stub of the gas key on top, only enough to keep the bolt aligned in the receiver. Without it, the bolt could rotate in the upper receiver (it is basically just a long cylinder) and that would be bad.

Case thrust is simple: chamber pressure times the cross section area of the case head, minus the frictional losses of case adhesion to the chamber wall. (The actual area of

thrust is the inside base of the case interior, but that is difficult to measure. Case adhesion is also difficult to measure, so we just ignore it for the initial estimation.)

The area of a circle is pi times radius squared. The 9mm has a nominal rim diameter of .394". The maximum chamber pressure is 36,000 PSI, so the maximum case thrust is 4,390 pounds. The actual is a lot less, as most 9mm rounds don't run at 36K, not even close. They might be more like 27K. And the case adhesion takes a

Colt makes the 9mm uppers on slickside receivers (obviously, A1) and includes a plastic gas shield with a shortened ejection port door.

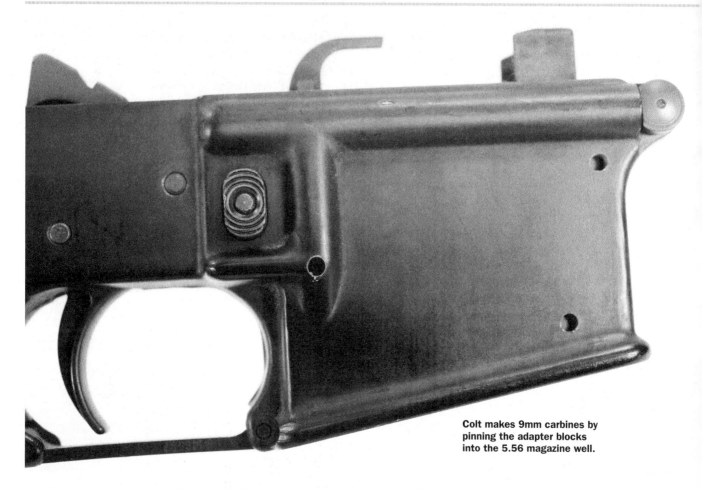

Colt makes 9mm carbines by pinning the adapter blocks into the 5.56 magazine well.

Below: The front block also includes a feed ramp to get the stubby 9mm rounds from the magazine up to the chamber.

bunch out of that. Let's call it one ton, just for a rough estimate.

Now, there is a new design coming out as I'm writing this, from CMMG. It is a delayed-blowback, using a rotating bolt. It is currently only in .45 ACP, which is great for those who want a big-bore PCC. But that's not so great for those who want to compete in PCC, because all the groups that have Divisions for it, score it Minor. That is, regardless of the power (assuming you meet or exceed the threshold), your PCC is scored as if it were a 9mm.

Oh, you can shoot a .40 or .45 PCC, but you won't get any better score for shooting something more powerful. That's just the way it is. So, from the start, a PCC for competition is in 9mm Parabellum.

ON TO THE MAGAZINES

These days, there are two main magazine choices. Back in the early days, there were more. My Olympic Arms 9mm conversion used Sten gun magazines. The Marlins used S&W 9mm hi-cap magazines. The Rugers used Ruger magazines. Now, the choice is Colt pattern or Glock.

The Colt magazine and PCC comes from the first of the 9mm PCCs, the Colt 9mm carbine. I first read about the Colt in an article by the late Frank James, a gunwriter I much later came to know and by whom I was honored to be considered one of the good guys. Frank was a curmudgeon, and if he didn't like someone he had no qualms about saying so.

The Colt uses modified Uzi magazines, and of the choices they had, they could not have done much worse. Well, the Sten gun mags were worse, but there weren't many others. The Colt mags did not use the same locking slot location as the Uzi smgs did, so the Colt ones had to have a different slot. One good thing Colt did was change the spine of the magazine tube, and it incorporated a bolt hold-open device. So, if you use modified Uzi mags (there was a time when they were common and cheap, and the Colts were expensive, and guys modified Uzi mags to fit a Colt), the bolt

won't lock back when you are empty.

Colt magazines will, most of the time. What Colt magazines also will do is spew rounds if you bump the magazine. Drop a Colt magazine and you can easily see five to fifteen rounds, lemming-like, leave the tube. I've seen Colt magazines spontaneously spew rounds. If they are so bad, what is the alternative? Glock magazines. The good point is, the Glocks do not spew. The bad point is, they feed from a single location. The Colt magazines feed from alternating sides of the feed lips.

This, combined with the angle of the magazine, means that your PCC has to start with one or the other. You cannot swap between them. You cannot use a Colt bolt, in an upper, on a lower meant for Glock magazines. And vice-versa. You go with one, and that's what it is.

Currently, there are choices for Colt-pattern magazines. When Colt was the only source,

The 9mm ejector is a blade pinned to the rear adapter block.

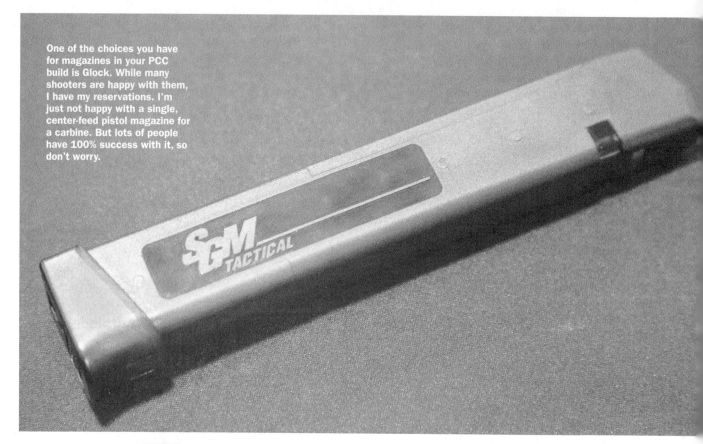

One of the choices you have for magazines in your PCC build is Glock. While many shooters are happy with them, I have my reservations. I'm just not happy with a single, center-feed pistol magazine for a carbine. But lots of people have 100% success with it, so don't worry.

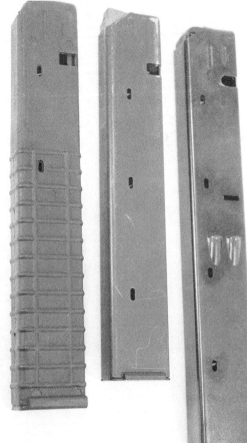

The standard is the Colt, in the center. You can cut a slot at the right location and use Uzi mags, and for practice the polymer Pro-Mag will work.

they were expensive, and they spewed. Now, we have other makers, and they are both more reliable (a Colt-pattern PCC can take some tuning) and less expensive.

Colt made their 9mm smgs (the first ones were sub machine guns, the semi carbines came later) the good old fashioned way: on the cheap, by cobbling parts together at the lowest possible cost. Colt makes a 9mm by pinning two blocks into the lower, to create a magazine well that is the correct size for the 9mm magazine. So, if you have a Colt, you now know the reason for those holes and pins and the extra blocks. Colt can do it cheaply, and doesn't have to pay for a new magazine well broach.

The blocks that are pinned in place contain the extra feed ramp needed to coax a 9mm into the chamber and the ejector (which is a hooked blade pinned to the rear block), and thwacking the fired case through a slot in the bolt face.

The bolt is also a compromise. It is a carrier with the front end not bored out, but instead machined to be a breechface. There is no separate bolt on a Colt or Colt-style 9mm.

In the lower receiver, the hammer is a different hammer than that of the .223/5.56 AR, as part of the engineering to work with the blowback system. Also, the buffer weight is different in the Colt, being heavier, since all the carbine has is mass to work with. And obviously there is no gas tube up over the barrel. There is, however, the stub of a gas tube, because without one the handguards might turn from your holding the handguards, and loosen the barrel nut. Think not? I've done it.

PINNED CONVERSION

Now, Colt still makes the PCC/smg this way. But you can make a regular AR lower into a 9mm Colt-pattern PCC by simply assembling it with a Hahn conversion block. They make two: one that installs from the top, and one that installs from the bottom.

Install the conversion, slap a 9mm upper onto the lower, and start feeding it with Colt-pattern magazines.

They are also made by Colt themselves, as well as by Rock River. Typically, the adapters use the magazine catch of the .223/5.56 receiver to hold the adapter block in place. In this instance, the top-install Hahn is a bit more secure. It has small lips on it to keep it from falling out the bottom. Of course, if you really wanted to be secure, you could go the "belt and suspender" route.

Install your adapter block. Make sure it functions as you expect it to, and with the reliability you need. Translation: 100%. Then, with the block in place, locate an unused portion of the block and receiver, drill it and pin it.

In an era of $40 AR-15 lowers, you can even drill and tap the block (in place, in the receiver) and bolt the block in place. It may not be the prettiest (then again, it could be, if you are careful), but it is your rifle, your PCC, and if you are winning matches, the rest of the shooters won't care about looks.

NON-PINNED

What if we have a crazy idea and decide to not cobble together a PCC by pinning in blocks? What if we actually sprang for the money to make a new broach? Why, then we'd have the Rock River PCC. What they

did was simple, really. They took the dimensions of the Colt lower, with the blocks in it, and simply broach the forged lower to that spec. Then, they pinned in the feed ramp (steel, to take the impact) and the ejector blade (again, steel, same reason, but even more-needed) and built a proper 9mm PCC on that.

Voila, solid 9mm PCC. It still uses the Colt-pattern magazines, but with the new manufacturers (Brownells, Metalform, and CProducts Defense company in metal, and ProMag in polymer), the Colt pattern is a lot more dependable than it was decades ago.

To build this, you need a 9mm bolt and barrel, a conversion block or Rock River lower, and all the rest is normal, standard AR parts. You can have a 9mm barrel as short as 4.5" and up to 16". I don't know of any 20" 9mm barrels, but not many want that, and I haven't really looked. I mean, what's the point?

The rest of the build is whatever AR your heart desires. If you want this or that handguard or stock, go for it. The handguard attachments are unchanged, as are the stock options. (That seems odd, using the phrase "stock options" in a firearms publication. Oh well.)

One point on the upper: Colt uses a shorter than normal ejection port door, with a plastic "gas diverter" behind it. You can do that, but you don't need it. If you want to use an M4 or an A1 upper, knock yourself out. The PCC won't care.

NON-PINNED GLOCK

OK, there is one advantage to using the Glock magazine: .45 ACP. Not everyone who wants a PCC wants it for competition. And, a lot of people like the .45 ACP (go figure). Those who make ARs built to use the Glock magazines in 9mm, 40 and .45 do so with properly-broached receivers. This has the advantage of ensuring that the round being fed is properly positioned for the journey. It has the disadvantage of being a Glock magazine, and feeding from the center. But, Glock magazines are everywhere, they are inexpensive, and if you break, lose or otherwise damage one, there is no angst involved.

What you will find, however, is that those who make PCCs built for Glocks tend to build complete rifles. So you will be less making your own 9mm than buying one ready to go, built to your specs.

But, the .45 ACP looms large here. The previous problems with a .45 PCC were magazines. As in, there weren't any that were suitable. The oldie but goodie, the M3 Grease gun magazine, was too wide. An alternative, the Uzi in .45, worked in the AR lower as it wasn't as fat as the M3, but there was one big problem with it: the Uzi magazine was really, really, tight on acceptable length. Decades ago I had a PCC built to use the Uzi .45 magazines (sold, it, wish I hadn't) and it seemed like half the factory 230 FMJ available was too long to fit into the magazine.

The Glock magazine doesn't have that problem.

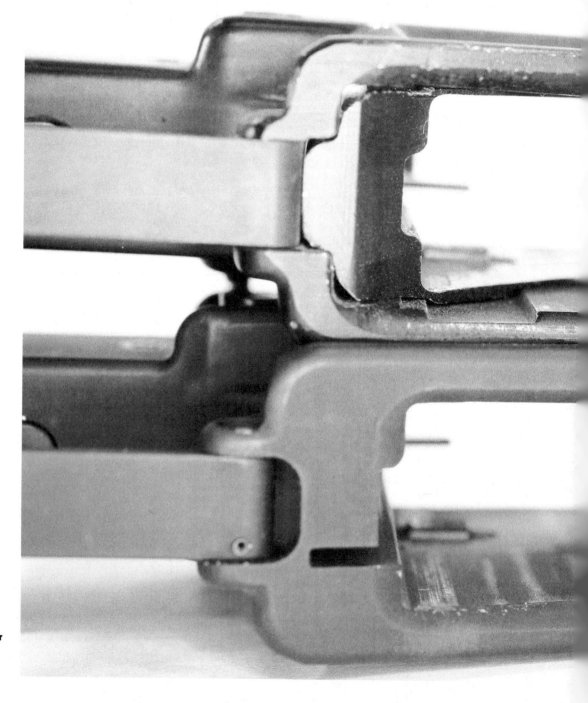

On top, a Colt receiver with the pinned-in blocks, and below it a Rock River receiver. The RRA receiver has the magazine well properly broached for the 9mm magazine. No adapter blocks here.

UPPERS DIFFERENCES

One thing you will not right away see is that Colt makes the 9mm PCC in 9mm only (even in the height of the use of the .40 they did not make one, and never a .45), and for the longest time only with an A1 upper. And not just any A1 upper, but a slickside, lacking a forward assist. They have recently changed, offering a flat-top, but it is still a slickside, with the funky plastic gas diverter, no forward assist and no ejector lump. This also means it has the short ejection port door.

Most of those you see from Colt will be the old A1 slickside, and those from anyone else will be an M4 clone, with a full-sized ejection port cover, ejector lump and forward assist.

The differences are also internal. The Colt 9mm upper will not have a recess milled inside of the upper, the recess being the location the bolt cam tips into. Since the Colt has no cam, there was no need for Colt to mill it. This matters only if you get the clever idea of using a Colt 9mm upper as the basis for an early M16 retro build. Can't be done.

Everyone else who is using an M4 upper uses a real, honest-to-goodness 5.56 upper, and you could, if you wanted to, go back to 5.56 from 9mm.

And you can, obviously, build a 9mm PCC from parts, based on an upper and lower receiver set for .223/5.56.

COMPETITION SETUP

OK, you have a 100% reliable PCC, or plans to build one. You want to make it slick and ready for competition. What to do? The first thing to consider is speed and balance. You need a PCC that you can move quickly through a stage. You do not want an anvil, but for each of us there is a limit, and a too-light rifle will hurt your scores just as surely as a too-heavy one will.

On this, you are on your own. You have to decide what is too light, what is too heavy, and what is too bulky.

You'll want a set of iron sights that you find to be fast and accurate, or better yet, a red-dot sight. The USPSA, when they

Here is a Colt/C-Products 32-round 9mm magazine with a Taylor Free-lance magazine extension on it. The end result is a 9mm carbine that holds 43 rounds, 42 of them in the magazine.

adopted PCC, went full-bore into the 21st century. Red-dots are allowed on PCC, and you really should be using one if you expect to do well. That said, if you show up with your PCC sporting iron sights, you can use the first few matches to fine-tune your gear. See what others are using (it can change overnight, if a new RDS becomes the hot thing), and see what breaks and what doesn't.

What you won't need is a muzzle brake. Oh, they are allowed, but the gas pressure at the muzzle is so insignificant that you won't gain anything by having one. You won't even need a flash hider (but you'll probably want one, just because) since, again, the end of a 16" barrel is not a busy place on a 9mm carbine.

You can use a shorter barrel if you want, with some caveats. You'll have to

Here is a USPSA Open gun with magnifying optic, red dot close-range sight and a comp. Oh, and a humongo magazine, holding an afternoon's worth of ammo. However, this is not a PCC, and you can't use it in PCC Division, even though it is an AR, just like your PCC.

Above: The options for a PCC have greatly increased of late. This is the Sig, but you can't build it, only buy it.

Opposite Page: This is the winning PCC at the USPSA Nationals, a carbine built from parts. Photo courtesy Taylor Freelance.

register/paper it as SBR, just to stay kosher. You can shoot an AR pistol, but you can't use an arm brace on it, not because the match organizers hate them, but because the national body has to have rules that work across the country. Some places no-doubt hate them, and so the USPSA nixes them. That's not to say that your local gun club will. If your club is OK with them, and the match organizer is willing to risk the tsk, tsk, of the USPSA, knock yourself out.

Make sure that your favorite load for the PCC does not exceed 1,600 fps. Again, the USPSA is looking out for the clubs, and if a club is still using steel that is not full-up armor plate, your 1,750 fps load might dent it. That would be bad.

You can't use magazine couplers. Those are the gizmos that lash a pair of magazines together. That's fine, since two 32-round magazines add a lot of weight, and you won't benefit from it.

What you can do is go to Taylor Freelance and see about magazine extensions. Sooner or later, you will run into a 35-40-round stage, and your 32-round magazine will require that you reload. Or, the stage is 30 rounds and you need more than two make-up shots. TF offers extensions that get you up to 40 rounds, in some magazine designs.

Last, a laser. Wait, what? Yep, a laser. You see, at the closest, fastest distances, and when shooting from odd positions, you can get hits really fast with a laser. What you need, however, is one that can be mounted as close to the bore line as possible. Trying to shoot at warp speed while trying to calculate the hold-off from your laser being 2-3-4 inches off the bore axis does not compute.

ADDENDA

The advantages of a PCC are many: low recoil, cost, easy on steel, indoor-friendly, and best of all, they are giggle-worthy fun in a match. Plus, if you practice and do well, no one can knock how it looks.

If you've built a PCC, you'll find it grand fun to install a suppressor and do a lot of really quiet plinking. As a blowback system, you don't have to worry about gas dwell time and gas blowback from using a suppressor. You'll be the life of the party on family range day, as people line up to shoot the quiet carbine. Subsonic ammo will make it even more fun.

Just don't show up at a PCC match with it. Suppressors aren't allowed.

I was outraged when I read that. What? No suppressors? I asked the match organizers and found out the simple reason: the shot timers have a hard time hearing the sound of the shot when suppressed. It made match scoring too difficult. If the Range Officer was even just a few feet farther away than normal, trying to catch up

as a competitor fired their last shot, the timer might not hear it. That would shave time off their run and muddy the scores.

So, no suppressors. Hey, these are fun enough as it is.

PCC AMMUNITION

Being a blowback system, the PCC is sensitive to changes in bullet weight and

velocity. A lot of shooters think that, because they are putting their pistol ammunition into a carbine, the 16" barrel may double their velocity. Alas, it just isn't so. The problem is the expansion ratio. That is, the volume of the case and barrel to the muzzle, compared to that of the case. (Actually, what we start with is the "combustion chamber," the volume of the case inside, below the bullet. But for a first estimate, we just use the case.)

The volume of a 9mm case is the radius squared, times pi, times the height. The famous "pi-r-squared" times the length of the cylinder. So, we have a .394" case, .754" long. That gives us, with the arithmetic out of the way, a volume of 0.092 cubic inches.

The 9mm bullet is .355" in diameter, so if we use that as our first, rough, estimate for our 16" barrel, we end up with a bore (chamber and barrel) volume of 1.584 cubic inches. The ratio is 17.2 to 1. The ideal gas law tells us that as a volume expands, the pressure inside of it decreases, so the ratios of the two will remain the same.

If we take the chamber pressure as the maximum for a 9mm, at 36,000 PSI, the expansion ratio tells us that at the muzzle the remaining pressure in the bore will be....ta da... 2,093 PSI.

Essentially, the net effect of the gases pushing has stopped, back at the 10" point, and the bullet is coasting, or even being slowed down by friction.

Add to that the fact that the powders used in your 9mm have been formulated and selected to be fully-burned and give all they can in a 5" pistol barrel. There's no residual push left, after 10".

So, your PCC will show a boost of some kind, but unless you find a really dense and slow-burning (for a handgun) powder to load with, you won't get much. And what you get, your PCC will pay for, as the momentum generated slings the bolt back with more force.

Use standard ammo and avoid the +P and +P+ loads, you pay a big price for the marginal increase in performance.

You can't get something for nothing. ■

CHAPTER 24

Big Bores

The .458 Socom barrel from Brownells comes with its own bolt (it has to, the 5.56 you have won't fit) and a muzzle brake, which is a very good idea on the .458.

What's the biggest bore you can get in an AR? Why, .50, of course. Any bigger and it becomes a "Destructive Device," something the ATF keeps a tight handle on. The biggest is the .50 Beowulf from Alexander Arms. But that is a complete upper, there's no other way to get a .50. So, if you want the .50, you ring up AA and order one. But the biggest to build is a .458 Socom, and you can do that.

The .458 Socom comes from Marty ter Weeme of Teppu Jutsu. The parent case is the .50 AE base stock, but not actual .50 AE cases. They would be too short. Really, you don't make cases, you just get ammo or cases ready to go.

The bore is, obviously, .458, and the case is necked down from the .50 to hold the .458" bullets. The end result is a round just short enough to fit inside the AR-15 magazine, but it will only stack as a singe-stack, not double. This means you have limited magazine capacity, but who cares? You have an AR that is the functional and ballistic equivalent of a .45-70.

A barrel can be had from Brownells, yes, just the one, but it comes with a head-spaced bolt, the muzzle threaded, and with a muzzle brake.

Building is simple. You plug the barrel into a receiver, just like any other barrel. The gas system is carbine length, so you can use a low-profile gas block and tube under than handguards, or you can install a regular A2 front sight base. You won't have the option of using cross-pins, however, and the recoil of the .458 is stout. I would recommend going low-profile, and dimpling the barrel for the setscrews.

You can use the muzzle brake, or install a flash hider. The muzzle threads are ¾" x 24, so finding a suitable flash hider, or a mount for a suppressor, might be difficult. As most .45 suppressors are made for the .45 ACP, they won't be suitable (and might not even stand up to the use) for installation. And the .50 cans are made for the .50 BMG, so they will be as long as your forearm and

The .458 Socom is a singe-stack fit in regular AR magazines.

weight 3 pounds. There are makers of suppressors for the .458 Socom, but they aren't nearly as common as the standard calibers.

The recoil is stout. You do not want to think in terms of a lightweight build. Your standard M4gery will likely tip the scales at 7 to 7.5 pounds. If you make a .458 Socom that weighs less than 9 pounds, be prepared for a world of hurt. Unless, of course, you have an effective muzzle brake on it. Then the guys on either side of you on the firing line will hate you.

The big advantage here is that the .458 Socom can be built on a standard AR-15, and does not need an AR-10 of one kind or another.

.458 SOCOM

The .458 build gets the ubiquitous M4 upper, and the Brownells .458 barrel and headspaced bolt, complete with muzzle brake. This gets a Midwest Industries handguard as its enclosure, and a Sig Romeo4 red-dot sight. I suspect I'll experiment with various buis irons, folding of course, before I settle on something, and I will probably get into serious suppressor-search mode to find a .458-compatable suppressor, just because. ∎

Left: The two big bores, the .50 Beowulf on the left and the .458 Socom on the right.

CHAPTER 25

Rimfire for Practice and Varmints

The Alexander Arms .17 rimfire uses proprietary magazines.

.22LR

Despite the increase in the cost of rimfire ammo, it is still the cheapest actual firearm practice you can get. Getting an AR to shoot .22LR isn't too difficult. Improving the experience is easy.

You need a .22 LR conversion kit. This consists of a replacement bolt and chamber adapter, and a .22LR-specific magazine.

Open your AR, remove the bolt and car-

rier. Slide in the .22LR adapter, load the .22 magazine and get shooting. How can this be anything but fun? Not so fast.

The .22LR bolt assembly replaces the .223 bolt assembly, and has its own recoil spring. It does not need the regular buffer and spring for anything but keeping the new bolt from falling back into the tube.

It is the other end that causes problems. First of all, the cartridge-shaped extension, on the front of the conversions, is there

to fill the chamber of the .223 barrel. That part is smooth, not rifled. Then, there is the jump from that extension to the actual rifled portion of the barrel. Now, if you have a high-volume .223/5.56 barrel on there, the throat is likely to be all heated up and cracked. This is called "alligator skin" because that's what it looks like magnified.

Finally, your bullet reaches the rifling, and the problems are not over with. The nominal bore of a .22LR is .221", while that of the .223/5.56 is .224". The rifling of the AR may be from 1/12 to 1/7. The .22LR is expecting a 1/16 twist.

So, after the long slide in a smooth bore and the rough transition to the rifling, the bullet finds itself in a too-fast twist and oversized bore. Most shooters don't notice this, because for plinking and just having a grand time at low cost and low noise, it doesn't matter. But if you are using your .22 conversion for practice to improve skills, this matters. You need to upgrade.

The upgrade is easy. You simply get a dedicated .22LR barrel. Mine came from CMMG.

A dedicated .22LR barrel differs from the .223 barrel in your AR in a number of respects. First of all, it is the proper bore size and rifling twist for the .22LR. There's no gas port, since the .22LR is a blowback round, and this is a blowback system. It has a proper .22LR chamber, not a cobbled-together arrangement of adapters and compromises.

It is also longer.

The last part is for a good reason: in order to use the dedicated .22LR barrel, you have to remove the .223 case-shaped extension from the conversion assembly. This is easy, because it is designed to be removed. Just gently pry apart the bars that clip onto it, and pull off the extension.

The .22LR barrel is longer than the regular one because you have removed the extension, and the barrel has to come back to fill that gap. In fact, it has to come back all the way to the rear of the standard bar-

rel extension, and then some. As a result, a .22LR carbine with a 16" barrel in .22LR will actually be an inch shorter than a .223 carbine with a 16" barrel.

You'll be able to tell the two apart simply by looking into the ejection port. If you see nothing but carrier or open port, then it is your .223 upper. If you see a "carrier" with an extractor in it, or when the bolt is back a stub of a barrel, then it is your .22LR upper.

Oh, and the .22LR upper will not lock open when it is empty.

By using a dedicated .22LR barrel, you do a couple of things. First of all, you increase reliability, as the moving parts have less to do. You improve accuracy, as the bullet is not now skidding down the extension before rudely encountering the rifling. And, you decrease cleaning and fouling. The .224" bore is likely to collect more lead and powder residue, which will have to be scrubbed out before you use .223 again. And, the gas port of the .223 can collect crud, since you are shoving a pure lead bullet with a wax coating on it past the gas port when you shoot .22LR.

All these advantages also come with better magazines. In the earliest iteration of conversions, the magazines were pretty bad. They were either the Air Force conversion kits, which used a magazine installed into the stripped shell of a 20-round 5.56 magazine; or they were a skinny .22LR magazine, with a sheet

Not that you need the faster cooling rate, but the AA .17 comes with a fluted barrel.

To lighten weight and free-float the barrel, Alexander Arms uses their own carbon fiber tube handguard.

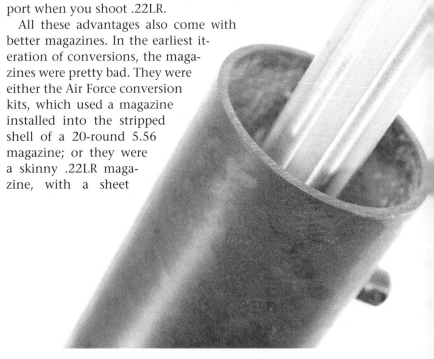

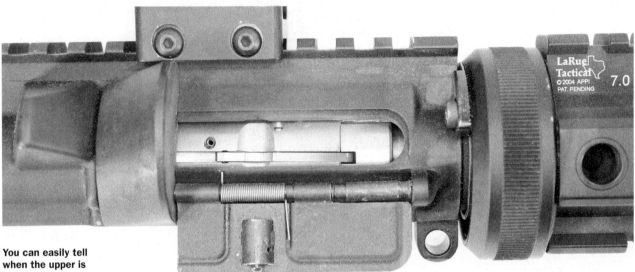

You can easily tell when the upper is a .22LR, the rear of the barrel sticks back and is visible in the ejection port. That and the extractor are the clues.

On top, a carbine in 5.56; bottom, a carbine in .22LR. Both barrels measure 16" and a fraction, but because the rimfire barrel starts farther back in the upper receiver, the end result is a shorter overall length.

metal housing tack-welded to it, so you could use it in an unaltered AR lower.

Black Dog LLC makes magazines for the .22LR conversions that are solid, look like AR mags, and work reliably. They are made by bolting a shell together, and the shell contains the parts for a .22LR magazine.

To build a dedicated .22LR AR, you need the barrel and conversion kit (mine came from CMG, there are others), a magazine or magazines, and an upper to build on. The parts fit into an upper like any other, so there is nothing special here. You do not need to go to extra lengths to bed the barrel into the receiver unless you have some crazy idea of using a .22LR AR as a rimfire Service Rifle trainer. If you do, you're in for a program of testing various .22LR ammo, to see what shoots the best.

The conversion upper does not need anything special in the lower, unless you are looking to improve the trigger pull. The conversion bolt does not use the buffer and spring as anything but spacers, to keep the .22LR from falling back into the tube. If you were building a dedicated rifle and not just an upper, you could see about replacing those parts with a solid plastic rod, just to fill the gap. I'm not sure what advantage it would give you, and it would make it more work to use the lower with a centerfire later, but you could.

.17 HMR

The .17 HMR conversion is less of a build and more of an acquisition. This comes to us from Alexander Arms. The conversion is a complete upper, and a spacer block and magazines for the lower. The .17 HMR is essentially a .22 Magnum necked down to use .177" bullets, which is why it cannot use the Black Dog .22LR magazines. A con-

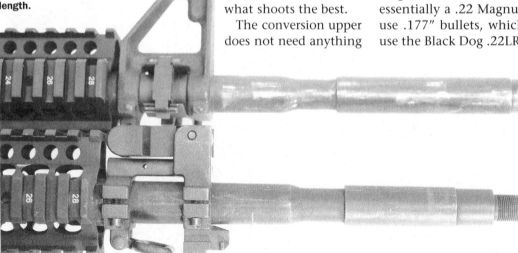

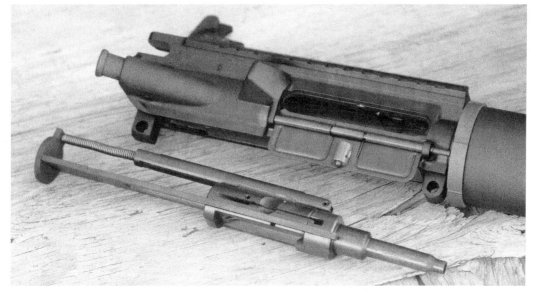

The rimfire conversion does not require a buffer and spring, except to keep the conversion from falling back into the buffer tube. The rimfire has its won recoil spring.

verted AR, chambered in .17 Mach 2, could, since it is a .22LR necked to .17. Alas, the only barrels to be seen in .17 Mach 2 are conversions for the Ruger 10/22, and the extra barrels for the Sako Quad.

The AA .17 HMR is a complete upper, so you simply install the conversion block into your lower, install the upper on it, load magazines and shoot.

What you get for this is a lot more speed, less recoil, a flatter trajectory, and a jacketed bullet that wont foul the bore. The muzzle velocity is up over 2,300 fps for a 17- or 20-grain bullet, and being jacketed

it has a better ballistic coefficient. This gives you less drop, and better close- and medium-range results on varmints. The .17 HMR is not so energetic that you can't find a suppressor for it. The supersonic crack won't go away, but you'd still have that with any high-speed .22LR, anyway.

The .17 HMR comes with either a carbon fiber free-float cylinder handguard, or the Manticore tactical handguard. As the whole thing is built on standard AR parts, you could disassemble the upper and rebuild it into any configuration you wanted, if those two were not to your liking. ∎

The beauty of a rimfire AR is that you can build it on a regular upper receiver, and you can use any receiver you want to. So, an M4 flat-top rimfire? No problem.

CHAPTER 26

Suppressors Uber Alles

Suppressors are hot, especially after a couple of magazines have been pumped through them. Don't get too crazy about which its the "best" or "quietest." All modern suppressors are good, and they will all usually improve accuracy. And yes, Virginia, they are worth the money and the wait.

LEGAL AND PROCEDURAL

Suppressors are the hot new thing, and I'd like to take some of the credit. What I can't take credit for, is why. Back in 1986, the Firearms Owners Protection Act was about to be passed. It prohibited local jurisdictions, which may happen to be anti-gun, from prosecuting travelers who happened to be traversing their locale. Driving through an anti-gun city where the mayor and police would enforce their Catch 22 was to be prohibited.

Catch 22? It is a novel, and it refers to something like this: You are arrested in Central City for owning an unregistered handgun. It was locked in the trunk of your car. The catch is, you weren't a resident of Central City, and therefore had no grounds on which to apply for it to be registered. You break a law for which there is no provision for you to conform.

Well, at the literal last minute, in a voice vote and ignoring requests for a roll-call vote, the bill to be known as FOPA 86, had an amendment added. The Hughes Amendment prohibited the future production of select-fire firearms. Machine guns. Those in existence could be bought and sold, but no new ones could be made. And, none found, uncovered, or otherwise brought to light, could be registered. So, all those WWI and WWII bring-backs hidden in attics, barns and god knows where else, had to remain hidden or be destroyed.

At the time of FOPA 86, a select-fire AR, either a re-built/converted one or a real-deal M16, sold for about $100 more than a semi-auto-only AR. Not a lot of people cared for them, and there were a lot of states where they weren't allowed. Add in the $200 transfer tax, and why bother? Ditto with suppressors and SBRs, short-barreled rifles.

As an example of Econ 101, the price of transferables (as those not in LE or government service, and with proper registration, are known) began to move up in price. Forty years of inflation, and wear and tear (if a transferable is used-up and unrepairable, it cannot be replaced) brought the values to absurd heights. I have recounted it before, seeing a transferable M16 on the wall of a gun shop for $25,000. The big, belt-fed machine guns go for more. I saw an unfired, in the box, FN M-240 listed for $80,000.

Suppressors suddenly became a lot more affordable. A suppressor that cost $1,000 in 1986 cost, gee, $1,000 in 2016. And the inflationary effect on the $200 transfer tax was in the negative. What cost $200 in 1986, inflation had eaten away, and the tax now seemed reasonable.

A quick thank-you on the lack of prescience in lawmakers. The tax was enacted in 1934, the controlling legislation being the National Firearms Act of 1934, aka NFA. Had they pegged it to inflation then (not that anyone would have even thought of it in 1934), the tax would now be close to $3,800 per transfer. Ouch. Had they thought to peg it to inflation in 1986, it would now be $450. Not as painful, but still an impediment. You can also see the huge barrier thrown up to the taxpayer ownership of machine guns, in 1934. $200 was a lot of money back then, and more than a lot of the firearms in question sold for at retail.

Today, you can easily shoot $200 worth of ammunition on a weekend at the range or the cabin up north.

The cost of a transferable has brought a lot more shooters to the realization that an SBR or a suppressor is a lot more fun for the money. The cost is reasonable, the tax is bearable, and the changes in firearms laws over the last two decades have made them a lot more common.

The only real impediment these days is the paperwork time. It takes months to get your application approved. This is due to two things: volume and the nature of the process. Volume, as there are only so many agents checking the paperwork and diving into the databases to check you out. Each examiner has a literal stack of forms on their desk, stacks they are grinding through.

So, if you are curious about where yours is, don't call. That's right, don't call and pester them. It won't get yours any faster, and the time they spend looking for your form is time they can't spend processing forms.

The second reason is the check itself. When you buy a vanilla-plain firearm, you undergo what is called a NICS check. Basically, the dealer shoots your name and identifying info off to the FBI, who does what is called in LE a "wants and warrants check." They also check to see if you have any disqualifying incidents in your background, but that's pretty much it. DQI? Sure, have you ever been arrested for a felony, and what happened there? Have you ever had a domestic violence complaint filed, and what happened to it? Plus, if your name is common, which of the five, fifteen or fifty people with that name are you, really?

The form application for your suppressor (or your SBR build) is a bit more involved. It includes the W&W check and the incidents check, but then goes on to add a couple of other checks as well. Is there actually a manufacturer of suppressors by that name? A dealer? Does the description of the item make sense? I've had examiners phone or

There's a lot more that goes along with a high-end military rifle than just a suppressor. If you are serious about building, and you want to really be the talk of the gun club, you not only build it and suppress it, but you box it with all the extras as well. If you want to show off, don't do it halfway.

email me, asking about such things. "Is that barrel actually that length?" (An uncommon length, yes.) "Was there a transposition of the markings to be made?" (As a matter of fact, yes, that one slipped past the spell-check and two sets of eyes. Thank you.)

The transfer is also complicated by the nature of the transfer itself. A NICS check is just a "yes or no" check on you. The product being transferred is assumed to be a plain old firearm, and which one it is in particular doesn't matter.

The transfer form also looks at what is being transferred and where, which is why we have the occasional approval of a build of a select-fire firearm. Someone overlooked that, and approved building a new machine gun. As soon as it is discovered, it is rescinded. Is suppressor ownership allowed in the state

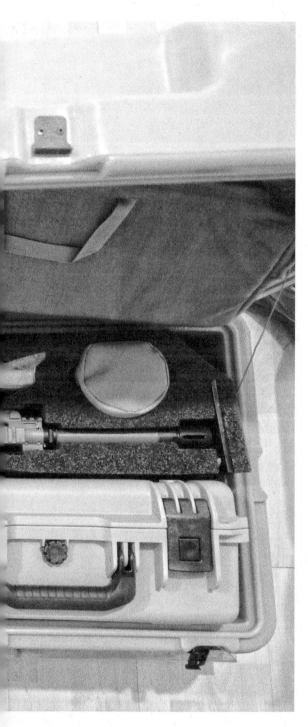

Once owned, no, you do not give up your Fourth Amendment rights to search and seizure. That's an old urban legend. Yes, you would be in big trouble if you lost it or it was stolen, and you can't loan it to someone, but other than that it is just another firearm. If the ATFE really needs to see it, they'll phone you up and ask. You can even take it down to the local office, with your attorney if you wish, to let them look at it.

The possession part is important. Yes, you can go to the range and let your friends, relatives and fellow gun club members shoot it. But you have to be there. Which is only prudent.

MECHANICAL

Mounting a suppressor can be involved, but the manufacturers include instructions and materials. A gas-operated rifle such as the AR will have some problems. The effect of a suppressor is to make the barrel length longer. This increases what is known as "gas dwell time" and can over-drive the system. It does not "increase back-pressure," it simply increases the time it works.

You can deal with this various ways. You can build a rifle that is meant to run suppressed only. If you take the suppressor off, the rifle lacks gas pressure to run and becomes marginally- or un-reliable. You can install an adjustable gas block, to throttle the gas back when the suppressor is on. Or, you can build it with a piston system, and use the adjustable gas settings to throttle the gas back.

You can increase the weight of the buffer. Or, live with the sharper cycling, the extra gas back, and just chalk it up to the cost of having a suppressor.

The advantage of the AR is that you can have two uppers for your AR. One is a regular one, and one is a gas-restricted, suppressor-only upper. You can swap them as you need them. Also, you can still practice and compete with the regular upper, while you undertake the effort to re-tune the other upper for use with a suppressor only.

Just be careful. It won't take too much (well, it will take time and money) to find yourself with a rack full of ARs, in various calibers, all of which are suppressed.

Welcome to the club. ∎

from which you are applying? Nope, then no-go on the transfer, here's your money back.

And the approval is for a particular item, from a particular dealer, to a particular person, you, at this time. You can't change your mind. Once the NICS approval comes through, you can buy anything in the shop. Once this form comes back approved, you get to take home the item listed, and nothing else of an NFA nature.

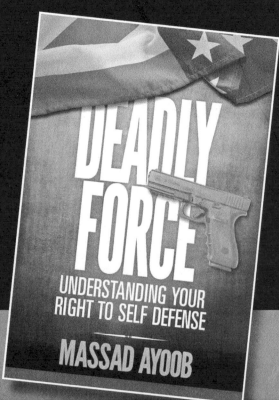